A guide to the Thames Path

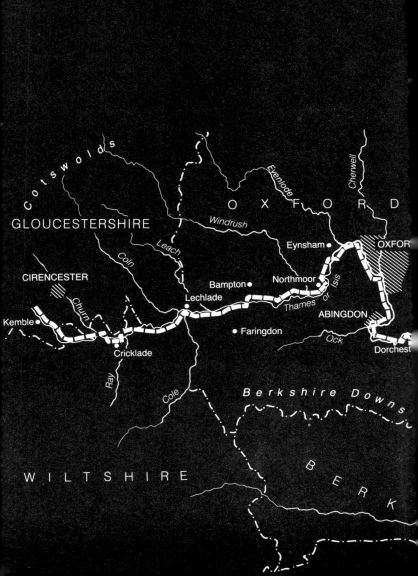

Miles Jebb

A guide to the Thames Path

Constable London

First published in Great Britain 1988
by Constable and Company Limited
10 Orange Street, London WC2H 7EG
Copyright © 1988 Miles Jebb
Set in Linotron Times 9 pt by
Rowland Phototypesetting Limited
Bury St Edmunds, Suffolk
Printed in Great Britain by
The Bath Press, Avon

British Library CIP data
Jebb, Miles
A guide to the Thames path.
1. Thames, River, Region (England) –
Description and travel – Guide-books
I. Title
914.22′04858   DA670.T2

ISBN 0 09 466950 3

Contents

Illustrations and Maps

Maps

The photographs were all taken by the author. **The maps** were prepared by John Mitchell.

Acknowledgements

I wish to make acknowledgement to the following for extracts quoted from their books: to Heinemann and Max Beerbohm for *Zuleika Dobson*; to Herbert Jenkins and Martin Briggs for *Down the Thames*; to David and Charles and Patricia Burstall for *The Golden Age of the Thames*; to Weidenfeld and Nicolson and A. P. Herbert for *The Thames*; to Herbert Jenkins and P. G. Wodehouse for *Summer Moonshine*; to J. M. Dent and Robert Gibbings for *Sweet Thames Run Softly* and *Till I End My Song*; to The Architectural Press and Eric de Maré for *Time on the Thames*; to Cassel and Florence Lennon for *Lewis Carroll*; to Batsford and L. T. C. Rolt for *The Thames*; to MacMillan and Osbert Sitwell for *The Scarlet Tree*; to Thomas Nelson and H. G. Wells for *The History of Mr Polly*; to Duckworth and Alfred Williams for *Round About the Upper Thames*; to John Murray and John Betjeman for the poetry from 'Henley-on-Thames', in John Betjeman's *Collected Poems*, quoted on page 126; and to John Pitt for the poetry from 'The River Thames from Source to Mouth' quoted on pages 19 and 177.

My thanks go to Jenny Blair of the Countryside Commission for useful advice, and to my editor, Prudence Fay.

M.J.
1987

Introduction

This is an unofficial guide to an official path. Or, rather, to a path that is about to become official. Britain already has fifteen official long-distance footpaths of superb quality totalling over 2,000 miles. The Countryside Commission, which authorizes and funds them, is now recommending a route along the Thames.

At the time of writing in 1987 they have issued their Draft Report, which proposes a route of 180 miles, to be called the Thames Path. The proposed Thames Path will start at the source and follow the river downstream, on one bank or the other, 144 miles to Kingston. Here it will continue through London to the Thames Barrier for 36 miles, plus a further 20 miles on the opposite bank. This is the happy outcome of decades of lobbying by the River Thames Society and the Ramblers' Association, whose guide *The Thames Walk* outlined the way.

An unofficial guide can take its own line, and I have quite arbitrarily decided to exclude all the tidal Thames below Kew, with a single-bank route between Kingston and Kew, giving 152 miles. Below Kew the banks of the Thames are virtually all urban in character and utterly different from the non-tidal river. Buildings are large and dominating, traffic and noise impinge closely, and the route is unable to keep to the embankment. So the official Thames Path is really two quite separate entities. Fortunately, a companion title in the Constable Guide series, *London's Riverside* by Suzanne Ebel and Doreen Impey, already gives a comprehensive description of the tidal Thames, and when reissued will include specifics of the lower Thames Path.

From the source to Kew the proposed route is very largely along existing rights of way, but there are several points or sections where rights or links still need to be created. *In all such instances I have shown the section in italics. It is important to realize that until authorization is granted anyone walking on sections without rights will be trespassing: so these must be avoided until affirmed by official Thames Path waymarking, and the alternative route used meanwhile.* It is also possible that the finally authorized route may at points differ from the proposed route; but so much consultation has already taken place that differences should be negligible.

Long-distance walking routes are linear: they do not lead conveniently back to the starting point. In this lies their special attraction, and also their disadvantage. The attraction is that one can walk as little or as much as one likes, and can go on walking for several days. Also, for the equivalent distance, one tends to see much more of the country than on a circular route. The disadvantage is that one must either retrace one's steps or arrange transport or accommodation at the far end. There are many who are not prepared to do this, and for them I have included six circular routes with a total additional distance of 26 miles. But this book is mainly intended for linear walkers, short or long; and, ultimately, nothing can compare with the sense of achievement in walking the full length of a long-distance trail, especially if it is done consecutively and without intervening transport, so that one perceives the changing scene in all its full variety. For myself, I have walked consecutively from Windsor to Lechlade in a week, not a particularly strenuous walk but unforgettably exhilarating.

I have divided the route into fifteen Stages. The Strip Charts show the separate and cumulative distances, and the Specifics amplify the route directions for each Stage. Once the path is waymarked it will be self-evident and far easier to follow than other trails because of all the obvious check-points, and the river alongside. My lists of pubs, restaurants and accommodation are only selective, but they show how easily and comfortably the Thames Path may be walked, with a maximum distance between pubs of 6 miles, and between places to stay of 16 miles. Prices at some of the restaurants and hotels can be extremely high, but the pubs all provide good bar food at lunch-time and give a most congenial extra dimension to this long-distance path.

A RIVER PATH

The Thames Path is an exception, even a contradiction. For where else in the world can one walk pleasurably for hundreds of miles strictly along the banks of a river from end to end? The banks of large rivers in their natural state are covered with thick vegetation and broken by unbridged tributaries. Civilization brings intensive agriculture and enclosures where walkers are not welcome; and finally villages and towns and bank-hugging roads and even railways. Rivers often start in gorges and end in deltas; they are liable to flood; many are bordered with mud. There may certainly be pleasant paths along them for comparatively short stretches – but hardly for their whole length.

The traffic-free path beside the Thames from source to tide is thus a precious rarity, and provides a walking experience virtually unique. To travel the length of a great river is to see and feel its organic change, its transformation between infancy and maturity, its eternal transition and renewal. Certainly, this is usually best done from a boat, and preferably an unpowered boat where skill and muscle are pitted against the force of the water. But along the placid Thames, where few challenges await even oarsmen or canoeists, walkers are now equally able to share this special experience and identification, for they can observe the river just as well, if not better, and their physical effort is just as great, if not greater. What is more, they can penetrate to the very source, where the Thames bubbles out of the grass. Doing this is rather like climbing a horizontal mountain, progressing from the broad and easy to the narrow and difficult, and it is one reason why I have decided to write my descriptions in an upstream direction, for all rivers were first explored upstream, not downstream.

The essential basis for this remarkable facility is the old towpath, which attained its most extensive coverage and greatest use in the early nineteenth century immediately before the arrival of steam-power and the construction of the railways. The Thames was then at its peak as a great commercial highway, and barges had to be towed. The towing was done by teams of men or horses, and a heavy barge might need as many as forty men (known as 'halers') or five horses to go upstream, pulling in single file the rope secured to the barge's mast. All the same, the towpath was never completely continuous. Obstructive landlords blocked it at several points and there the barges had to be poled or winched up. And the towpath changed banks constantly, by means of bridges or horse ferries. Upstream it went as far as Lechlade and the entrance of the Thames and Severn Canal: downstream it lost its importance in the tidal reaches, culminating at Putney. Streams and small channels often had to be forded, and in times of flooding whole sections were submerged.

But towpaths of this sort were established along many navigable rivers, and gangs of men pulling boats have been a feature of the riverine scene since time immemorial, their monotonous toil reflected in the sombre strains of the 'Song of the Volga Boatmen'. What makes these towpaths different from that of the Thames is that today they have largely disappeared or else been improved into roads, especially when on large embankments or dykes or on the slopes of hills. The Thames towpath, however, was never totally abandoned and nowhere became a road. It was kept in use for pleasure when it had ceased to be of use for commerce. And it was saved from becoming a road by the peculiarities of geography. From early times settlements and towns were generally kept away from the banks of the Thames as it meandered and spilt its way along its shallow clay valley, and by the time the towpath was created there was no need to convert it to a road because of the comprehensive network of other roads behind it. Besides, the dimensions were all so small – of the towpath, the embankment, and the Thames itself. So the towpath was preserved with its distinctive sequence of grey swing gates, though its continuity was broken with the closure of all the old towpath ferries, and its quality deteriorated with neglect and erosion.

Meanwhile towpaths continue to exist as secluded paths along old canals; and the modern Thames does indeed have some of the characteristics of a canal. Its flow is scientifically regulated by means of reservoirs and weirs: there are 44 weir systems along its length of 124 miles (and its drop of 69 m) between Lechlade and Teddington. Its water is siphoned off at several points to provide piped water to a large part of southern England (and then, as sewage, is cleansed and returned to the river). Its embankments are fortified against floods. In effect, despite its natural appearance, there is much that is artificial about the Thames.

A COUNTRY PATH

Walking the Thames Path is like walking through a gigantic garden, for the whole of rural southern England may be compared to a garden, and ours is the lushest and leafiest path through it. Great gardens are often designed with separate divisions, each with its own theme, and one moves from one to another as from room to room. They are also linked intimately to architecture, to the principal house, to walls, to cottages and potting-sheds and greenhouses, and they always have ornamental water as an attractive feature. So it is with the Thames Path, with the bridges acting as gates in garden walls, copses as beds of flowering shrubs, old villages as potting-sheds, great complexes like Windsor and Oxford as palatial entities, and the Thames itself as a perpetual length of ornamental water. And, of course, all the time the real flowers, the wild flowers of the meadows and the cultivated flowers of the gardens (especially in the well-tended lock gardens), brighten the path.

This garden-like quality is what makes the Thames Path so different from our other official walking trails. They usually follow the ridges or the coasts, the open country or the distant views, in an attempt to escape from the garden. On them the sense of change emanates from slowly unfolding panoramas. But the Thames Path, though completely flat, is one of rapid visual change, so that every five or ten minutes the scene alters completely, often to our delight. As the girl says to William Morris in *News from Nowhere*, 'The smallness of the scale of everything, the short reaches, and the speedy change of the banks, give one a feeling of going somewhere, of coming to something strange . . .' As we come upon some bridge or church appearing around a bend in the river, we experience that special quality of the gradual approach which walkers, more than any others, can best appreciate, whereby everything appears within its true setting and each arrival is the culmination of satiated energy.

The character of the Thames Path changes completely from end to end. For much of the way from Kew to Windsor one is constantly passing housing of one sort or another, and on the Middle Thames as far as Oxford housing is a recurrent feature. But this is not to say that the lower reaches are merely urban, for one is frequently astonished by enclaves of greenery; the path is virtually always quiet and secluded, and everywhere there are trees. Indeed, there is a far wider selection of trees than on any other of our national trails, all the more impressive for not being massed in great woods or forests, but standing alone or in small clumps. In the gardens are weeping willows, acacias and occasional cedars; in the countryside beeches and chestnuts and oaks; and throughout along the banks are alders, many varieties of willows, and various poplars, notably the tall and narrow Lombardy poplars. Below them are the bushes, hazels and thorns, which encase our path recurrently from the very start at Kew, and garden hedges of box and yew, beech and holly.

A rich selection of wildlife is all around us when we walk. The river birds are the most visible, from the large mute swans and Canada geese to the moorhens, the grebes and ducks – teal, wigeon and mallard. Of the fish-eating birds the most evident is the heron and the most elusive the kingfisher. As for the fish themselves, notices at the locks list the full range for permitted fishing: barbel, bleak, bream, carp, chub, dace, flounders, gudgeon, perch, pike, roach, rudd, tench and trout. To this may in time be added salmon, which have already been successfully rehabilitated into Stages 1 and 2. Other birds which enliven the scene throughout the year are blackbirds, thrushes, tits, robins, jays, chaffinches and pheasants, joined in summer by swallows and sandpipers. And, for the more observant, there are the water insects, water beetles, bugs and scorpions with their amazing versatility of existence.

A PLEASURE PATH

Walkers share the Thames with many others seeking pleasure. On the river itself are excursionists in launches, people in motor-cruisers or small powerboats, rowers and dinghy sailors. On its banks are fishers, bird-watchers, picnickers and sunbathers. On the path are joggers and, in some places, cyclists. On a summer weekend on the lower reaches the path is far from solitary.

But this rather daunting vision of humanity is not typical of the Thames Path, for two reasons. The crowds are packed into certain places, mostly near towns or close to car-parks. And only a fraction of them are to be seen outside the summer months. The

motor-cruisers, in particular, are nearly all moored unused from
October through to April, and their hibernation in their extensive
marinas makes a great difference, for on summer weekends the
chronic diesel hum of the cruiser procession inevitably detracts from
the natural scene. And apart from the visual shock of the larger
cruisers with their pretentious superstructures (one wonders how
some of them would fare if really out to sea) it is distressing to see
the wash they make, which is causing an inexorable erosion of the
river banks, besides driving off small rowing boats and punts and
disturbing the natural life.

These marked seasonal peaks and troughs in river usage are good
for walkers, who can enjoy their recreation equally well at any time,
and nowhere are the relative advantages of walking in the colder
months greater than on the Thames Path. There are really no
dangers of getting lost or perishing from exposure, as do apply in
upland trails in winter. The river itself is more impressive, especially
when in spate; a purposeful mass of gunmetal grey, with swirling
eddies and flotsam of twigs, silent except for the roar of the weirs.
Even in fog or mist there is always something interesting to observe,
and a clear, bright, frosty February day is best of all.

A HISTORICAL PATH

When we walk along the Thames, we walk into history, for no other
long-distance trail in the world has such rich and varied connections
with the past. For geology, the West Highland Way or the South
West Peninsular Coastal Path may be vastly more exciting; for
pre-history, the Ridgeway or the South Downs Way; but for
history, the story of men and women and their social, economic or
political structures, the Thames Path is supreme.

The institution of the English nation-state centred on the Thames
Valley; and so consistently successful has that institution been that
its heartland by the Thames has for a thousand years been spared
war and pillage to an unparalleled extent. Since 1066 no invading
armies have marched through it, and the Civil War and era of
religious strife were relatively mild affairs here in comparison to the
rest of Northern Europe. As a result, a wealth of architecture has
been preserved, from medieval to Victorian extravaganzas,

together with much in the way of furnishings and works of art: and, above all, the sequence of churches provides a profound visual and spiritual link with all those past centuries.

What is more, the harsh realities of nineteenth-century industrialization were fortunately kept at arm's length from the non-tidal Thames. This was thanks to the railways, which diverted commercial traffic away from rivers and canals. And since historical buildings and their surrounding landscapes are now conserved more rigorously than ever before, we can today see and visit them in better circumstances than in the past. In any case, some of them would not yet have existed.

An important key to the past is the understanding of place names, so throughout I have briefly indicated the original meaning. Some are fairly obvious, others obscure: nearly all are Anglo-Saxon, most of them habitation names preceded by a personal name. But the Thames itself is a word of much earlier origin, one which philologists generally agree to come from *teme*, meaning dark, and the common source of several other British river names – Teme, Team, Tam, Tame, Thame, Tamar and Taff. And beside the Thame, most of the Thames' other tributaries' names are also pre-Saxon – Churn, Colne, Ock, Kennet, Lodden, Windrush and Wey.

The Thames itself has its own local history, of which a constant theme has been the facilitation of navigation on its waters. The main impediment to navigation came originally from the millers who dammed the river with weirs to secure a head of water. Barges and other boats could be winched up or shot down through the weir by flash locks only with the consent of the millers, who often charged exorbitant tolls. Other impediments lay in the severe fluctuations of water-flow and in the fishing weirs which obtruded into the mainstream. Despite a series of statutes nothing could effectively be done until the construction of the pound locks. Three were built downstream of Oxford in the 1620s and '30s, but it was not till the 1770s that several more were built on the Middle Thames, or till the 1800s that the entire river downstream of Lechlade was satisfactorily controlled by the Thames Commissioners. In the mid-nineteenth century it was the task of the new Thames Conservancy to preserve navigation for pleasure rather than commerce, a task now undertaken by the Thames Water Authority.

From monarchs in their palaces to lock-keepers in their cottages, from knights battling on the banks to couples necking in punts, the whole tapestry of the past is here beside the Thames. So it is not surprising that the Thames has been more written about than any other river in the world. A recent selective bibliography lists 342 titles of a general historical or literary nature, plus hundreds of others on specialized subjects such as bridges, navigation and natural history. Among them are several classics; and since the Thames has also often featured in biography and fiction I have decided to draw on some of the best of all this literature by means of a topographical anthology to balance my own factual descriptions, in partial emulation of the Constable Travellers' Companions to famous cities. All my quotations refer to our immediate route, and virtually all to outdoor scenes.

I have also quoted a few verses from the hefty corpus of Thames poetry, ranging from the truly poetic to the simplest versification. One particular *tour de force* is John William Pitt's 'The River Thames from Source to Mouth' (published privately in 1939), a guidebook written entirely in verse. In his introduction he says:

> But England's longest waterways, the Severn, Thames, and
>   Trent,
> Seem merely narrow ditches when compared to the extent
> Of many foreign rivers distant from the British Isles,
> Brazil's enormous Amazon, in length four thousand miles,
> The Mississippi and Missouri rivers (USA),
> Vast Russia's Volga, and the Danube, Europe's waterway.
> However, none of these huge rivers own such scenic gems
> As can be claimed by little British rivers like the Thames.

Path Upstream

In the traditional manner, '*left*' and '*right*' refer to the downstream direction, as if flowing with the river, throughout; so when walking upstream the 'left' bank of the Thames appears on the right, and the 'right' bank appears on the left.

'*Bank*' refers to the self-evident riverside path, which sometimes goes behind houses or along lock cuts.

Check points: all locks and all bridges over the mainstream up to Cricklade; above Cricklade selected points.

Italics: these sections may not yet be authorized or practicable for all or part of their length; if not authorized and waymarked, the alternative route must be taken.

CHECK POINTS	DISTANCES			
	between each check point		cumulative	
	miles	km	miles	km
Stage 1				
Kew Bridge	0.0	0.0	0.0	0.0
right bank				
Richmond Half Tide Lock	2.4	3.9	2.4	3.9
right bank				
Twickenham Bridge	0.2	0.3	2.6	4.2
right bank				
Richmond railway bridge	0.1	0.1	2.7	4.3
right bank				
Richmond Bridge	0.3	0.5	3.0	4.8
right bank, passing near Petersham and Ham				
Teddington Lock	2.7	4.4	5.7	9.2
right bank				
Kingston railway bridge	1.7	2.7	7.4	11.9
right bank				
Kingston Bridge	0.2	0.3	7.6	12.2
left bank				

	DISTANCES			
CHECK POINTS	between each check point		cumulative	
	miles	km	miles	km
Stage 2				
Hampton Court Bridge	2.8	4.6	10.4	16.8
right bank				
Molesey Lock	0.2	0.3	10.6	17.1
right bank				
Sunbury Lock	3.0	4.7	13.6	21.8
right bank				
Walton Bridge	1.7	2.8	15.3	24.6
right bank, then along Desborough Cut, under the first bridge and over the second (see text for alternative route)				
Proposed footbridge	1.1	1.8	16.4	26.4
left bank (see text for alternative route)				
Shepperton Lock	0.5	0.8	16.9	27.2
left bank				
Stage 3				
Chertsey Bridge	1.8	2.9	18.7	30.1
left bank				
Chertsey Lock	0.2	0.3	18.9	30.4
left bank				
M3 Bridge	0.2	0.4	19.1	30.8
left bank, passing Laleham				
Penton Hook Lock	1.7	2.8	20.8	33.6
left bank				
Staines railway bridge	1.5	2.4	22.3	36.0
left bank, initially around buildings				
Staines Bridge	0.4	0.6	22.7	36.6
right bank				
M25 Bridge and joint A30 Bridge	0.9	1.4	23.6	38.0
right bank				
Bell Lock	0.2	0.3	23.8	38.3
right bank, passing Runnymede				
Old Windsor Lock	2.9	4.7	26.7	43.0
right bank, initially in long lock cut				

CHECK POINTS	DISTANCES			
	between each check point		cumulative	
	miles	km	miles	km
Albert Bridge	0.9	1.5	27.6	44.5
left bank, passing Datchet (see text, and for alternative route)				
Victoria Bridge	1.6	2.5	29.2	47.0
right bank				
Windsor (SR) railway bridge	0.4	0.7	29.6	47.7
right bank				
Romney Lock	0.3	0.4	29.9	48.1
right bank, initially through boatyard and later right on to enclosed path				

Stage 4

Eton Bridge, Windsor	0.5	0.8	30.4	48.9
left bank, initially down Brocas Street				
Windsor (GWR) railway bridge	0.5	0.7	30.9	49.6
left bank				
Windsor Queen Elizabeth Bridge	0.2	0.4	31.1	50.0
left bank				
Boveney Lock	1.2	2.0	32.3	52.0
left bank, passing near Dorney				
M4 Bridge	2.9	4.6	35.2	56.6
left bank				
Bray Lock	0.3	0.5	35.5	57.1
left bank				
Maidenhead railway bridge	1.2	2.0	36.7	59.1
left bank				
Maidenhead Bridge	0.2	0.4	36.9	59.5
right bank				
Boulter's Lock	0.7	1.1	37.6	60.6
right bank, then inland (see text), by-passing Cookham Lock				

Stage 5

Cookham Bridge	2.6	4.2	40.2	64.8
right bank				
Bourne End railway bridge (and proposed footbridge)	1.1	1.7	41.3	66.5
left bank (see text for alternative route)				

CHECK POINTS	DISTANCES			
	between each check point		cumulative	
	miles	km	miles	km
Marlow A404 Bridge	2.4	3.9	43.7	70.4
left bank (see text)				
Marlow Lock	0.3	0.5	44.0	70.9
left bank (see text)				
Marlow Bridge	0.4	0.7	44.4	71.6
left bank (see text for alternative route)				
Temple Lock	1.3	2.1	45.7	73.7
left bank (see text for alternative route)				
Proposed footbridge	0.1	0.1	45.8	73.8
right bank				
Hurley Lock	0.5	0.8	46.3	74.6
right bank, part inland (see text)				
Hambleden Lock	3.9	6.2	50.2	80.8
right bank				

Stage 6

Henley Bridge	2.3	3.7	52.5	84.5
left bank				
Marsh Lock	0.9	1.5	53.4	86.0
left bank, part inland (see text, and for alternative route)				
Shiplake railway bridge	2.8	4.5	56.2	90.5
left bank (see text, and for alternative route)				
Shiplake Lock	0.3	0.4	56.5	90.9
left bank				
Sonning Bridge	2.6	4.2	59.1	95.1
right bank				
Sonning Lock	0.3	0.5	59.4	95.6
right bank				
Caversham Lock	2.6	4.2	62.0	99.8
right bank				

Stage 7

Reading Bridge	0.1	0.2	62.1	100.0
right bank				
Caversham Bridge	0.5	0.8	62.6	100.8
right bank, then inland (see text, and for alternative route)				

CHECK POINTS	DISTANCES			
	between each check point		cumulative	
	miles	km	miles	km
Mapledurham Lock	4.0	6.4	66.6	107.2
right bank, ending at Pangbourne				
Whitchurch Bridge	2.2	3.6	68.8	110.8
left bank, at first inland (see text), by-passing Whitchurch Lock				
Basildon Railway Bridge	2.9	4.6	71.7	115.4
left bank, ending at Goring				

Stage 8

Streatley Bridge	1.3	2.1	73.0	117.5
right bank, via Streatley Church, and by-passing Goring Lock				
Cleeve Lock	0.9	1.5	73.9	119.0
right bank, then inland (see text, and for alternative route)				
Moulsford Railway Bridge	2.2	3.6	76.1	122.6
right bank (see text, and for alternative route)				
Wallingford Bridge	3.4	5.4	79.5	128.0
right bank (see text for alternative route)				
Benson Lock	1.3	2.0	80.8	130.0
left bank, via Benson Lane				

Stage 9

Shillingford Bridge	1.4	2.3	82.2	132.3
right bank, inland (see text)				
Little Wittenham footbridge	2.3	3.8	84.5	136.1
left bank, passing near Dorchester (see text for alternative route)				
Day's Lock	0.1	0.2	84.6	136.3
right bank (see text for alternative route)				
Clifton Hampden Bridge	2.5	4.0	87.1	140.3
left bank				
Clifton Lock	0.4	0.7	87.5	141.0
left bank, at first in long lock cut				
Appleford railway bridge	1.5	2.4	89.0	143.4
left bank				
Sutton Bridge, by Culham Lock	0.9	1.5	89.9	144.9
left bank, at first in long lock cut, passing near Sutton Courteny				

CHECK POINTS	DISTANCES			
	between each check point		cumulative	
	miles	km	miles	km

Stage 10

Abingdon Bridge	2.2	3.4	92.1	148.3
left bank				
Abingdon Lock	0.5	0.8	92.6	149.1
right bank, at first over footbridge and keeping right on paths				
Nuneham Railway Bridge	1.6	2.5	94.2	151.6
right bank				
Sandford Lock	3.2	5.1	97.4	156.7
right bank				
Kennington railway bridge	1.1	1.8	98.5	158.5
right bank				
Oxford A423 (Donnington) Bridge	0.2	0.4	98.7	158.9
right bank				
Iffley Lock	0.3	0.5	99.0	159.4
right bank				
Oxford Hinksey Bridge	0.5	0.7	99.5	160.1
right bank				

Stage 11

Oxford Folly Bridge	0.9	1.5	100.4	161.6
right bank				
Oxford (former gasworks) footbridge	0.2	0.3	100.6	161.9
right bank				
Oxford (former railway) footbridge	0.1	0.2	100.7	162.1
right bank				
Oxford railway bridge	0.2	0.3	100.9	162.4
right bank				
Osney Lock	0.3	0.5	101.2	162.9
right bank				
Osney Bridge	0.3	0.5	101.5	163.4
left bank				
Medley Footbridge	0.9	1.4	102.4	164.8
right bank				
Godstow Lock	1.3	2.2	103.7	167.0
right bank				

CHECK POINTS	DISTANCES			
	between each check point		cumulative	
	miles	km	miles	km
Godstow Bridge	0.2	0.3	103.9	167.3
right bank				
Oxford A34 Bridge	0.2	0.3	104.1	167.6
right bank				
King's Lock	0.6	1.0	104.7	168.6
right bank				
Eynsham Lock	2.4	3.9	107.1	172.5
right bank				
Swinford Bridge near Eynsham	0.1	0.2	107.2	172.7
right bank, behind properties at Pinkhill				
Pinkhill Lock	1.4	2.2	108.6	174.9
left bank, inland (see text)				

Stage 12

Bablock Hythe (former ferry point, near Northmoor)	2.6	4.2	111.2	179.1
left bank				
Northmoor Lock	1.5	2.4	112.7	181.5
left bank				
Hart's Weir footbridge	1.0	1.6	113.7	183.1
left bank				
Newbridge	1.1	1.8	114.8	184.9
right bank				
Proposed footbridge, by Shifford Lock	2.4	3.9	117.2	188.8
left bank, at first along lock cut (see text for alternative route)				
Tenfoot footbridge	1.5	2.4	118.7	191.2
left bank				

Stage 13

Tadpole Bridge (near Bampton)	1.9	3.0	120.6	194.2
left bank				
Rushey Lock	0.8	1.3	121.4	195.5
right bank				

CHECK POINTS	DISTANCES			
	between each check point		cumulative	
	miles	km	miles	km
Old Man's footbridge right bank	1.9	3.0	123.3	198.5
Radcot Lock right bank	0.2	0.3	123.5	198.8
Radcot Bridge left bank	0.9	1.5	124.4	200.3
Grafton Lock left bank, passing near Kelmscot	1.2	1.9	125.6	202.2
Eaton footbridge left bank	1.8	3.0	127.4	205.2
Buscot Lock *right bank, behind Buscot Church* (see text for alternative route)	1.2	2.0	128.6	207.2
St John's Bridge right bank	1.1	1.7	129.7	208.9
Lechlade (St John's) Lock right bank	0.1	0.1	129.8	209.0

Stage 14

Lechlade (Halfpenny) Bridge right bank	0.6	1.0	130.4	210.0
Inglesham footbridge *right bank, then inland* (see text, and for alternative route)	0.6	1.0	131.0	211.0
Hannington Bridge right bank, inland (see text)	3.4	5.5	134.4	216.5
Castle Eaton Bridge *right bank* (see text for alternative route)	2.0	3.2	136.4	219.7
Water Eaton footbridge left bank	2.4	3.8	138.8	223.5
Eysey footbridge right bank	0.7	1.2	139.5	224.7
Cricklade A419 Bridge right bank, ending through farm into Abingdon Court Lane	0.3	0.5	139.8	225.2

CHECK POINTS	DISTANCES			
	between each check point		cumulative	
	miles	km	miles	km

Stage 15

Cricklade High Bridge	0.5	0.8	140.3	226.0
along the line of the Thames (see text, and for alternative route)				
Former railway bridge	1.4	2.2	141.7	228.2
(see text)				
Waterhay Bridge	2.5	4.1	144.2	232.3
(see text)				
Church Walk, Ashton Keynes	1.2	2.0	145.4	234.3
along the line of the Thames (see text)				
Neigh Bridge, Somerford Keynes	1.9	3.0	147.3	237.3
along the line of the Thames (see text, and for alternative route)				
Parker's Bridge, Kemble-Ewen road	2.7	4.3	150.0	241.6
along the line of the Thames (see text)				
Source	1.8	2.9	151.8	244.5

Path Downstream

In the traditional manner, '*left*' and '*right*' refer to the downstream direction, as if flowing with the river, throughout.

'*Bank*' refers to the self-evident riverside path, which sometimes goes behind houses or along lock cuts.

Check points: all locks and all bridges over the mainstream down from Cricklade; above Cricklade selected points.

Italics: these sections may not yet be authorized or practicable for all or part of their length; if not authorized and waymarked, the alternative route must be taken.

| CHECK POINTS | DISTANCES | | | |
| | between each check point | | cumulative | |
	miles	km	miles	km
Stage 15				
Source	0.0	0.0	0.0	0.0
along the line of the Thames (see text)				
Parker's Bridge, Kemble-Ewen road	1.8	2.9	1.8	2.9
along the line of the Thames (see text, and for alternative route)				
Neigh Bridge, Somerford Keynes	2.7	4.3	4.5	7.2
along the line of the Thames (see text)				
Church Walk, Ashton Keynes	1.9	3.0	6.4	10.2
(see text)				
Waterhay Bridge	1.2	2.0	7.6	12.2
(see text)				
Former railway bridge	2.5	4.1	10.1	16.3
along the line of the Thames (see text, and for alternative route)				
Stage 14				
Cricklade High Bridge	1.4	2.2	11.5	18.5
right bank, at first by Abingdon Court Lane and through farm				
Cricklade A419 Bridge	0.5	0.8	12.0	19.3
right bank				
Eysey footbridge	0.3	0.5	12.3	19.8
left bank				
Water Eaton footbridge	0.7	1.2	13.0	21.0
right bank (see text for alternative route)				

CHECK POINTS	DISTANCES			
	between each check point		cumulative	
	miles	km	miles	km
Castle Eaton Bridge right bank, inland (see text)	2.4	3.8	15.4	24.8
Hannington Bridge *right bank, at first inland* (see text, and for alternative route)	2.0	3.2	17.4	28.0
Inglesham footbridge right bank	3.4	5.5	20.8	33.5

Stage 13

Lechlade (Halfpenny) Bridge right bank	0.6	1.0	21.4	34.5
Lechlade (St John's) Lock right bank	0.6	1.0	22.0	35.5
St John's Bridge *right bank, inland behind Buscot Church* (see text for alternative route)	0.1	0.1	22.1	35.6
Buscot Lock left bank	1.1	1.7	23.2	37.3
Eaton footbridge left bank, passing near Kelmscot	1.2	2.0	24.4	39.3
Grafton Lock left bank	1.8	3.0	26.2	42.3
Radcot Bridge right bank	1.2	1.9	27.4	44.2
Radcot Lock right bank	0.9	1.5	28.3	45.7
Old Man's footbridge right bank	0.2	0.3	28.5	46.0
Rushey Lock left bank	1.9	3.0	30.4	49.0

Stage 12

Tadpole Bridge (near Bampton) left bank	0.8	1.3	31.2	50.3
Tenfoot footbridge *left bank, ending in lock cut* (see text for alternative route)	1.9	3.0	33.1	53.3

CHECK POINTS	DISTANCES			
	between each check point		cumulative	
	miles	km	miles	km
Proposed footbridge, by Shifford Lock	1.5	2.4	34.6	55.7
right bank				
Newbridge	2.4	3.9	37.0	59.6
left bank				
Hart's Weir footbridge	1.1	1.8	38.1	61.4
left bank				
Northmoor Lock	1.0	1.6	39.1	63.0
left bank				

Stage 11

Bablock Hythe (former ferry point, near Northmoor)	1.5	2.4	40.6	65.4
left bank, inland (see text)				
Pinkhill Lock	2.6	4.2	43.2	69.6
right bank, behind properties at Pinkhill				
Swinford Bridge near Eynsham	1.4	2.2	44.6	71.8
right bank				
Eynsham Lock	0.1	0.2	44.7	72.0
right bank				
King's Lock	2.4	3.9	47.1	75.9
right bank				
Oxford A34 Bridge	0.6	1.0	47.7	76.9
right bank				
Godstow Bridge	0.2	0.3	47.9	77.2
right bank				
Godstow Lock	0.2	0.3	48.1	77.5
right bank				
Medley footbridge	1.3	2.2	49.4	79.7
left bank				
Osney Bridge	0.4	1.4	50.3	81.1
right bank				
Osney Lock	0.3	0.5	50.6	81.6
right bank				

CHECK POINTS	DISTANCES			
	between each check point		cumulative	
	miles	km	miles	km
Oxford railway bridge right bank	0.3	0.5	50.9	82.1
Oxford (former railway) footbridge right bank	0.2	0.3	51.1	82.4
Oxford (former gasworks) footbridge right bank	0.1	0.2	51.2	82.6

Stage 10

Oxford Folly Bridge right bank	0.2	0.3	51.4	82.9
Oxford Hinksey Bridge right bank	0.9	1.5	52.3	84.4
Iffley Lock right bank	0.5	0.7	52.8	85.1
Oxford A423 (Donnington) Bridge right bank	0.3	0.5	53.1	85.6
Kennington railway bridge right bank	0.2	0.4	53.3	86.0
Sandford Lock right bank	1.1	1.8	54.4	87.8
Nuneham railway bridge right bank, ending inland, on path and keeping left over footbridge	3.2	5.1	57.6	92.9
Abingdon Lock left bank	1.6	2.5	59.2	95.4

Stage 9

Abingdon Bridge left bank, ending in long lock cut, passing near Sutton Courtenay	0.5	0.8	59.7	96.2
Sutton Bridge, by Culham Lock left bank	2.2	3.4	61.9	99.6
Appleford railway bridge left bank, ending in long lock cut	0.9	1.5	62.8	101.1
Clifton Lock left bank	1.5	2.4	64.3	103.5

CHECK POINTS	DISTANCES			
	between each check point		cumulative	
	miles	km	miles	km
Clifton Hampden Bridge	0.4	0.7	64.7	104.2
right bank (see text for alternative route)				
Day's Lock	2.5	4.0	67.2	108.2
left bank, passing Dorchester (see text for alternative route)				
Little Wittenham footbridge	0.1	0.2	67.3	108.4
right bank, inland (see text)				

Stage 8

Shillingford Bridge	2.3	3.8	69.6	112.2
left bank, ending in Benson Lane				
Benson Lock	1.4	2.3	71.0	114.5
right bank (see text for alternative route)				
Wallingford Bridge	1.3	2.0	72.3	116.5
right bank (see text, and for alternative route)				
Moulsford railway bridge	3.4	5.4	75.7	121.9
right bank, at first inland (see text, and for alternative route)				
Cleeve Lock	2.2	3.6	77.9	125.5
right bank, ending via Streatley Church, and by-passing Goring Lock				

Stage 7

Streatley Bridge	0.9	1.5	78.8	127.0
left bank, starting at Goring				
Basildon railway bridge	1.3	2.1	80.1	129.1
left bank, then inland (see text), by-passing Whitchurch Lock				
Whitchurch Bridge	2.9	4.6	83.0	133.7
right bank, starting at Pangbourne				
Mapledurham Lock	2.2	3.6	85.2	137.3
right bank, at first inland (see text, and for alternative route)				
Caversham Bridge	4.0	6.4	89.2	143.7
right bank				

Stage 6

Reading Bridge	0.5	0.8	89.7	144.5
right bank				

CHECK POINTS	DISTANCES			
	between each check point		cumulative	
	miles	km	miles	km
Caversham Lock right bank	0.1	0.2	89.8	144.7
Sonning Lock right bank	2.6	4.2	92.4	148.9
Sonning Bridge left bank	0.3	0.5	92.7	149.4
Shiplake Lock *left bank* (see text and for alternative route)	2.6	4.2	95.3	153.6
Shiplake railway bridge *left bank, part inland* (see text, and for alternative route)	0.3	0.4	95.6	154.0
Marsh Lock left bank	2.8	4.5	98.4	158.5

Stage 5

Henley Bridge right bank	0.9	1.5	99.3	160.0
Hambleden Lock right bank, part inland (see text)	2.3	3.7	101.6	163.7
Hurley Lock right bank	3.9	6.2	105.5	169.9
Proposed footbridge *left bank* (see text for alternative route)	0.5	0.8	106.0	170.7
Temple Lock *left bank* (see text for alternative route)	0.1	0.1	106.1	170.8
Marlow Bridge left bank (see text)	1.3	2.1	107.4	172.9
Marlow Lock left bank (see text)	0.4	0.7	107.8	173.6
Marlow A404 Bridge *left bank* (see text for alternative route)	0.3	0.5	108.1	174.1

Bourne End railway bridge
    (and proposed footbridge)
    right bank
	2.4	3.9	110.5	178.0

CHECK POINTS	DISTANCES			
	between each check point		cumulative	
	miles	km	miles	km

Stage 4

Cookham Bridge	1.1	1.7	111.6	179.7
right bank, at first inland (see text), by-passing Cookham Lock				
Boulter's Lock	2.6	4.2	114.2	183.9
right bank				
Maidenhead Bridge	0.7	1.1	114.9	185.0
left bank				
Maidenhead railway bridge	0.2	0.4	115.1	185.4
left bank				
Bray Lock	1.2	2.0	116.3	187.4
left bank				
M4 Bridge	0.3	0.5	116.6	187.9
left bank, passing near Dorney				
Boveney Lock	2.9	4.6	119.5	192.5
left bank				
Windsor Queen Elizabeth Bridge	1.2	2.0	120.7	194.5
left bank				
Windsor (GWR) railway bridge	0.2	0.4	120.9	194.9
left bank				

Stage 3

Eton Bridge, Windsor	0.5	0.7	121.4	195.6
right bank, ending along enclosed path and through boatyard				
Romney Lock	0.5	0.8	121.9	196.4
right bank				
Windsor (SR) railway bridge	0.3	0.4	122.2	196.8
right bank				
Victoria Bridge	0.4	0.7	122.6	197.5
left bank, passing Datchet (see text, and for alternative route)				
Albert Bridge	1.6	2.5	124.2	200.0
right bank, ending in long lock cut				
Old Windsor Lock	0.9	1.5	125.1	201.5
right bank, passing Runnymede				
Bell Lock	2.9	4.7	128.0	206.2
right bank				

CHECK POINTS	DISTANCES			
	between each check point		cumulative	
	miles	km	miles	km
M25 Bridge and joint A30 Bridge right bank	0.2	0.3	128.2	206.5
Staines Bridge left bank, ending around buildings	0.9	1.4	129.1	207.9
Staines railway bridge left bank	0.4	0.6	129.5	208.5
Penton Hook Lock left bank, passing Laleham	1.5	2.4	131.0	210.9
M3 Bridge left bank	1.7	2.8	132.7	213.7
Chertsey Lock left bank	0.2	0.4	132.9	214.1

Stage 2

Chertsey Bridge left bank	0.2	0.3	133.1	214.4
Shepperton Lock *left bank* (see text for alternative route)	1.8	2.9	134.9	217.3

Proposed footbridge
    right bank, immediately right across bridge over Desborough Cut and
    along the cut (see text for alternative route)
	0.5	0.8	135.4	218.1

Walton Bridge right bank	1.1	1.8	136.5	219.9
Sunbury Lock right bank	1.7	2.8	138.2	222.7
Molesey Lock right bank	3.0	4.7	141.2	227.4

Stage 1

Hampton Court Bridge left bank	0.2	0.3	141.4	227.7
Kingston Bridge right bank	2.8	4.6	144.2	232.3
Kingston railway bridge right bank	0.2	0.3	144.4	232.6

CHECK POINTS	DISTANCES			
	between each check point		cumulative	
	miles	km	miles	km
Teddington Lock	1.7	2.7	146.1	235.3
right bank, passing near Ham and Petersham				
Richmond Bridge	2.7	4.4	148.8	239.7
right bank				
Richmond railway bridge	0.3	0.5	149.1	240.2
right bank				
Twickenham Bridge	0.1	0.1	149.2	240.3
right bank				
Richmond Half Tide Lock	0.2	0.3	149.4	240.6
right bank				
Kew Bridge	2.4	3.9	151.8	244.5

Useful facts

ACCESSIBILITY: all Stages of the Path are easily accessible by private or public transport, except that public transport is not convenient for Stage 12. British Rail services from London to Reading, Didcot, Oxford and Swindon provide rapid transit towards many of the Stages. All points can be reached within two hours' drive from Central London, and many within one hour.

ACCOMMODATION: only one hotel or guesthouse is listed in each locality, and all those listed appear in the 1987 English Tourist Board's *Where to Stay*. All are on or near the route, though several are up to a mile or so off course.

CAMPING: permission to camp may be obtained locally, though only with difficulty on the lower river. But the authorized campsites are better placed on the lower river, so that it is quite possible for backpacking campers to walk the whole route.

CATTLE: cattle encountered in the fields will generally be quite harmless, though they may gather around accompanying dogs. It is illegal for farmers to put dairy-breed bulls of over ten months old in fields with rights of way, since these are the most aggressive, but watch out for bulls anyway.

CHURCHES: some are open, some closed: keys are sometimes obtainable. Visitors to churches should be generous in donations.

COUNTRY CODE: all users of the countryside should observe the Country Code which is: (1) Guard against all risk of fire (2) Fasten all gates (3) Keep dogs under close control (4) Keep to public paths across farmland (5) Use gates and stiles to cross fences, hedges and walls (6) Leave livestock, crops and machinery alone (7) Take litter home (8) Help to keep all water clean (9) Protect wildlife, plants and trees (10) Take special care on country roads (11) Make no unnecessary noise.

CYCLING: three sections have been proposed for cycling status: Runnymede (Stage 3) to Eton Bridge (Stage 3); Sonning Bridge (Stage 6) to Caversham Bridge (Stage 7); and the A423 Donnington Bridge (Stage 10) to Godstow Bridge (Stage 11). The remainder of the route is not suitable for cycling, and numerous gates and stiles make it impracticable anyway.

LINKS TO OTHER LONG-DISTANCE PATHS: at Goring the Thames Path crosses the Ridgeway Path, an official national path of 85 miles, which follows broadly the line of the Icknield Way between Avebury in Wiltshire and Ivinghoe in Buckinghamshire. At Henley the Thames Path joins the Oxfordshire Way, an unofficial path of 62 miles between Henley and Bourton-in-the-Water. Between Windsor and Marlow the Thames Path marches with the London Countryway, an unofficial path of 205 miles around London, which itself links to the North Downs Way. And at various points the Thames Path bumps against the Thames Valley Heritage Walk, an unofficial route of 107 miles between Westminster and Woodstock.

MAPS: the relevant Ordnance Survey Landranger 1:50,000 Series Maps are numbers 176 for Stages 1–3, 175 for Stages 4–7 and part of Stage 8, 164 for Stages 9–11 and part of Stages 8 and 12, and 163 for Stages 13–15 and part of Stage 12.

REFRESHMENT: only one pub or restaurant is listed in each locality; some of the pubs have restaurants and some of the restaurants have bars. All are on or close by the route except for three pubs slightly off course – the Pineapple at Dorney (0.8 miles), the Fleur de Lys at Dorchester (0.7 miles), and the Red Lion at Northmoor (1.0 miles). The welcome will be all the greater if muddy boots are taken off on entering.

TIMINGS: the Thames Path is entirely flat and for nearly all the way the going is smooth and easy. So for normal walking allow an average of 2.5 miles an hour, with the following exceptions. 1) in Stage 15 between Waterhay Bridge and the Source, where the route is largely across fields and so rather rougher and occasionally flooded. 2) on certain sections of the Upper River where the local highway authorities may not yet have cleared the Path: such sections may include Stage 12 between Newbridge and Tadpole Bridge, Stage 13 between Eaton Footbridge and Buscot Lock, and the greater part of Stage 14 between Inglesham and Eysey Footbridge.

USEFUL NUMBERS: Boat services: Salters, Oxford (0865–243421) and Windsor (0753–65832); Turks, Kingston (01–5462434).

British Rail travel enquiries (01-2626767). British Travel Centre, 12 Regent Street, London SW1Y 4PQ (01-7303400).

Bus travel enquiries: Green Line (01-6687261); London Link (0734-794875); London Transport (01-2221234); Oxford Bus (0865-791579).

Long Distance Walkers' Association: Membership Secretary, Lodgefield Cottage, High Street, Slimwell, Wadhurst TN5 7PA (0580-87341).

Ramblers' Association, 1 Wandsworth Road, London SW8 2LJ (01-5826826).

South East England Tourist Board, 1 Warwick Road, Tunbridge Wells TN2 5TA (0892-40766).

Thames and Chilterns Tourist Board, 8 Market Square, Abingdon OX14 3UD (0235-22711).

Weather forecast for Thames Valley: (01-2468090).

Youth Hostels' Association, 8 St Stephen's Hill, St Albans, Hertfordshire (0727-55215).

THE THAMES PATH

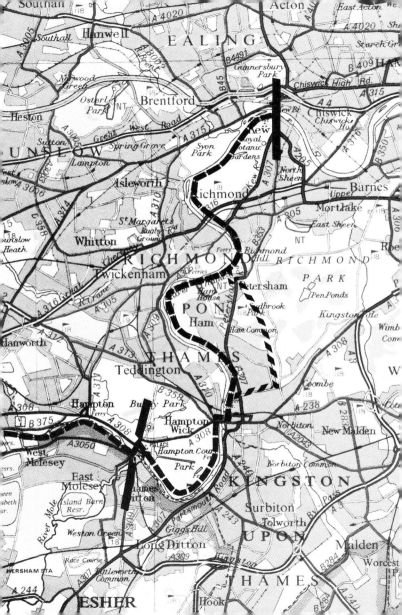

Stage 1 **Kew to Hampton** 10.4 miles (16.8 km)

Stage 1 provides a magnificent country walk within Greater London and leads directly past Kew Gardens, Ham House and Hampton Court Palace. For the entire length the path lies between the river and attractive open spaces, except for 2 miles by the waterfronts of Richmond and Kingston. But the farther bank is mostly covered by residential housing. The path is metalled or firmly gravelled as far as Richmond. Between Richmond and Kingston there are sections on earth; after Kingston the path is gravel or earth.

Path Upstream and Downstream: see Strip Charts

Approach by car
At start: Kew is in South-West London, near the M4 exit 1; car-park at Brentford Gate. *At end*: Hampton is in South-West London, 3 miles from the M3 exit 1; car-park at Hampton Court Palace. *Also*: at Richmond, car-park; at Ham House, car-park; and at Kingston, car-park.

Approach by other transport
Train: London Transport stations at Kew Bridge and Kew; London Transport and British Rail stations at Richmond; British Rail stations at Kingston and Hampton. *Bus*: from Central London, Green Line to Kingston and Hampton, also local London Transport buses. *Boat*: summer services at Kew, Richmond, Kingston and Hampton Court. *Taxi*: London Radio Taxis (01-286 0286)

Refreshment
Pubs: Coach and Horses, Kew Green; White Cross, Cholmondley Walk, Richmond; Bishop out of Residence, Thames Street, Kingston; Cardinal Wolsey, The Green, Hampton Court.
Restaurants: Le Province, Kew; Down by the Riverside, Canbury Gardens, Kingston; Mitre Hotel, Hampton Court Bridge.

Accommodation
Hotels: Petersham Hotel, Richmond Hill, Richmond upon Thames
TW10 6RP (01-940 7471); Liongate Hotel, Hampton Court Road,
Hampton Court KT8 9DD (01-977 8121). *Guest houses and small
hotels*: Chase Lodge, 10 Park Road, Hampton Wick KT1 4AS
(01-943 1862).

Admission
Royal Botanic Gardens, Kew, open daily (no dogs); Ham House,
Tuesdays to Sundays year round; Hampton Court Palace, weekdays
year round and also Sundays April to September.

Stage 1 **Kew to Hampton** 10.4 miles (16.8 km)

If it be true that the first step is what counts, our initial step on
descending from Kew Bridge has a special significance. For, given
the requisite determination, it should be able to set us on a
pendulate motion all the way to the dubious source of the Thames
on Trewsbury Mead 152 miles ahead. But Hilaire Belloc, in a
lengthy dissertation in *The Path to Rome*, contends that it is not the
first but the five-hundredth step that really counts; and I think his
contention is specially valid for walkers of the Thames Path who
start upstream from Kew Bridge. After some five hundred to a
thousand paces the terraces and towers, the bricks and concrete,
oppressive or fascinating according to our personal point of view,
but all recognizably London, draw away from both banks, so that
we have the unequivocal impression of leaving the city and entering
the country.

Not that we should overlook several interesting buildings in this
initial half-mile. Kew Bridge itself, though no beauty, is worth a
backward glance: it was built in 1903, of granite from Cornwall and
Aberdeen. Beside us are the gardens of houses facing Kew Green.
Several were built for courtiers in attendance on the Hanoverian
royalty at Kew (whose name derives from an Old English word
denoting a projecting piece of land). Ferry Lane leads up to the
green, where are St Anne's Church, with the graves of the artists
Gainsborough and Zoffany, and the ornamental entrance to Kew
Gardens.

Kew Gardens originated as the garden of the royal residences of
Frederick, Prince of Wales and his wife Princess Augusta, and later
their son George III. Father and son came to Kew to escape from
the stifling formalities of their London palaces, and also for the
hunting in Richmond Park; and George III and his Queen Charlotte
led a very domesticated life with their numerous children when at
the Dutch House, which we see from our path. Built in 1631, it had
belonged to a Dutch merchant, and was one of the first houses in
England with rounded gables and bricks laid with sides and ends
alternating. But when the King began to exhibit signs of madness,

domestic happiness gave way to tension and stress: Fanny Burney, a lady-in-waiting to the Queen, had an unnerving experience when walking in the gardens (1, page 57).

Today the Royal Botanic Garden is the most exciting place in Britain for the observation of plants. The initial enthusiasm of Princess Augusta and Lord Bute, and the early professionalism of Joseph Banks and William Hooker, laid the foundations of a national institution which is much more than merely a garden: it is a world centre for plant identification, distribution and conservation. The herbarium houses one of the largest collections of dried and pressed plants in the world. The various hot-houses contain all sorts of exotic plants, especially the Palm House, an immense glass structure of 1848, designed by Richard Turner as engineer and Decimus Burton as architect. But for Thames Path walkers who may decide to deviate into Kew Gardens by the river entrance, the natural scene is what will impress most: the extensive lawns, glades and vistas which lead the eye towards astonishing displays of flowers or impressive groups of trees, as well as to ornamental temples and the pagoda. In spring, acres of snowdrops, crocuses, primroses, daffodils and bluebells; in early summer rhododendrons; and all year round bamboos, deodars and ilexes.

On the far bank the Grand Union Canal, together with the Brent, flows into the Thames at Brentford. Then, after a final concentration of housing, the scene is transformed as *Syon House* comes into view. What makes this set piece so impressive is not just the sturdy, honey-coloured house, crenellated and turreted, but its setting among the water-meadows, whose banks are entirely natural, washed twice daily by the tide. So looking at Syon we observe a scene virtually unchanged from when painted by Richard Wilson in the eighteenth century, except that his long-dressed figures would now be in jeans. As to the house, it was originally a nunnery, but at the time of the premature death of Edward VI was owned by the powerful Duke of Northumberland, who from it attempted to launch his daughter-in-law, Jane Grey, on to the throne; literally so, since she was dispatched from Syon in a barge to

Low tide at Isleworth

be rowed down to Westminster and proclaimed Queen.

Soon a second cynosure appears across the water, the village of *Isleworth* (Gishere's farm). Flanked by Syon Pavilion, a gorgeous Georgian boathouse designed by James Wyatt, and the arboreal Isleworth Eyot, it gives an illusion of the past broken only by the modern church. The pub, the London Apprentice, is named after the apprentices who used to row up here in their clinker racing-boats.

On our bank Kew Gardens has given way to the Old Deer Park, now a golf course. In it is the Observatory, built in 1769 by William Chambers: close by our path are three obelisks which acted as meridian markers. The Observatory is on the site of another royal residence, one that Walter Scott had in mind when, in *The Heart of Midlothian*, he brought his heroine, Jeanie Deans, before Queen Caroline, wife of George II. Jeanie has walked from Edinburgh, and when the Queen asks her how far she can walk in a day, she replies 'Five-and-twenty miles and a bittock', a bittock being interpreted as about five miles more. The bonnie Scottish lassie, who has undertaken this long walk to seek a reprieve for her unfortunate sister, then proceeds to advise the Queen in forthright fashion: 'May your Leddyship never hae sae weary a heart, that ye canna be sensible of the weariness of the limbs.'

Richmond Lock was London's first tentative attempt at a Thames Barrier. The effect of spring tides backing up against the swollen stream was always a hazard, especially after 1832 when the massive starlings of Old London Bridge were replaced by the wide arches of the New: the tidal effect at Richmond became more pronounced, the Thames sometimes flooding, sometimes reduced to a trickle. To regulate this a half-tide weir was built in 1894, the barrier being raised or lowered as required: beside it is a pound lock which, of course, only has to be used occasionally, and above it a footbridge.

Twickenham Bridge is a ferro-concrete structure of 1933, whose brutal lines suggest strength but not elegance; it is surprising to learn that the arches ride on layers of compressed cork. Immediately beyond it is Richmond railway bridge, whose piers and abutments date from 1848 (designed by Joseph Locke), but the steel arches are 1908.

The waterfront of *Richmond* consists of a series of disconnected buildings, starting with Asgill House, a fine stone mansion of 1758. Here was once the principal royal palace upstream from London. In medieval times it was called Shene: a Norman manor grew into successive Plantagenet complexes. On the site Henry VII, formerly Duke of Richmond, built a new palace covering nearly ten acres and commanding the river front from what is now Old Palace Lane to Water Lane. The Hapsburg Emperor Charles V visited him here, and here he eventually died, as did his grand-daughter Elizabeth I. But then in the Civil War it was 'slighted' by the Parliamentarians, and later declined in favour of Windsor and Hampton Court; and now all that remains of it is the old gateway leading to Kew Green.

By contrast the little town that grew around the palace continued to thrive, and in Georgian times Richmond was certainly the most fashionable place near London. The great came here in summer, often for short visits, and the concept of the weekend away from town virtually originated at Richmond. For us by the river the principal monument of those days is Richmond Bridge. Since London has replaced all its pre-nineteenth-century bridges, this graceful construction of white Portland stone, opened in 1776, is all the more exceptional. Though widened (upstream) in 1937, the original facing stones were all put back, so that the whole appearance, with the five semi-circular river arches, is just as it was when originally designed by James Paine.

Emerging on to Petersham Meadows we see at ground level the foreground of the classic view of the Thames enjoyed by those up on the terrace on Richmond Hill behind us. Richmond Terrace, like Richmond Green, is English domestic architecture at its very best, now slightly deadened by the architecturally dull Star and Garter Home at one end. Charles Dickens, who besides being a writer was a compulsive walker, used often to stay at the old inn here, and in *Pickwick Papers* describes Mr Tupman walking on the terrace 'with a youthful and jaunty air which has rendered him the admiration of the numerous elderly ladies of single condition who reside in the vicinity'. To Richmond Hill came artists such as Turner and Reynolds to paint the sweep of the river, poets such as James Thompson to soliloquize about the natural scene, and thousands to

admire the view and dream about the Sweet Lass of Richmond Hill as in the popular song. They also came to walk in Richmond Park and to enjoy, as we can still do, the sight of the herds of red and fallow deer browsing amid the bracken and the oaks.

Tucked away at the foot of the hill beyond the cattle-grazed meadows, is *Petersham* (Peohtric's dry ground), a Georgian gem cut in half by a busy road. This was once the most exclusive of the summer resorts near London, with several dukes all living in one street. Many of these aristocrats are buried in the churchyard of St Peter's, where is also the grave of Captain George Vancouver, explorer of Canada's West Coast. This exquisite church is remarkable for its eighteenth-century interior with box-pews, two-decker pulpit and galleries.

Now come two great houses set among trees. On the further bank is Marble Hill, built by George II for his mistress, Henrietta Howard, Countess of Suffolk. Around it are ilexes and what is claimed to be the tallest Lombardy poplar in England. On our bank is Ham House, a great mansion owned in the late seventeenth century by a vulgar but powerful couple, the Countess of Dysart and her husband the Duke of Lauderdale, both red-haired. It is rich in paintings, tapestries, furnishings, plaster and woodwork. Behind is a walled garden, now lovingly replanted in its original formality; and in front is the site of the extensive avenues once known as Ham Walks. A perambulatory ghost apparently haunts this stretch of towpath. Elliott O'Donnell, in *Great Thames Mysteries*, describes how once when walking here in an evening in late autumn he heard footsteps behind him and called out, 'Who are you? Why do you follow me?' 'There was no reply, but as I stood there the footsteps came right up to me and passed me by, so close that, had the author of them been a living person, he must have brushed against me.'

The ferry which still operates from Hammerton's Boatyard near Marble Hill has been running for two centuries since it broke the monopoly of the Dysarts' earlier ferry just upstream, below Eel Pie Island. This island has definitely gone down-market. At the turn of the century it was largely undeveloped, a favourite place for tying

The Thames from Richmond Hill

up punts or skiffs, for spooning and smooching as described by the
astonished American visitor, Henry Wellington Wack (2, page
59). But after the First World War there came a jazz club, then a
community centre for drop-outs, and now a shamble of bungalows,
house-boats, and corrugated-iron shacks.

Eel Pie Island is linked by bridge to *Twickenham* on the far shore.
Twickenham (Twicca's dry ground) was once as charming and
fashionable as Richmond, and its more talented residents included
Horace Walpole, Alexander Pope, Jonathan Swift, Henry Fielding,
John Gay and William Chambers. But not much remains of that
former Twickenham, and certainly from the river there is little to
attract. Walpole's Strawberry Hill is out of sight, and Pope's Villa is
no more, though part of his famous grotto (3, page 60) remains:
the acid little poet had an excellent eye for landscaping.

An obelisk beside the path marks the precise point of
demarcation between the Port of London Authority and the
Thames Water Authority. It presages the enormous Teddington
Lock. For this is where the last vestiges of the tide yield to the flow
of fresh water over the weir – as much as 7 billion litres at peak daily
flow. Behind us are 66 miles of tidal Thames: ahead are 142 miles of
freshwater river. There are three locks: the Barge Lock, nearly
200 m long, enough for a tug and six barges; the Old, or Launch
Lock; and the tiny Skiff, or Coffin Lock; and then, a quarter-mile
upstream, the weir. All can be seen well from the footbridge, as also
from the glass terraces of the Thames Television Studios on the far
bank.

Kingston is approached under the shadow of the power station
and the cast-iron ribs of the railway bridge (1863). The Thames here
looks purposeful, with mooring rafts on our side and a timber yard
on the other side in Hampton Wick. From the mooring rafts at
Kingston Jerome K. Jerome embarked on his river expedition,
famously described in *Three Men in a Boat*. From Burgoine's yard
at Hampton Wick in 1914 floats were fitted to Tom Sopwith's
Schneider Trophy seaplane, which was tested here on the Thames.

Kingston has shamefully destroyed nearly all its old buildings, but

Connaught leaving Teddington Lock

just by the approach to the bridge is All Saints' Church, with medieval elements; and by it is a block of grey sandstone believed to have been a coronation stone for Saxon kings. Kingston (King's tun, or royal manor) was then an important market centre, geographically significant because it was the lowest point on the Thames that was consistently fordable: London was then by no means dominant. Later a wooden bridge was built, and for 500 years it was the nearest upstream from London Bridge. As such, it was strategically important during the Wars of the Roses and the Civil War. It was also the last recorded place in England where a ducking-stool was used – in 1745 for a woman who kept the King's Head Inn, to punish her for scolding!

The present Kingston Bridge is similar in style to Richmond Bridge, though built half a century later. On it we cross the silent Thames, though the roar of traffic makes it more like crossing some dangerous mountain torrent. We regain tranquillity on Barge Walk. This splendid three-mile embankment takes the left bank around the loop to Hampton Court. Beside the wide grass verge a thick hedge, succeeded by a wall, borders Hampton Court Park, in which sheep graze and fallow-deer browse. Cedars, poplars and willows and clumps of thorns complete the natural scene. But on the far bank the houses and roads of Kingston and Thames Ditton destroy any illusion of being in the country. We pass the little Raven's Eyot, tightly packed with boats and boating tackle; and later, after rounding the bend, the rather larger Thames Ditton Island, entirely built over.

On the river are boats of all varieties, from racing eights to large launches with hundreds aboard, from the occasional barge which has penetrated from the tideway to the many cabin cruisers about to penetrate upstream. But this river traffic is orderly and restrained compared to the bustle and muscle of 300 years ago, when the Thames was still the great highway and the bridges had not yet been built. Along our path came cart-horses pulling the Western barges, flat-bottomed, vertical-sided, square-ended, with central mast and with rudder hung from long projecting fin. Most numerous were the

Hampton Court Bridge seen through the Tijou screen

wherries, little clinker boats with long pointed bows and broad rounded sterns, sort of river-taxis capable of carrying eight passengers, their long oars propelled sometimes by a single sculler, sometimes with two auxiliary oarsmen rowing 'randan'. And then, more rarely, there passed the state barges of the great, with double ranks of liveried watermen, and gilded poops, plying their way on the tide to Hampton Court. As the Stuart monarchs wafted thus past Thames Ditton, I wonder if they spared a thought for their ancestor Charles I who, on the night of 11 November 1647, escaped from house arrest at Hampton Court by crossing the river about here in a wherry?

Eventually we become aware of *Hampton Court Palace*, though we cannot at first see it clearly; rather, terraces and formal lines of limes and yews indicate it. Then, through the lovely lace-like wrought-iron Tijou screens, we glimpse the upper levels of Wren's south façade, the ranks of chimneys, the balustraded cornices, the windows square and round, the white stone set in the red brick. A pavilion right against our path (the Banqueting House) brings us nearer to the Tudor frontage.

All this should not prevent us from noticing across the river the mouth of the Mole. The Mole provided great opportunities for the pastoral poets. Its name suggested, quite erroneously, that in its journey from the North Downs it ran underground in fissures in the chalk: hence Milton's 'sullen Mole, that runneth underneath'. Then, because the Thames was tidal here, the fancy was that he dilly-dallied for love of his new-found girl-friend, and we have Drayton's 'soft and gentle Mole'.

And so to the palace, or rather, the palaces – the palace of Wolsey augmented by his capricious master Henry VIII, and the renaissance palace of William III. Both are architectural manifestations of power. To pass from one to the other is like going from Fontainebleau to Versailles, or, in poetic terms, from Shakespeare to Pope. And the contrast is equally marked in the gardens, the Tudor Knot Garden and Sunken Garden contrasting with the Broad Walk and the Great Fountain. But the palaces are welded by their common use of red brick, as by their common shelter of the great picture collection; and on leaving them eventually by the Trophy Gates our final impression is of a complex red mass of towers and chimneys, a structure of majestic frame.

ANTHOLOGY
(1) George III pursues his Queen's lady-in-waiting in Kew Gardens: from Fanny Burney's diary for 2 February 1789.

Taking, therefore, the time I had most at command, I strolled into the gardens. I had proceeded, in my quick way, nearly half the round, when I suddenly perceived, through some trees, two or three figures. Relying on the instructions of Dr John, I concluded them to be workmen or gardeners; yet tried to look sharp, and in so doing, as they were less shaded, I thought I saw the person of His Majesty!

Alarmed past all possible expression, I waited not to know more, but turning back, ran off with all my might. But what was my terror to hear myself pursued! – to hear the voice of the King himself loudly and hoarsely calling after me, 'Miss Burney! Miss Burney!'

I protest I was ready to die. I knew not in what state he might be at the time; I only knew the orders to keep out his way were universal; that the Queen would highly disapprove my unauthorized meeting, and that the very action of my running away might deeply, in his present state, offend him. Nevertheless, on I ran, too terrified to stop, and in search of some short passage, for the garden is full of little labyrinths, by which I might escape. The steps still pursued me, and still the poor hoarse and altered voice rang in my ears: – more and more footsteps resounded frightfully behind me, – the attendants all running, to catch their eager master, and the voices of the two Dr Willises loudly exhorting him not to heat himself so unmercifully.

Heavens, how I ran! I do not think I should have felt the hot lava from Vesuvius – at least not the hot cinders – had I so run during its eruption. My feet were not sensible that they even touched the ground.

Soon after, I heard other voices, shriller, though less nervous, call out, 'Stop! stop! stop!'

I could by no means consent: I knew not what was purposed, but

I recollected fully my agreement with Dr John that very morning, that I should decamp if surprised, and not be named.

My own fears and repugnance, also, after a flight and disobedience like this, were doubled in the thought of not escaping; I knew not to what I might be exposed, should the malady be then high, and take the turn of resentment. Still, therefore, on I flew; and such was my speed, so almost incredible to relate or recollect, that I fairly believe no one of the whole party could have overtaken me, if these words, from one of the attendants, had not reached me: 'Dr Willis begs you to stop!'

'I cannot! I cannot!' I answered, still flying on, when he called out, 'You must, ma'am; it hurts the King to run.'

Then, indeed, I stopped – in a fear really amounting to agony. I turned round, I saw the two Doctors had got the King between them, and three attendants of Dr Willis's were hovering about. They all slackened their pace, as they saw me stand still; but such was the excess of my alarm, that I was wholly insensible to the effects of a race which, at any other time, would have required an hour's recruit.

As they approached, some little presence of mind happily came to my command: it occurred to me that, to appease the wrath of my flight, I must now show some confidence; I therefore faced them as undauntedly as I was able, only charging the nearest of the attendants to stand by my side.

When they were within a few yards of me, the King called out, 'Why did you run away?'

(2) An American visitor marvels at English permissiveness around Teddington: from Henry Wellington Wack's *In Thamesland*, 1906.

The author spent two pleasant summers in the neighbourhood of Teddington and Kingston, and wandered many times over the length and breadth of the valley and the river between Kew and Hampton Court. There are few, if any spots in the world which

Heron at Teddington

afford so much of history and life, so much of the latter's variety, such natural, unconscious display of a nation's simpler characteristics, as this tiny bit of toyland beside the Thames.

On a fresh, cool Sunday morning, as the sun looms up over the darkly verdured undulations of Richmond Hill and plashes its sheen flatly upon the quiet stream, one may sit upon its banks and watch the kaleidoscope form and reform, expand, enliven, and finally blaze with the colours of frocks and parasols, of ribboned children and loosely, sensibly attired young men and old men, all moving up stream in craft laden with hampers and tea baskets, pillows, books, mandolins, guitars, banjos, and sometimes with enough *impedimenta* to furnish a farm.

Move up with them and drop into the backwaters of Teddington about luncheon or tea time. You will see hundreds of punts wherein the occupants are laying their picnic meal, making tea, popping soda bottles, and generally proceeding daintily to their little feast under the swaying willows, amongst the swans which here abound. In an hour look again and you will find the tables cleared and neither punter nor puntee visible above the rim of the punt-pit. Everyone is lying full length in various chamber attitudes, in defiance of all so-called propriety, of every gaze, every expression of wonderment which a foreigner might venture to utter. This river, this island called England, these picnic habits, this love dalliance afloat, these lispings and kissings and woodland spooning belong to the swains of Teddington, and no foreigner, habitually living in terror of his own country's police, need waste one gasp in surprise at the sights and sounds, by day or by night, in a Teddington backwater.

(3) The high priest of garden design describes his riverside grotto at Twickenham: from Alexander Pope's letter to Edward Blount, 2 June 1725.

Let the young ladies be assured I make nothing new in my gardens without wishing to see the print of their fairy steps in every part of them. I have put the last hand to my works of this kind, in happily finishing the subterraneous way and grotto. I there found a spring of the clearest water, which falls in a perpetual rill, that echoes through the cavern day and night. From the river Thames, you see through my arch up a walk of the wilderness, to a kind of open temple, wholly composed of shells in the rustic manner; and from that distance under the temple you look down through a sloping arcade of trees, and see the sails on the river passing suddenly and vanishing as through a perspective glass. When you shut the doors of this grotto it becomes on the instant, from a luminous room, a *Camera obscura*, on the walls of which all the objects of the river, hills, woods, and boats, are forming a moving picture in their visible radiations; and when you have a mind to light it up, it affords you a very different scene. It is furnished with shells interspersed with pieces of looking-glass in angular forms; and in the ceiling is a star of the same material, at which when a lamp, of an orbicular figure of thin alabaster, is hung in the middle, a thousand pointed rays glitter, and are reflected over the place. There are connected to this grotto by a narrower passage two porches with niches and seats – one towards the river, of smooth stones, full of light, and open; the other towards the arch of trees, rough with shells, flints, and iron-ore. The bottom is paved with simple pebble, as the adjoining walk up to the wilderness to the temple is to be cockle-shells, in the natural taste, agreeing not ill with the little dripping murmur, and the aquatic idea of the whole place.

Stage 2 **Hampton to Chertsey** 8.3 miles (13.3 km)

In Stage 2 the banks of the Thames are bordered by residential housing of one sort or another for virtually all the way, though the path also passes several open spaces. The buildings vary from bungalows to apartment blocks, and include, on the far bank, the old frontages of Hampton and Sunbury. There is nearly a mile on small roads. The surface of the path is predominantly gravel or metal.

Path Upstream: see also Strip Chart
Walton Bridge to Shepperton Lock: alternative route 1.8 miles (2.9 km)
   (This unsatisfactory alternative may be avoided if the ferry just below Shepperton Lock is operating: to reach this, continue up the right bank beyond the Desborough Cut). Cross Walton Bridge to the left side of the Thames and follow the B376 ahead: left along the B375, turning left through Old Shepperton, then left again to Shepperton Lock.

Path Downstream: see also Strip Chart
Shepperton Lock to Walton Bridge: alternative route 1.8 miles (2.9 km)
   (This unsatisfactory route may be avoided if the ferry just below Shepperton Lock is operating, from which a path leads along the right bank to the Desborough Cut.) Follow the road past the lock around to its end. Turn right on to the B375 through Old Shepperton, later following the road to the right at a fork. Then right again on the B376 to cross Walton Bridge and regain the right bank.

Approach by car
At start: Hampton is in South-West London, 3 miles from the M3 exit 1; car-park at Hampton Court Palace. *At end*: Chertsey is in Surrey, 1 mile from the M3 exit 2 and the M25 exit 12; park near the bridge. *Also*: at Walton, car-park by the bridge.

Approach by other transport

Train: British Rail stations at Hampton, Walton, Weybridge and Chertsey. *Bus*: from London, Green Line to Hampton. *Boat*: summer service at Hampton Court. *Taxi*: Walton, Studio Car Hire (0932-222222); Chertsey, Station Taxis (0932-562206).

Refreshment

Pubs: Cardinal Wolsey, The Green, Hampton Court; Weir, Sunbury Lock; Swan, Manor Road, Walton; Bridge Hotel, Chertsey. *Restaurant*: Mitre Hotel, Hampton Court Bridge.

Accommodation

Hotels: Liongate Hotel, Hampton Court Road, Hampton Court TW10 6RP (01-940 7471); Ashley Park Hotel, Walton on Thames KT12 1JR (0932-220196). *Guest houses and small hotels*: Russets, Osborne Road, Walton on Thames KT12 2RL (0932-229285). *Camping*: Camping and Caravaning Club Site, Field Common Lane, Walton on Thames KT12 3QG (0932-220392); Camping Club International Site, Bridge Road, Chertsey KT16 0JX (0932-862405).

Admission

Hampton Court Palace, weekdays year round and also Sundays April to September.

Stage 2 **Hampton to Chertsey** 8.3 miles (13.3 km)

Hampton Court Bridge, opened by the Prince of Wales in 1933, was designed by Lutyens. It is concrete but, so as to blend with the palace, is faced with narrow red bricks and great quantities of Portland stone for dressings and balustrades, a formula he used later for his Runnymede Bridge. It is the fourth bridge on this site, one of which was a rococo fancy of seven white wooden arches, each humped on top, flanked with trellises and separated by pagoda-like turrets.

At *Molesey* (Mul's island), and now in Surrey, we get a close look at the lock though we cannot see the fall of the weir which was painted from the far bank by Sisley in a famous blue and white picture. This is as good a spot as any to inspect a Thames lock, its granite-edged walls and heavy wooden doors and beams, its smooth bollards and its white steps. The principle of the pound lock is beautifully simple, and it is surprising that it was only properly developed in the late fifteenth century. The whole object is to arrange for the minimum of water loss whilst raising boats. Some control was first achieved on Chinese and Dutch canals by the use of stop-log gates: but it was in Italy that the mitre gate was first used. Obviously, the size of the lock must be as small as is consonant with the type of boat and amount of traffic, which is why Thames locks are much smaller than on some Continental rivers and canals. All Thames locks below Oxford are now equipped with hydraulic mechanisms, but Dr Plot's description of them still applies (37, page 204). The Lower Thames locks were first constructed in the early nineteenth century, and before them the river was tidal to Staines.

Two eyots pass in quick succession: Ash Island, connected to Molesey Weir, and Tagg's Island. Tagg's island had its time of glory early this century. An impresario called Frederick Westcott, better known as Fred Karno, financed a leisure complex on this island, comprising a theatre, hotel and restaurant, dance-hall and casino. It was dubbed the Karsino. The architecture was ornate, the comedy shows were slapstick, and the atmosphere was raffish. All that now remains is a Swiss chalet on the far bank beyond the island.

Fred also commissioned an enormous houseboat, the *Astoria*, and moored it alongside. Among its facilities was a marble-clad bathroom and its upper deck was a dance floor. However, the *Astoria* was not the largest houseboat on the Thames. That honour went to the *Satsuma*, a leviathan built at Tagg's Boat House. The wooden *Satsuma* went in two sections, each of which could just get through a Lower Thames lock. Put together they provided a sumptuous residence whose showpiece was a large drawing-room with a grand piano and all sorts of heavy furniture and china. The *Satsuma* was attended by *Tom Tug*, named after Tom Tagg. *Tom Tug* acted as a tug or a launch, and provided a kitchen and quarters for servants and crew. Originally built for private use, *Satsuma* came to be hired for parties: despite a ban on smoking, it was destroyed by fire. Faint images of the *Astoria* and the *Satsuma* are stirred by the smaller double-decker houseboats that still moor on Tagg's Island.

Hurst Park, now partly a green space and partly a housing estate, was till recently a race track, and was the setting for one of Dickens' very best set-pieces (4, page 71), a splendid example of the use of words to galvanize the mind to visual images. Another vivid account of a scene at Hurst Park comes from the memoirs of George Sanger (5, page 74). Prizefighting, that bloody, bare-fisted boxing, was by this time illegal but had been performed here since the days when Regency dandies drove down from London in their phaetons to bet on champions such as Mendoza. The park also saw less violent sports and was one of the earliest centres for cricket.

On the far bank is *Hampton* (village on dry ground), clustered around its church, St Mary's. A few hundred metres downstream of the church is the Shakespeare Temple. This is an octagonal domed structure with a portico, built to house a statue of the bard to the orders of David Garrick when he lived at Hampton House, just behind. Garrick was a great actor who revolutionized the English stage. He had a gift for friendship and when he retired here in financial security a flow of fashionable people came to visit him. There were *fêtes champetres* and *conversaziones*, and the

The Shakespeare Temple at Hampton

Gentleman's Magazine of 1774 records that 'the Temple of Shakespeare, and the gardens, were illuminated with 6,000 lamps and a Forge of Vulcan made a splendid appearance'.

Next comes Platt's Eyot. On this little island was Thorneycroft's Hampton Launch Works. Fast diesel-engined torpedo-boats were urgently needed by the Admiralty in 1914, and Thorneycroft's built some of them here. There was jubilation when Motor Boat No 4, commanded by Lt. A. S. Agar, torpedoed and sank the cruiser *Oleg* at Kronstadt in the Baltic, for which he was awarded the Victoria Cross.

A long brown-brick wall with intervening pilasters makes for a secluded but not unpleasant stretch of towpath. Behind it are Thames Water reservoirs, and there are more on the far bank. Blackberry bushes and Dad's Army tank barriers provide variety. A charming view of old *Sunbury* (Sunna's village) precedes Sunbury Locks, for there are two, the smaller Old Lock (1886) and the larger New Lock (1925).

Walton Reach has a mile and a half of riverside dwellings. What is there to be said about these, in this most urbanized of all our 15 Stages? It would be easy to make fun of the garden gnomes, the pretentious or silly names, the ridiculous designs, the perilous floodability of these bungalows, villas and chalets. But, on reflection, Alan Herbert must be right in his assessment (6, page 76), even though not all the occupiers bother to look their best or care what passers-by may see or think.

Walton Bridge is surely the ugliest on the river, a steel affair resembling a wartime Bailey bridge, though it is soon to be replaced. It was set beside the previous bridge, whose brick viaduct is still in use. The original brick bridge, painted by Turner, was in its turn preceded by a famous wooden bridge, built in 1750 for a local landowner and so designed that every timber was arranged as a tangent to a circle, and each could be removed and replaced without disturbing any other. Canaletto, that cosmopolitan Venetian, came down to rustic Walton to paint this 'mathematical' or 'perpetual' bridge, gleaming white against a cloudy sky and with a coach and four trotting over it.

Two hundred metres upstream from Walton Bridge there was

once a ford. A line of wooden stakes sunk in the mud excited antiquarian curiosity. They were known as the Cowey, or causeway, Stakes, and, without any evidence, they were associated with the advance of the Romans led by Julius Caesar across the Thames in 54 BC to defeat the British leader Cassivellaunus. Brentford or Kingston, or even Staines, are equally possible sites, but the Cowey Stakes can at any rate stake their claim, so here I shall append Caesar's own account (7, page 76). Walton (probably meaning the settlement of the Britons, or the British serfs) can certainly claim one undisputed piece of very ancient timber: an almost complete dugout canoe, hewn out of an oak, was recently discovered in the reach below the bridge. And, as evidence of prehistoric settlement here, several grave-mounds were levelled for the construction of the bridge.

Now the Thames divides, or, more accurately, reunites after a division. The straight channel is the Desborough Cut (1935): the twister is the mainstream, which passes by *Shepperton* (shepherds' settlement) on the far bank. There follows a complicated section of water. Another eyot (D'Oyly Carte Island, once owned by the impresario of Gilbert and Sullivan) precedes a point where five streams unite in a large pool below a weir much favoured by canoeists and kayakers, testing their skills in the restricted turbulence. From the left they are the River Wey; the Wey Navigation Canal; the Thames mainstream below its weir; another stream of the Thames falling from its weir; and the Shepperton Lock Cut. The Wey rises in Sussex, cutting through the downs; hence, with poetic licence Pope could refer to 'the chalky Wey, that rolls a milky wave'. The canal was built to connect with the Arun and hence the south coast, an important commercial and strategic link before the railway age.

Above Shepperton Lock the river flows around Pharoah's Eyot after its stately sweep down from *Chertsey* (Cerot's island), past Chertsey Meads. These meadows, with their waving expanses of long grass, have mercifully been protected from gravelling, and are spoilt only by the dominating and forbidding lines of pylons striding across like giants. They figure in a local legend which would have been long forgotten had not Rose H. Thorpe written her

once-popular poem 'Curfew shall not ring tonight'. In brief, the story goes that during the Wars of the Roses one of the Neville family was captured by the Yorkists and condemned to die on Chertsey Meads as soon as the curfew bell was sounded. The execution party waited impatiently on the meadow for the bell to ring, but it didn't. Instead a messenger eventually galloped up with a royal reprieve. When they all got back to the town it was found that Blanche Herriot, a beautiful local girl, had fatally fastened herself to the clapper of the bell to prevent it ringing, all for the love of Neville. It seems a most improbable story to me, I must say. Why could not Blanche have tied sacking or padding around the bell? Why should the execution have been at curfew time, surely most unusual? Perhaps the legend grew around the simple fact that St Peter's, Chertsey (a mile off our course) continued to ring its curfew bell each evening long after the curfew had been abolished.

So we come to Chertsey Bridge and the end of this Stage. Immediately before it we have to imagine a 'solitary house: all ruinous and decayed'; for at this precise point Dickens placed a scene in *Oliver Twist*. The unfortunate Oliver has been taken by Bill Sikes to rob a house in Chertsey. They travel from Whitechapel mostly on foot, and I calculate that Oliver had to walk fourteen miles through the night. Just before Chertsey Bridge they turn down to the river bank where Sikes' confederate, Toby Crackit, awaits them: and after some blustering discussion and a nap, they proceed to the scene of the crime.

ANTHOLOGY
(4) The animated scene at Hampton race-course: from Charles Dickens's *Nicholas Nickleby*, 1839.

The little race-course at Hampton was in the full tide and height of its gaiety, the day as dazzling as day could be, the sun high in the cloudless sky and shining in its fullest splendour. Every gaudy colour that fluttered in the air from carriage seat and garish tent top,

Shepperton Weir

shone out in its gaudiest hues. Old dingy flags grew new again, faded gilding was re-burnished, stained rotten canvas looked a snowy white; the very beggars' rags were freshened up, and sentiment quite forgot its charity in its fervent admiration of poverty so picturesque.

It was one of those scenes of life and animation, caught in its very brightest and freshest moments, which can scarcely fail to please; for if the eye be tired of show and glare, or the ear be weary with a ceaseless round of noise, the one may repose, turn almost where it will, on eager, happy, and expectant faces, and the other deaden all consciousness of more annoying sounds in those of mirth and exhilaration. Even the sunburnt faces of gipsey children, half naked though they be, suggest a drop of comfort. It is a pleasant thing to see that the sun has been there; to know that the air and light are on them every day; to feel that they *are* children and lead childrens' lives; that if their pillows be damp, it is with the dews of Heaven, and not with tears; that the limbs of the girls are free, and that they are not crippled by distortions imposing an unnatural and horrible penance upon their sex; that their lives are spent from day to day at least among the waving trees, and not in the midst of dreadful engines which make young children old before they know what childhood is, and give them the exhaustion and infirmity of age, without, like age, the privilege to die. God send that old nursery tales were true, and that gipsies stole such children by the score!

The great race of the day had just been run; and the close lines of people on either side of the course suddenly breaking up and pouring into it, imparted a new liveliness to the scene, which was again all busy movement. Some hurried eagerly to catch a glimpse of the winning horse; others darted to and fro searching no less eagerly for the carriages they had left in search of better stations. Here a little knot gathered round a pea and thimble table to watch the plucking of some unhappy greenhorn; and there another proprietor with his confederates in various disguises – one man in spectacles, another with an eye-glass and a stylish hat, a third dressed as a farmer well to do in the world, with his top-coat over

Cruisers in Walton Marina

his arm and his flash notes in a large leathern pocket-book, and all with heavy-handled whips to represent most innocent country fellows who had trotted there on horseback – sought, by loud and noisy talk and pretended play, to entrap some unwary customer, while the gentlemen confederates (of more villanous aspect still, in clean linen and good clothes) betrayed their close interest in the concern by the anxious furtive glance they cast on all new comers. These would be hanging on the outskirts of a wide circle of people assembled round some itinerant juggler, opposed in his turn by a noisy band of music, or the classic game of 'Ring the Bull', while ventriloquists holding dialogue with wooden dolls, and fortune-telling women smothering the cries of real babies, divided with them, and many more, the general attention of the company. Drinking-tents were full, glasses began to clink in carriages, hampers to be unpacked, tempting provisions to be set forth, knives and forks to rattle, champagne corks to fly, eyes to brighten that were not dull before, and pickpockets to count their gains during the last heat. The attention so recently strained on one object of interest, was now divided among a hundred; and look where you would, was a motley assemblage of feasting, laughing, talking, begging, gambling, and mummery.

(5) A prize fight at Hampton race-course develops into a general affray: from George Sanger's *Seventy years a Showman*, 1910.

Presently a roar went up as two lithe figures stripped to the waist, their bodies shining like old ivory in the summer sunshine, stepped out on the green grass and faced each other. There was a pause. Then another roar, and as I sat on my perch and trembled with excitement I saw a quick flash of sinewy arms, two jumping, dodging bodies, now close together, now apart again, and knew that the big fight had begun.

How that crowd round the battling men did yell and sway, the ring of brightly dressed gipsies keeping a clear space for the combatants with their swinging 'livetts'. I yelled and shouted with the rest as the pugilists dashed at each other with their iron fists, jabbed, countered, closed, and broke away, each grimly determined not to yield to the other as long as he could stand upon his legs. A brutal sight, you might say; but, oh, the excitement of it!

I suppose some five punishing rounds had been fought when there came from the crowd about the ring a mightier roar than ever. Louder and louder rose the babel of voices, the ring with the struggling men in the centre grew smaller and smaller as the mass of forms swayed hither and thither about it. Then I saw that the gipsies, no longer in a circle, but in a compact body, were battering with their heavy 'livetts' at a knot of men who were pushing towards the place where the pugilists still battled. The sun gleamed on a row of hard hats. It was the police who had arrived to stop the fight!

They did, so far as the battle of the gipsey champions was concerned, for the ring was broken up, and the pugilists were separated in the jostling, pushing crowd. But another fight infinitely more brutal and damaging was at once in progress. The gipsies, infuriated by their interference, attacked the police, who were very few in number, in the most merciless fashion. Bash! bash! bash! went the heavy 'livetts' on the tall hats and blue-coated shoulders, as, vainly endeavouring to retaliate with their short batons, the representatives of law and order were driven, many of them streaming with blood, towards the river.

'My God, boy! There will be murder done this day!' said my father, who had climbed on the roundabout to my side, and it certainly looked like it. We saw the police with many of the frightened spectators scrambling towards the two big ferry-boats. Behind them pressed the gipsies with those terrible 'livetts', beneath which men went down like pole-axed oxen. Still forms were distinguishable here and there on the river-bank stretched out dead or insensible. It was like a battlefield for its action and its clamour, and I shall never forget the scene or the white faces of that other crowd that, deathly still, watched it with ourselves from the vantage place of the showground.

At last, just as the ferry-boats, overladen with fugitives, had sunk and thrown their freight of frightened and wounded men into the river, luckily very shallow at that point, there was a cessation of hostilities almost startling in its suddenness. As if at a signal, the attacking gipsies stopped striking at their beaten foes, and, turning round, made for their camps.

(6) Happiness among the bungalows: from A. P. Herbert's
The Thames, 1966.

From Windsor to Teddington there is a pattern too. It is a pattern of close building and living, of 'commuters', of suburbia, of 'timbered' houses, large and small, of villa and bungalow and holiday dwellings built against the floods and used in summer only, of smart public houses that serve the town as much as the country – Wraysbury, Staines, Penton Hook, Laleham, Chertsey, Shepperton, Weybridge, Walton, Sunbury, Hampton Court, Molesey, Thames Ditton, Kingston and Teddington. But the scene is not to be despised. The poets do not write about it or the painters paint it: there is little real beauty, perhaps, but there is prettiness everywhere, and, not unimportant, contentment. Even where the villas and bungalows are thickest, as you come near to London, I like to look at them, for in each one there are signs of happiness. The tiny lawns are well kept, there is colour in every garden; every one has its own pet ornaments, a cannon, an artificial stork, a little pool, a marble terrace, bright tables or umbrellas, a raft, a diving-board, even a tiny boat. Every resident, one feels, is proud of his domain and has said to himself: 'We are not alone. The river sees us. We must look our best.'

(7) The Roman army forces its passage across the Thames in 54BC: from Julius Caesar's *De Bello Gallico* (translation T. Rice Holmes).

Having ascertained the enemy's plans, Caesar led his army to the Thames, into the territories of Cassivellaunus. The river can only be forded at one spot, and there with difficulty. On reaching this place, he observed that the enemy were drawn up in great force near the opposite bank of the river. The bank was fenced by sharp stakes planted along its edge; and similar stakes were fixed under water and concealed by the river. Having learned these facts from prisoners and deserters, Caesar sent his cavalry out in front, and ordered the legions to follow them speedily; but the men advanced with such swiftness and dash, though they only had their heads above the water, that the enemy, unable to withstand the combined onset of infantry and cavalry, quitted the bank and fled.

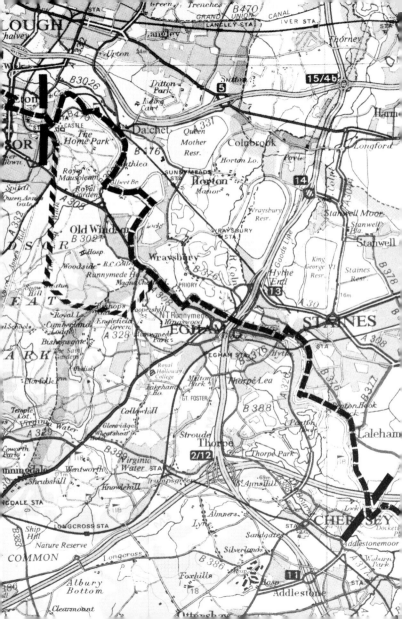

Stage 3 **Chertsey to Windsor** 11.7 miles (18.8 km)

SPECIFICS

Stage 3, like Stage 2, is almost entirely bordered by a wide range of domestic habitation. Only for less than 2 miles do open spaces line the route, at Runnymede and Windsor Home Park. The path is gravelled or metalled for much of the way, with sections on earth or grass, especially at Runnymede. Windsor and Eton together provide an imposing destination.

Path Upstream: see also Strip Chart
Albert Bridge to Victoria Bridge
   After 0.3 miles by the left bank, the path turns inland and gains the road. Left on to the B3021 into Datchet and ahead on the B470 towards Windsor. Where the Datchet housing ends, *regain the left bank on a path*. The alternative route sticks to the two roads throughout.

Path Downstream
Victoria Bridge to Albert Bridge
   After 0.4 miles by the left bank, the path turns inland and gains the B470. Enter Datchet, then ahead out of it on the B3021 towards Old Windsor. *Then right on to a path to regain the left bank*. The alternative route sticks to the two roads throughout.

Approach by car
At start: Chertsey is in Surrey, 1 mile from the M3 exit 2 and the M25 exit 12; park near the bridge. *At end*: Windsor is in Berkshire, 1 mile from the M4 exit 6; River Street car-park. *Also*: at Staines, car-parks; and at Runnymede, National Trust car-park.

Approach by other transport
Train: British Rail stations at Chertsey, Staines and Windsor. *Bus*: from London, Green Line to Staines and Windsor. *Boat*: summer services at Runnymede and Windsor. *Taxi*: Chertsey, Station Taxis (0932-562206); Staines, Runnymede Cars (0784-36162); Windsor, Castle Taxis (0753-861416).

Refreshment
Pubs: Bridge Hotel, Chertsey; Ship, The Causeway, Staines; Bells of Ouzeley, Old Windsor; Adam and Eve, Thames Street, Windsor. *Restaurants*: Barnaby's Carving Rooms, Staines; House on the Bridge, High Street, Eton; Wine Bar, High Street, Eton.

Accommodation
Hotels: Runnymede Hotel, Windsor Road, Egham TW20 0AG (0784-36171); Manor Hotel, The Green, Datchet SL3 9EA (0753-43442); Wren's Old House, Thames Street, Windsor SL4 1PX (0753-861354). *Guest houses and small hotels*: Swan Hotel, The Hythe, Staines TW18 3JB (0784-52494); White Close Guest House, 59 Montague Road, Datchet SL3 9DR (0753-41086); Clarence Hotel, Clarence Road, Windsor SL4 5AE (0753-864436). *Youth Hostel*: Edgeworth House, Mill Lane, Windsor SL4 5JE (0753-861710). *Camping*: Camping Club International Site, Bridge Road, Chertsey KT16 0JY (0932-862405).

Admission
Windsor Castle Precincts, daily; Windsor Castle State Apartments, weekdays and on summer Sundays, but closed during periods of royal residence; Windsor Royalty and Empire Exhibition, daily; Eton College, afternoons April to September.

Stage 3 **Chertsey to Windsor** 11.7 miles (18.8 km)

Stage 3 passes by more Thames bridges than any other – nine in all – and from its start at Chertsey Bridge we already see and hear the M3 motorway bridge only 600 m ahead. Chertsey Bridge was built in 1785, but badly. It was not long before the piers began to settle, the parapet to collapse, the outer walls to bulge and the stone facing to break away. Tie-bars were driven through and the centre arch reconstructed. Now, after 200 years, although the traffic over it is still heavy, its burden has been eased by the M3 bridge, which one imagines will last till the end of the world, with its 2,794 cubic m of concrete piers and abutments and its 1,361 tonnes of high-tensile steel superstructure.

In between these two bridges, which form a sort of visual lock, is Chertsey Lock and Weir, built in 1913. The weir did worse than Chertsey Bridge and actually collapsed (or 'blew') in 1955: while it was being repaired, the Thames charged straight through the lock which had both sets of gates open.

Just below the weir on the far bank a stream joins the river. It is not a tributary but a branch of the Thames emanating at Penton Hook, and is called the Abbey River because it brought water to the former Chertsey Abbey, whose site is half a mile to our left. This Benedictine monastery was in Saxon times as important as Westminster. After total destruction by the Danes in the ninth century it was recolonized under Norman rule and progressively enriched with gifts of land; it gets a mention in history and in Shakespeare because the body of the saintly Henry VI was sent by the Yorkist usurper Edward IV to be buried here – 'Come now towards Chertsey with your holy load.' But the Abbey, which had survived the Danes, was unable to survive the Reformation; and Chertsey had the indignity of being systematically dismantled, with many of its best stones floated down river to be used for Hampton Court.

Beyond the motorway bridge is an area of gravel pits and reservoirs till reaching *Laleham* (settlement by the willows). Laleham House, a neo-classical pile set among trees, is now a

religious community but was once the seat of the Earls of Lucan, a title associated with misfortune, the third earl giving the disastrous order to the Light Brigade to attack at Balaclava in 1855, and the seventh earl still missing after a murder in 1974. Just where the main road veers away there was once a ferry, and on the far bank is the former ferryman's cottage. This is also where cattle from Laleham were sent to swim over to what were water-meadows. Laleham's most famous resident was Thomas Arnold, the great headmaster of Rugby, who was appointed to that position largely on the reputation built up in his small private school here (1819–28). Thomas Arnold describes how he would walk to Staines up the river bank 'which, though it be perfectly flat, has yet a great charm from its entire loneliness, there being not a house anywhere near it'. Alas, for us the prospect is quite the reverse, for until Runnymede four and a half miles on there is scarcely any break in the housing that lines both banks. Still, along this water-street, besides trees and gardens, there are several objects of interest.

The first is Penton Hook, where the Thames doubles back on itself, though we cut the loop beside the lock, so missing the entrance to a marina and yet more bungalows, one of them once owned by the famous actress Ellen Terry. Later, as we come into *Staines* and the houses have graduated to blocks of flats – happily, no tower blocks are visible – the scene is varied by the late-Victorian church of St Peter.

After the iron railway bridge we cross the mouth of the tiny River Colne, immediately followed by Staines (stones) Bridge. Opened with great ceremony by William IV in 1832, and designed by John Rennie and his son George, this bridge represents the conclusion of an embarrassing episode in British civil engineering, for no less than four preceding bridges had had to be demolished on the site (or, to be accurate, on a site 200 m downstream) within the previous fifty years. First the old medieval wooden bridge had to go; then its wooden successor cracked; so did an iron bridge which replaced it; and a compromise bridge, part timber and part iron, failed miserably also.

Swans near the London Stone, Staines

Above Staines Bridge and the little Church Island, hidden behind houseboats and willows on the far bank, is a curiosity, the London Stone. On a grey stone plinth of 1857 is a white stone pedestal of 1781, on which sits a sandstone block carved with 'God Preserve ye Citty of London' and the very unconvincing date of 1285. This marked the upper end of the jurisdiction of the City of London on the Thames. It was the highest point where the tide could (if only occasionally) be discerned, 80 miles above its mouth at the Nore. Control of the tidal river, with all its commerce, was deemed essential to the interests of the capital city, though London's influence also extended all the way upstream. The tide provided easy transit in both directions for goods and passengers, and the tidal Thames was kept clear of obstructions such as private fishing kidels or eel-bucks; a relic from those days is the fact that fishing rights below the London Stone on the Thames are not held by riparian owners. The Lord Mayor once held an annual inspection of London's river by being rowed down it in his state barge. Before he embarked, a ceremony took place by the London Stone, which later degenerated into scenes of buffoonery (8, page 90). Just above this point we first enter Berkshire.

Finally, as objects of interest in this water-street, the M25 and A30 road bridges, separated by only 3 m, together provide a width of 80 m which we walk beneath as if in some vast building. The downstream bridge (M25) was built in 1978, entirely of concrete; the upstream one (A30) in 1961, to a design of twenty years earlier by Lutyens. It too is mostly concrete, though the main span is stiffened by steel girders, and its sides are disguised behind red brick and Portland stone. During the construction of these overwhelming structures, bearing their endless traffic of encapsulated humans, archaeologists uncovered a Bronze Age settlement site yielding pottery and metalwork; and it overlaid a far older Neolithic site. Shortly beyond the bridges comes Bell Weir Lock, and then the housing ceases as we round a bend where once stood the Benedictine nunnery of Ankerwycke.

Runnymede is a well-tended grass lawn extending for more than a mile beside the river, and owned by the National Trust. A road runs through it, and at each end are lodges and columns designed by

Lutyens in the same red-brick and stone as his nearby bridge. The whole area, besides being a pleasant place to sit or stroll in, is also a sort of open-air shrine to democracy. Although the ordinary people of the day got nothing from Magna Carta, it was a precursor of our democratic rights and as such is venerated wherever English law is practised. As to what really happened on 15 June 1215, we know no more than the bare facts given by Roger of Wendover (9, page 91). There is no evidence that the charter was sealed on the so-called Magna Carta Island (despite the fact that Runnymede means council-island meadow), nor of the disposition of the parties. So as we walk along Runnymede we may as well leave the scene to our imagination – the sulky, bearded King, the mediating bishops, and the bluff, angry barons with their threatening 'sign or resign' gestures.

The Magna Carta memorial, a small circular temple at the foot of Coopers Hills beside the meadow, was presented by the American Bar Association; and near it is a memorial to President Kennedy. At the crest of the hill is the Royal Air Force Memorial, surmounted by a golden star.

Just beyond Coopers Hill lies Windsor Great Park, and the whole area was once part of Windsor Forest, a royal hunting-ground. In his poem 'Windsor Forest', written 1704–13, Alexander Pope paints a brilliant scene, with reference to Father Thames and his tributaries. He includes three couplets on the fishermen whom we still see, silent and motionless here as elsewhere along the bank:

> In genial spring, beneath the quivering shade,
> Where cooling vapours breathe along the mead,
> The patient fisher takes his silent stand,
> Intent, his angle trembling in his hand:
> With looks unmoved, he hopes the scaly breed,
> And eyes the dancing cork, and bending reed.

Runnymede is succeeded by a further half-mile of the street paved with water, with *Old Windsor* on our side and Wraysbury (Wigric's village) on the other. Just before it, hidden to our left, is Beaumont, the Roman Catholic public school: also, prominent beside us, the

Bells of Ouzely pub, where one of the first German V2
rocket-bombs exploded in September 1944. At the far end of the
street is the village nucleus of Old Windsor, approached by way of
an enclosed path just by a towpath bridge, leading to the church, St
Peter's. In the churchyard is the tomb of Mary Robinson, a talented
beauty and actress known as 'Perdita' who was seduced by the
future George IV when he was Prince of Wales. She also had poetry
published, and became something of a legend, and the old man in
the graveyard in the 1850s regaled Samuel and Anna Hall with what
must have been a well-rehearsed routine (10, page 92). Just by the
church is the site of a Saxon royal residence: also a house once
owned by King Farouk of Egypt.

The cut past Old Windsor Lock brings us to the Albert Bridge,
from where we find our way past *Datchet*, whose name is of
uncertain origin. William Herschel lived here for three years
(1782–5) when appointed astronomer to George III following his
discovery of Uranus, and devoted his time here to observation of
the night sky, setting his telescopes out of doors in his garden.
Datchet Church (St Mary's) is Victorian, with an octagonal tower.

A street in Datchet comes to the riverside road at a point where
two cottages stand on the Windsor bank: and here was once a
bridge. Before it was taken down Datchet Bridge was a strange
sight because the Berkshire half was iron and the Buckinghamshire
half was wooden, and the dividing line went right down the middle
of the central arch. But this bastard soon gave way to twins: for it
was decided to replace Datchet Bridge, which led to a road through
Windsor Home Park, with the Albert and Victoria Bridges, whose
road avoided it. Originally (in 1851) they were identical, but then
Albert was rebuilt in 1928 and Victoria in 1963, to different designs,
though both retain their seated embrasures and painted iron
plaques.

In Windsor Home Park is *Frogmore*, which features in *The Merry
Wives of Windsor* as a place of assignment: 'Go through the fields
with me to Frogmore,' says the Host of the Garter Inn to Master
Caius, 'and I will bring thee to where Mistress Anne Page is, at a

Fisherman near Old Windsor

farm-house a-feasting, and thou shalt woo her.' In the Home Park also was Herne's Oak, traditionally believed to be where Herne the Hunter – a gamekeeper who was wounded by a stag and became insane, tied antlers to his head and ran naked through the forest – hanged himself: and here Shakespeare set the scene of Falstaff's final humiliation. An earlier humiliation for the fat knight was to be 'carried in a basket, like a barrow of butcher's offal' and thrown in the Thames at Datchet Mead.

After the Victoria Bridge comes the public part of the Home Park, in full sight of *Windsor Castle*. What we see of the Castle is partly medieval and partly an attempt by Wyatt and Wyattville to recapture the gothic magnificence of Edward III's castle. Likewise, our modern British monarchy apes the ritual of its distant Norman and Plantagenet forebears. The architecture and the monarchy are really not at all the same as they originally were, but that doesn't seem to matter as we contemplate the Round Tower and the enormous royal standard. As a quotation to bring to life the human sentiments that have stirred behind those forbidding walls, I have chosen an extract from Queen Victoria's diary which includes an account of a ride through Windsor Park with her first Prime Minister, Melbourne (11, page 94). It is also a most touching admission by a spirited and intelligent girl of eighteen of her intense admiration and love for a man of fifty-eight.

Once under the wrought-iron girders of the Black Potts Railway Bridge we enter the orbit of *Eton College* on the far bank, though the intervening lock island prevents us from seeing clearly the distant spires and antique towers that crown the watery glade – the view painted by so many, including Turner and Canaletto. Towering behind a dark-brick range are the pinnacles of the vast chapel, dedicated to the Virgin Mary by Henry VI, which for 500 years has stood in such close contrast to St George's Chapel in Windsor Castle. Eton (river settlement), the country's premier public school, has like all ancient institutions changed out of recognition, but its central buildings retain their original appearance. Between them and the river is Fellows' Eyot, from

Eton College and Luxmoore's garden

which crowds watch the traditional Procession of Boats and firework display at the school celebrations of the Fourth of June. But rather than a picture of Eton school life I have chosen two evocations of the natural scene at this spot. The first is a joyous greeting to a blustery spring by an Eton master, Henry Luxmoore, who created a beautiful garden on the riverbank here, largely with his own manual labour (12, page 94). The second is by Osbert Sitwell, who here represents a long tradition of Eton rebels, as, with lingering sentences of the style of Henry James, he records his morbid pleasure in watching a Thames flood when at school (13, page 95).

This Stage concludes along a channel of the river now occupied by Romney Lock but previously cut for the King's Engine, a pump which supplied water to the Castle, installed in 1681. The towpath used to go along the island, known as the Cobler at its upper end, which stretched almost to Windsor Bridge, and the horses then had to splash across the cut to our bank, where *Windsor* (probably meaning a landing-place with a windlass), with all its comforts and attractions, awaits us.

ANTHOLOGY
(8) Bumping the aldermen at the London Stone, Staines: from *The Illustrated London News*, 1846.

The State Barge being moored close to the edge of the meadow, a procession was formed of the Watermen, Lord Mayor, the Water Bailiff's eight Watermen in full Uniform bringing up the procession. The ceremony was commenced by walking round the Stone. Alderman Moon then ascended to its summit, and then drank 'God bless the Queen, and Prosperity to the City of London'. Three cheers were then given; the band played 'God save the Queen'; cake and wine were distributed among the Party, and small coin was thrown among the crowd. There is an old custom of bumping at the Stone the Sheriffs and Aldermen who have not been made 'Free of the Waters'; accordingly, four Watermen seized upon Sheriff Laurie, and while they were bumping the worthy Sheriff his colleague, Sheriff Chaplin, made his escape, and was followed by the Aldermen, with the exception of Alderman Hughes, who declined to answer his name when called, and had, indeed, refused to land from the Barge. Upon Alderman Moon descending from the Stone, he was instantly bumped. Those who had been so served then paid certain fees, and were declared Free Watermen of the River Thames. The Lord Mayor gave the usual direction that his name, as a record of his visit, should be painted on the Stone.

(9) Confrontation of king and barons at Runnymede, 1215: from Roger of Wendover, fourteenth century (translation J. A. Giles).

King John, when he saw that he was deserted by almost all so that out of his regal superabundance of followers he scarcely retained seven knights, was much alarmed lest the barons would attack his castles and reduce them without difficulty, as they would find no obstacle to their so doing; and he deceitfully pretended to make peace for a time with the aforesaid barons, and sent William Marshal earl of Pembroke, with other trustworthy messengers, to them, and told them that, for the sake of peace, and for the exaltation and honour of the kingdom, he would willingly grant them the laws and liberties they required; he also sent word to the barons by these same messengers, to appoint a fitting day and place to meet and carry all these matters into effect. The king's messengers then came in all haste to London, and without deceit reported to the barons all that had been deceitfully imposed on them; they in their great joy appointed the fifteenth of June for the king to meet them, at a field lying between Staines and Windsor. Accordingly, at the time and place pre-agreed on, the king and nobles came to the appointed conference, and when each party had stationed themselves apart from the other, they began a long discussion about terms of peace and the aforesaid liberties.

(10) A tear-jerker in Old Windsor churchyard: from Samuel and
Anna Hall *The Book of the Thames*, 1859.

In his youth the old man must have been conspicuous for strength
and beauty. He had withdrawn his hands from the barrow, and
wiped his furrowed brow with the remnant of a spotted
handkerchief. 'It be a goin' to rain,' he repeated, in answer to our
look of enquiry, 'though the clouds are drifting towards the castle,
and may break over there: but there's no telling at this time o' year
– they're here one minute, and gone the next. There's not much in
the churchyard to please you; only, maybe, like the rest of the
gentry, you want to see what we used to call the tomb of the Fair
Shepherdess. Lor! when that tomb was put up first, what numbers
came to see it! but there's nothing changes its object so much as
curiosity – what people think so much of to-day they don't care
about tomorrow. I've seen such loads of lords and gentlemen gazing
at that tomb – but not so many ladies. She was a play-actor once,
and they called her the Fair Perdita, which is shepherdess, you
understand, the fair shepherdess – but to see how one may go from
bad to worse! They say a king's love fell upon her like a mildew,
and, for all her beauty, withered her up; and then she died, poor
thing, – bad off enough too. And her daughter, – she has been to
see her mother's tomb often, as I know well, for I have been on the
spot, and opened the gate to her: and she'd bow and smile like a
real lady: but always – and I minded it well – always she came either
at early morning or in the gloom before night. She'd hang over the
railing, even in winter, like a wreath of snow: it always seemed as
though she loved, yet was ashamed of her; and she died just
eighteen years after her mother.'

The Magna Carta Memorial at Runnymede

(11) Happy days in Windsor Castle and Park: from Queen
Victoria's diary for 3 October 1837.

Got up at a ¼ to 9 and at ¼ p.10 I breakfasted with Mamma. Wrote
to dearest Uncle Leopold and my journal. Saw Sir H. Wheatley. At
½p.12 Lord Melbourne came to me and stayed with me till 5m. to 2.
He read to me some Despatches from Canada which are not very
satisfactory. Saw Princess Augusta. At ½p.3 I rode out with
Mamma, Lord Melbourne, Lord Palmerston, Lady Mary, Lord
Torrington, Mr Murray, Mr Brand, Col., Mrs and Miss Cavendish,
and Miss Murray, and came home at 6. We rode all round Virginia
Water, a beautiful ride, and cantered almost the whole way home.
It was the hottest summer evening that can be imagined, not a
breath of air, and hotter coming home than going out. Alas! it was
our last ride here! I am *very sorry* indeed to go! I passed such a very
pleasant time here; the pleasantest summer I EVER passed *in my life*,
and I shall never forget this first summer of my Reign. I have had
the *great* happiness of having my beloved Uncle and Aunt here with
me, I have had very pleasant people and kind friends staying with
me, and I have had *delicious* rides which have done me a world of
good. Lord Melbourne rode near me the whole time. The more I
see of him and the more I know of him, the more I like and
appreciate his fine and honest character. I have seen a great deal of
him, every day, these last 5 weeks, and I have always found him in
good humour, kind, good, and most agreeable; I have seen him in
my Closet for Political Affairs, I have ridden out with him (every
day), I have sat near him constantly at and after dinner, and talked
about all sorts of things, and have always found him a kind and most
excellent and very agreeable man. I am very fond of him.

(12) An Eton master salutes the English spring: from Henry
Luxmoore's letter to Lord Lytton, 20 May 1888.

But I throw up the window before I write and see the jolly dappled
sky with patches of blue between the sweeping showers, and the
Castle with its feet in town smoke and layer on layer of fresh green

between, here a fading apple-tree, there a wealth of tossing lilac, and sparkle of flame-coloured azalea and the like, but green that looks as if you could bury swim dive in it, billows in the elder, spray in the willows, foam on the hawthorne wet and soft and rich as heart could wish.

(13) An Eton boy welcomes the winter flood: from Osbert Sitwell's *The Scarlet Tree*, 1946.

In the winter, too, the river provided my principal, though brief, pleasure. The reader can imagine for himself with what eagerness I looked forward to the moment when the kindly Thames should overflow its banks again, thereby putting an end for a short span to the incessant playing of games. Further, water imparted to the look of the place, no less than to the life it sheltered, an agreeable sense of alteration, of change from the routine of every day. Usually, if I remember aright, the floods, which seemed then to recur regularly and without fail each year, would show their first sign of arrival about the 10th or 12th of December. At every break from school, I would run to the meadow's edge to watch with joy the encroaching sheets of water. Partly I welcomed them because of their direct usefulness to me, partly because of the suggestion that they brought of canals and of lagoons and, still more, because of the Dutch light thus created, directing at all objects that dared to impose themselves between the immense, shining, neutral spaces of sky and what had hitherto been earth a minute and scrupulous attention that omitted no detail, thus doubly focussed, of rough bark upon a tree or pitted brick in the construction of a house. Alas, these transient and shimmering meres, which brought to all things such an inhancement of their quality, seldom existed for more than four or five days. With a sorrow equal to my previous joy, with a sense, too, of life going flat again, I saw these calm and gentle waters begin to recede, until they had gone, leaving behind them only a thin layer of mud, and a lingering faint scent, enduring for a day or two, of moss and weed.

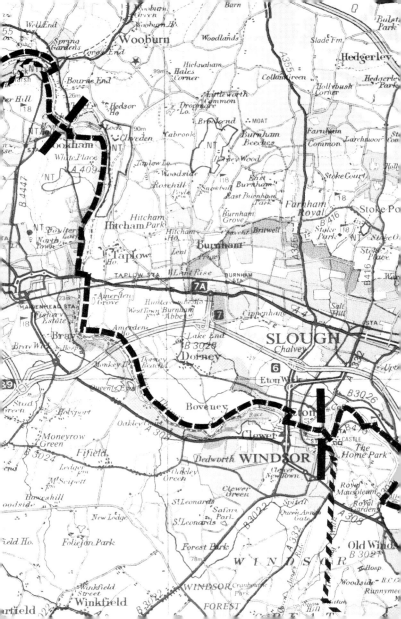

Stage 4 **Windsor to Cookham** 9.8 miles (15.9 km)

SPECIFICS

In Stage 4 we emerge from housing into countryside. Our path
passes housing for only 2 miles, and on the far bank only a further 4
miles is built up. From a starting point midway between Windsor
Castle and Eton College the route leads across flat ground till it
comes to the edge of the Chilterns and the imposing cliffs at
Cliveden. Bray, Maidenhead and Cookham all display fine
architecture. The path is easy throughout, over half of it metalled or
gravelled: 1 mile is on pavements beside roads.

Path Upstream: see also Strip Chart
Boulter's Lock to Cookham Bridge
   After 1.6 miles the towpath ends at a former ferry point. Left
along a path at the edge of a wood, then joining Mill Lane. At end,
right on to Sutton Road into Cookham, passing the entrance to the
High Street. Then, before reaching Cookham Bridge, left into
Church Approach. Cross the churchyard to regain the river.

Path Downstream: see also Strip Chart
Cookham Bridge to Boulter's Lock
   From Cookham Churchyard join Sutton Road 150 m from
Cookham Bridge. Right along Sutton Road, past the entrance to
the High Street, then left into Mill Lane. Then follow a path along a
belt of wood, regaining the river at a former ferry point. Then
follow the right bank down to Boulter's Lock.

Approach by car
At start: Windsor is in Berkshire, 1 mile from the M4 exit 6; River
Street car-park. *At end*: Cookham is in Berkshire, on the A4094
2 miles north of Maidenhead; car-park in Sutton Road. *Also*: at
Maidenhead, car-park near Boulter's Lock.

Approach by other transport
Train: British Rail stations at Windsor, Maidenhead and Cookham.

Bus: from London, Green Line to Windsor. *Boat*: summer service
at Windsor, Maidenhead and Cookham. *Taxi*: Windsor, Castle
Taxis (0753-861416); Maidenhead, AAA Taxis (0628-24446).

Refreshment
Pubs: Adam and Eve, Thames Street, Windsor; Pineapple,
Dorney; Riviera Hotel, Maidenhead Bridge; Bel and the Dragon,
High Street, Cookham. *Restaurants*: House on the Bridge, Eton
High Street; Wine Bar, Eton High Street; Franco's, Ray Mead
Road, Maidenhead; King's Arms, High Street, Cookham.

Accommodation
Hotels: Wren's Old House, Thames Street, Windsor SL4 1PX
(0753-861354); Monkey Island Hotel, Maidenhead SL6 2EE
(0628-23400); Boulter's Lock Inn, Maidenhead SL6 8PE
(0628-21291). *Guest houses and small hotels*: Clarence Hotel,
Clarence Road, Windsor SL4 5AE (0753-864436); Rookery Nook,
73 Ray Mill Road West, Maidenhead SL6 8SN (0628-33348). *Youth
Hostel*: Edgeworth House, Mill Lane, Windsor SL4 5JE
(0753-861710). *Camping*: Willows Riverside Park, Maidenhead
Road, Windsor SL4 5TR (0753-861785); Amerden Caravan and
Camping Site, Dorney Reach, Maidenhead SL6 0EE (0628-27461).

Admission
Windsor Castle Precincts, daily; Windsor Castle State Apartments,
weekdays and on summer Sundays, but closed during periods of
royal residence; Windsor Royalty and Empire Exhibition, daily;
Eton College, afternoons April to September; Dorney Court, June
to September, Sunday to Tuesday afternoons, and May to October,
Sunday afternoons; Stanley Spencer Gallery, Cookham, Easter to
October daily, and November to Easter Saturdays and Sundays.

Stage 4 **Windsor to Cookham** 9.8 miles (15.9 km)

Two civic victories have taken place on Eton Bridge, a fine iron structure of 1824. The first, nearly a century ago, was when Joseph Taylor of Eton contested the continuing right of Windsor Corporation to charge tolls – in a case which went to the House of Lords before he eventually won it. The second, ten years ago, was when motor traffic was banned. So it now provides a perfect pedestrian platform from which to view the hoary Thames wandering along his silver-winding way, and the enticing entrances to the ancient streets of *Windsor* and *Eton* with all their antique shops and restaurants. The grandest of these is the Old House, right beside us on the Windsor bank, associated with Christopher Wren: the oldest is the Cockpit in Eton High Street, formerly cottages and dating from 1420, or earlier.

Eton College lies less than half a mile off our course, and its influence is closely felt along this Stage because of its long tradition of rowing. Rowing, like walking, only became a leisure activity when it ceased to be a necessity. As with many other sports it originated in a disorganized way; in fact, until the 1840s the College put the river out of bounds to the boys. Before rowing was eventually recognized as an official sport, a curious compromise prevailed in a practice known as 'shirking'. If a master saw a boy heading for the river he took no action provided that the boy raised his arm in front of his face in a ritualistic gesture which indicated that he admitted he shouldn't be there. The boy was theoretically invisible to the master: nothing was said, honour was saved. When they reached the river the boys rowed about in clinker boats with fixed seats, boats which became narrower from the early 1860s when outriggers were introduced. But Eton was slow in adopting the radical American invention of sliding seats, which were only permitted from 1873 and then only with a six-inch slide. Finally clinkers gave way to skin constructions, bringing in the racing boat as we know it today.

Passing behind the college boathouses we emerge on to the Brocas and see the classic view of Windsor Castle. Rather like false

teeth, the castle walls are perfected imitations built on ancient foundations, and the prominent mansard roof of the Curfew Tower is actually less old than the railway bridge, a wrought-iron bowstring arch structure of 1849, designed by I. K. Brunel. Shortly after it comes the Queen Elizabeth road-bypass bridge (1966). This is the stretch where the Eton house fours used to position for their bumping races, the coxes holding on to a fixed bung until the start. On one occasion, after the sounding of the five-minute gun and then the minute gun, the treble voice of the small cox of Hope-Jones's boat was heard to cry, 'The bung has got stuck to the rudder!' Without hesitation the housemaster, William Hope-Jones, a well-known Eton eccentric, stripped off his formal clothes (these were the days of black coats and waistcoats, striped trousers, braces, stick-up collars and white ties) and swam out to release the rudder with only seconds to spare, to general applause. Another dramatic event, this time by two ten-oared clinker boats in the early days of rowing, is recorded on page 110 (14): the Lower and Upper Hopes referred to in that piece are the two sharp river bends just here.

On the far bank is Windsor race-course, technically an island with the small Clewer Mill Stream flowing beyond it: once a horse missed the sharp race-course bend by Upper Hope and plunged into the river. On our bank, we now enter Buckinghamshire for the first time.

Boveney Lock has rollers beside it for small boats; and soon after passing it comes the remote chapel of St Mary Magdalen, partly thirteenth-century. After the new Eton College boathouse (built upstream to avoid the crowded stretch around Windsor) the river takes a sharp turn opposite the site of Surley Hall. In the past, sumptuous entertainment was provided here for the clinker eights on the evening of the Fourth of June, after which they splashed downstream as best they could to the curious refrain of their famous boating song – 'We'll all swing together, with our bodies between our knees'.

Our path continues beside fields and a chestnut grove, but the

Windsor Castle

further bank bears a caravan site and marina, and then Oakley Court, surely the most fantastic of all Thames-side houses and now a hotel. Its tower and long mullioned windows, gloomy and dramatic in appearance, are framed by a fine collection of evergreens – Wellingtonias, cedars, yews, monkey-puzzles and hollies – but somehow one feels it would be more at home perched on a crag above the Rhine. The little island that soon follows is Queen's Eyot, owned by Eton College.

A hundred metres upstream from Queen's Eyot and just after our final view of Windsor Castle, a footpath to the right leads for half a mile to *Dorney* (bumble-bee island), a secluded haven beside the rush of the M4 and below the roar of the Heathrow flightpath. St James's church is rich in furnishings, and Dorney Court is the ancestral house of the Palmer family. The famous gardener, John Rose, supervised horticulture here; since he was the first to succeed in growing the pineapple in England, the pineapple motif is much in evidence and the pub is called the Pineapple. However, it must surely have been sheer coincidence that Jerome K. Jerome set his famous account of the battle with the tin of pineapple on the riverbank just here, 'a little below Monkey Island' (15, page 110).

Monkey Island gets its name from a series of charming frescoes in a house on it, built for the third Duke of Marlborough. They depict exotic scenes with monkeys dressed in the height of fashion as ladies and gentlemen of the day, indulging in sporting pastimes. An ornamental temple also on the island may have been designed by William Kent.

The M4 motorway bridge, with its vast, welded, high-tension steel-plate girders and hollow-section cross frames, was built in 1961, and also provides pedestrian crossings. The short stretch of ground between the bridge and Bray Lock is called the Amerden Bank, and was the subject of one of the most notorious obstructions to the early towpath by an obstinate landowner: at one period men and horses had to be ferried past it on barges.

The old centre of *Bray* (brow of a hill) is dominated by St Michael's church, externally mostly fifteenth-century and with a fine

Exotic trees at Oakley Court

tower. Bray is famous for the story of its vicar (16, page 112): a later version applied it to later times, in a popular ballad called 'The Trimming Parson' which started 'In good King Charles's golden reign'. But what matter, for the story is eternal and applies to place-holders everywhere.

The turn of the river above Bray was the scene, in 1891, of one of the most elaborate Venetian fêtes ever held on the Thames, with several firework set-pieces including a representation of the Battle of Trafalgar. The sequence of riverside villas on the further bank provides a bewildering range of architectural style, and, like Oakley Court, several seem palpably in exile. For instance, the one with the wooden shutters and surrounding first-floor verandah is shivering and pining for Jamaica, and that with the round turret and pepperpot roof is yearning for the Loire. But at the end of this stretch there is a structure that is so absolutely right for its setting and remarkable for its design that no one has faulted it despite all the changes in taste since it was built in 1838 – Brunel's Maidenhead railway bridge.

This bridge is entirely of brick and has the widest span yet achieved in pure brick construction, as well as the shallowest arch (39 m span and 7.4 m rise), and it leaps the river in two bounds. The trains glide over it at 125 mph: but even in its earliest days the broad-gauged Great Western Railway was noted for speed, and when Turner used this bridge as the setting for his painting *Rain, Steam and Speed*, trains were already doing 60 m.p.h. Today they have doubled that speed, and the bridge has also been doubled in width upstream to provide four tracks. A good shout while standing under it will give an exciting resonance.

The island on which rests the central pier of the railway bridge disguises the site of the former Guards Boat Club, which in Edwardian times was the most exclusive of all the social establishments on the river. The officers wore white flannels and dark-blue boating jackets with shining buttons, but occasionally shed their impeccable clothes as when they organized mop-fights from punts, or held amateur regattas with a military band on the

Maidenhead bridges

lawn playing a few bars of the regimental march of the winner of each race.

Just upstream is another beautiful bridge: Maidenhead Bridge. Designed by Robert Taylor and completed in 1777, it is made of Portland stone. Actually *Maidenhead*, although it means the maiden's landing-place, has its centre a mile away from the river, and so is not truly a riverside town.

Skindles Hotel, just beside Maidenhead Bridge, was, like the Guards Boat Club, a haunt of high society, and apt to appear in divorce proceedings as a place of assignation. Its very name had a raffish sound about it. Skindle had been a local lad with a good eye for business and the potentialities for fleecing Londoners here on pleasure bent; his patrons, as they tucked into whitebait, Aylesbury duckling, and strawberries and cream, washed down with dry champagne, could with feelings of superiority survey the lesser mortals on the river. But when they themselves got into their punts or rowing-boats they had to contend on equal terms, and acrimonious exchanges took place, especially when they entered the crowded Boulter's Lock.

Boulter's became the best-known lock on the river, immortalized in a painting by E. J. Gregory called *Boulter's Lock – Sunday Afternoon*, showing the tightly-packed assortment of boats eagerly emerging. The presiding genius at Boulter's was W. H. Turner the lock-keeper, an authoritative figure who was accepted, in that class-bound society, as one of 'nature's gentlemen'. He became a local legend, working for over 100 hours for weeks in succession, sometimes not even having time to go to bed, and always accompanied by his dog, Juggins.

Turner, in his cottage and well-kept garden on Boulter's Lock Island, had his upper-class counterpart in the grand personage of William Grenfell, Lord Desborough, who resided at Taplow Court high above the river bank. Grenfell was a formidable all-round athlete who had twice swum the Niagara rapids, thrice climbed the Matterhorn, sculled across the Channel, and became Amateur Punting Champion of the Upper Thames. He married a delightful wife who became one of the leading Liberal hostesses, and society flocked to their house: Kitchener once came down with their son

Julian to fish in the Thames before breakfast. With all these qualifications and advantages it was appropriate that Grenfell should be made Chairman of the Thames Conservancy, a position he took very conscientiously, overseeing many improvements in the river's navigation, including several new locks.

A steep chalk scarp now drops to the water. On it are hanging woods of beech and pine, and below it are little islands of willow and alder. This is our first encounter with the Chilterns, which here prevent the Thames from flowing east and force it south. *Taplow*, at the southern end of the hill, means Taeppa's burial mound; and though most such mounds were raided long ago, this one yielded one of the best Anglo-Saxon collections in England, now in the British Museum. At the northern end is Cliveden (valley by the cliffs) House, an enormous Italianate mansion by Charles Barry. It has twice been linked to scandal. The first occasion was when its owner George Villiers, Duke of Buckingham, the 'lord of useless thousands', killed his lover's husband, the Duke of Shrewsbury, in a duel, while the girl in question watched, disguised as a page. The second scandal occurred after the opening scenes of the Profumo affair took place here, as described in the plain-English report by Lord Denning (17, page 112): the ornate cottage on the far bank is where Stephen Ward held his parties. The Astors, who owned Cliveden for most of this century, were strong opponents of confrontation with Nazi Germany, and they and their supporters, known as the Cliveden Set, gathered here for weekends with people like Joachim Ribbentrop, the German Ambassador, and Geoffrey Dawson, editor of *The Times*.

We leave the river at My Lady Ferry, where the towpath changes banks: this ferry was the last to be abandoned by the Thames Conservancy, in the 1950s. Above My Lady Ferry is a complicated section of the river, where it divides into four streams, the nearest to us being the Lulle Brook, once a millstream: the house we pass is on the site of the mill.

In this way we enter *Cookham* (dry ground by a hill), a village which has retained several eighteenth-century buildings, of which Tarry Stone House is the finest. This is named after a sarsen, or vagrant, stone, placed here in a prominent position. Cookham

formed part of the dowry of the queens of England from Edward I's reign to Henry VIII's. Holy Trinity church has Norman and Early English architecture, and the tower dates from 1500. On the site of the Lady Chapel there once lived an anchoress, or female hermit. Cookham is also renowned for its local artist, Stanley Spencer (1891–1959), several of whose works are in a gallery in the High Street. Perhaps the most memorable is the unfinished *Christ preaching at Cookham Regatta*, but there are many other easily recognizable local scenes.

The Stage ends back by the river, close to Turk's Boatyard. Besides running its normal business of boat hire it is from here that John Turk supervises the control of the Middle Thames's population of swans, in his capacity as Royal Swan Keeper. These beautiful birds have enjoyed a special form of royal protection – originally for the royal kitchens – ever since they were introduced into England in the Middle Ages, supposedly from Cyprus at the time of the Crusades. They are the grandest animals of any sort we are likely to see on the Thames Path, and in the past, when legend was so much stronger than mere fact, were symbols of romance, as in the stories of Lohengrin, Leda, or Swan Lake. These are mute swans (*cygnus olor*) which cannot honk, though they can hiss, and there are several hundred of them on the river. They are under some threat from lead fishing-weights (when swallowed, these affect their muscular system and cause a lingering death) and from excessive river traffic (disturbing their habitat). The young cygnets have their beaks marked in an annual census called Swan Upping, conducted each July between Sunbury and Pangbourne by the Royal Swan Keeper together with the Swan Keepers of the two London livery companies, the Dyers and the Vintners.

Cliveden reach

ANTHOLOGY

(14) Smashing the rudder to win a race in 1827: from an account in *The Era*, 1856.

Kean's crew led in advance from the starting post to Lower Hope, as it was expected they would do. The night before the race a meeting of Taunton's crew was held in his room at Horsford's, where it was arranged that instead of following the usual plan of rounding the Lower Hope and clinging to the right bank between the two Hopes, the steerer of the Monarch, Robert Farquharson, was to cross straight over to the opposite side, and the crew were directed to pull (as best they could) through the enormous mass of weeds there collected with a stiff oar and a long stroke, without any attempt at feathering. When Kean's ten reached the Lower Hope they were about four boat's lengths in advance of the Monarch, which came up with her rival just as she was rounding the point. Here Farquharson struck the stern of Kean's boat, which materially assisted her in turning this point. Between the Lower and Upper Hope – a space perhaps of about 500 yards – the race was nearly equal, the boats being on opposite sides of the river, and Kean slightly in advance. In crossing from the Upper Hope to the side on which the Monarch's crew were pulling a collision took place, Kean's boat being on the outside, the Monarch within an oar's length of the bank. Taunton immediately directed No.9 on the bow side to smash the yoke of his opponent's rudder with the handle of the oar. This was done in a trice and so perfectly that little Paul (the steerer) was relieved of all further duty and responsibility. In the delirium of delight the Monarch's steerer rose from his seat and waved his hat in token of triumph. This, being against the rules, lost the race. All kinds of fouling were allowed, but neither rower nor steerer was permitted to rise from his seat.

(15) The battle with the tin of pineapple, near Monkey Island: from Jerome K. Jerome's *Three Men in a Boat*, 1889.

We are very fond of pineapple, all three of us. We looked at the picture on the tin; we thought of the juice. We smiled at one another, and Harris got a spoon ready.

Then we looked for the knife to open the tin with. We turned out everything in the hamper. We turned out the bags. We pulled up the boards at the bottom of the boat. We took everything out on to the bank and shook it. There was no tin-opener to be found.

Then Harris tried to open the tin with a pocket-knife, and broke the knife and cut himself badly; and George tried a pair of scissors, and the scissors flew up, and nearly put his eye out. While they were dressing their wounds, I tried to make a hole in the thing with the spiky end of the hitcher, and the hitcher slipped and jerked me out between the boat and the bank into two feet of muddy water, and the tin rolled over, uninjured, and broke a teacup.

Then we all got mad. We took that tin out on the bank, and Harris went up into the field and got a big sharp stone, and I went back into the boat and brought out the mast, and George held the tin and Harris held the sharp end of his stone against the top of it, and I took the mast and poised it high up in the air, and gathered all my strength and brought it down.

It was George's straw hat that saved his life that day. He keeps that hat now (what is left of it), and, of a winter's evening, when the pipes are lit and the boys are telling stretches about the dangers they have passed through, George brings it down and shows it round, and the stirring tale is told anew, with fresh exaggerations every time.

Harris got off with merely a flesh wound.

After that, I took the tin off myself, and hammered at it with the mast till I was worn out and sick at heart, whereupon Harris took it in hand.

We beat it out flat; we beat it square; we battered it into every form known to geometry – but we could not make a hole in it. Then George went at it, and knocked it into a shape, so strange, so weird, so unearthly in its wild hideousness, that he got frightened and threw away the mast. Then we all three sat around it on the grass and looked at it.

There was one great dent across the top that had the appearance of a mocking grin, and it drove us furious, so that Harris rushed at the thing, and caught it up, and flung it far into the middle of the river, and as it sank we hurled our curses at it, and we got into the boat and rowed away from the spot, and never paused till we reached Maidenhead.

(16) The Vicar of Bray: from Thomas Fuller's *History of the Worthies of England*, 1662.

The Vicar of Bray will be Vicar of Bray still. Bray, a village well known in this country, so called from the Bibroces, a kind of ancient Britons inhabiting thereabouts. The vivacious vicar hereof living under King Henry the Eighth, King Edward the Sixth, Queen Mary, and Queen Elizabeth, was first a papist, then a protestant, then a papist, then a protestant again. He had seen some martyrs burnt (two miles off) at Windsor, and found this fire too hot for his tender temper. This vicar being taxed by one for being a turncoat and an unconsistent changeling, 'Not so,' said he, 'for I always kept my principle, which is this, to live and die the vicar of Bray.' Such many nowadays, who though they cannot turn the wind, will turn their mills, and set them so, that wheresoever it bloweth their grist shall certainly be grinded.

(17) A weekend party at Cliveden: from Lord Denning's Report, 1963.

The weekend of Saturday, 8th July, 1961, to Sunday, 9th July, 1961, is of critical importance. Lord and Lady Astor had a large party of distinguished visitors to their great house at Cliveden. They included Mr Profumo, the Secretary of State for War, and his wife, Mrs Profumo, who stayed the weekend. Other visitors came to meals but did not stay the night. Stephen Ward entertained some young girls at his cottage. One of these was Christine Keeler, who was then living with him. Captain Ivanov came down on the Sunday. There is a fine swimming pool in the grounds at Cliveden near the main house, and Lord Astor, on occasions, allowed

Stephen Ward to use it with his friends so long as it did not clash with his own use of it.

On the Saturday, after nightfall, Stephen Ward and some of the girls were bathing in the swimming pool when one of them, Christine Keeler, whilst she was in the water, took off her bathing costume, threw it on the bank, and bathed naked. Soon afterwards Lord Astor and a party of his visitors walked down after dinner to the swimming pool to watch the bathing. Lord Astor and Mr Profumo walked ahead of Lady Astor, Mrs Profumo and the others. Christine Keeler rushed to get her swimming costume. Stephen Ward threw it on one side so that she could not get it at once and Christine seized a towel to hide herself. Lord Astor and Mr Profumo arrived at this moment, and it was all treated as a piece of fun – it was over in a few minutes, for the ladies saw nothing indecent at all. Stephen Ward and the girls afterwards got dressed and went up to the house and joined the party for a little while.

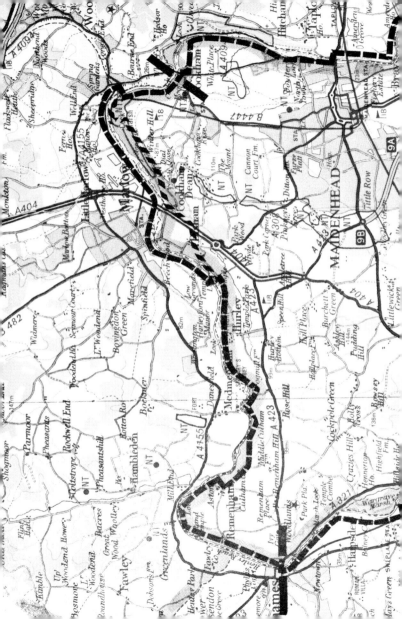

Stage 5 **Cookham to Henley** 12.3 miles (19.7 km)

Stage 5 is more rural than Stage 4: only about a mile is past housing, with another 2 miles built up on the farther bank. It passes directly by two charming towns, Marlow and Henley, as well as the village of Hurley which, though attractive in itself, is surrounded by an accumulation of cars, caravans, boat moorings and marinas. The hills add character to the scene. The route is easy throughout, mostly on earth and grass, but with long sections of gravel or metal.

Path Upstream: see also Strip Chart
Bourne End railway bridge to Marlow A404 bridge: alternative route 2.8 miles (4.5 km)
   Continue up the right bank for 0.6 miles, then follow the path behind houses and then left to the base of Winter Hill. Here turn right on a track uphill. At end, right along a road, ignoring crossing lanes, to the vantage point of Winter Hill. Beyond, turn right in front of Dial Place, then left on to a narrow path into beechwoods. At a fork bear right. At a road (Quarry Wood Road) turn downhill by a steep path, rejoining the road lower down at a corner. (Here the Bisham Loop diverts.) Right along the road for 300m: at the A404 embankment ascend the steps. Turn right to cross the river; then down steps to the right to the left bank.

Marlow A404 Bridge to Marlow Bridge
   After 0.4 miles, where the towpath ends at housing, turn from the river, then left along a road, passing Marlow Lock and a river view. Then turn left from the road into an enclosed path to St Peter's Street, then into another to reach Marlow Bridge.

Marlow Bridge to proposed footbridge: alternative route 2.3 miles (3.7 km)
   Cross Marlow Bridge to the right side of the Thames and follow the road to Bisham for 0.8 miles. Just after the entrance to the National Sports Centre and by a war memorial (where the Bisham Loop joins), take the small road to Temple. At Temple do not go

on to the island but continue ahead on a No Through Road and then a footpath, leading through woods. At the start of a surfaced farm road, turn right on to a footpath to the river at a point just upstream of the proposed footbridge, 0.5 miles downstream of Hurley Lock.

Hurley Lock to Hambleden Lock
   After 2.2 miles (0.6 miles after passing Medmenham on the far bank) the path leaves the river half left across a field. Turn along the right-hand track to where it bends left uphill after passing farm buildings. Here leave the track for a path across a field which leads through a garden between Culham Court and the river: then ahead across a further field, passing to the left of Holme Farm and down to a road. Turn right to the houses at Aston, then ahead down the lane to the river, and so up the right bank to Hambleden Lock.

Path Downstream: see also Strip Chart
Hambleden Lock to Hurley Lock
   After 0.5 miles turn right up the lane to Aston. 150 m on, left up a driveway and ahead on a path across a field. Pass through a garden between Culham Court and the river; then ahead across a further field to the upper corner of farm buildings. Here join a farm track downhill, to where a path leads across a field to the left to regain the river, and so along the bank to Hurley.

Proposed footbridge to Marlow Bridge: alternative route 2.3 miles (3.7 km)
   The towpath ends 0.5 miles downstream of Hurley Lock at the proposed footbridge. Just upstream of this, find a footpath leading from the river. 200 m on, turn left on to a path through woods to Temple. Continue ahead by the small road to Bisham, joining a larger road by a war memorial (where the Bisham Loop diverts). This leads through Bisham and to Marlow Bridge.

Marlow Bridge to Marlow A404 Bridge
   Take the enclosed footpath behind the church to St Peter's Street; then another to a road, where turn right, past the entrance to Marlow Lock, and on to where the housing ends: then right into a

field to regain the bank, which follow to the A404 bridge.

Marlow A404 Bridge to Bourne End railway bridge: alternative
route 2.8 miles (4.5 km)
   Ascend the A404 embankment by steps on the downstream side,
and cross the river. Then descend by steps to the left on to Quarry
Wood Road, and follow this for 300m, to where it turns sharply.
(Here the Bisham Loop joins.) Take a path steeply uphill from the
outside of the road bend. Where this meets the road again, go left
on the path, which contours through the wood and emerges at a
road. Left along this road, past the vantage point of Winter Hill. 0.6
miles on, ignoring crossing lanes, turn obliquely left down an
unpaved road to the base of the scarp. Left on to a path, which later
turns right and passes houses to regain the river, and so along the
bank to the railway bridge.

Approach by car
At start: Cookham is in Berkshire, on the A4094 2 miles north of
Maidenhead; car-park in Sutton Road. *At end*: Henley is in
Oxfordshire, 8 miles north of Reading, at the junction of the A423
and the A4155; car-park off Market Place. *Also*: at Marlow,
car-park off the High Street; and at Hurley (off the A423 between
Marlow and Henley), park by the church.

Approach by other transport
Train: British Rail stations at Cookham, Bourne End, Marlow and
Henley. *Bus*: from London, Oxford City Link to Henley. *Boat*:
summer service at Cookham, Marlow and Henley. *Taxi*: Marlow,
Marlow Taxis (0628-43955); Henley, AK Cabs (0491-572422).

Refreshment
Pubs: Bel and the Dragon, High Street, Cookham; Two Brewers,
St Peter's Street, Marlow; Flowerpot, Aston; Little White Hart,
Riverside, Henley. *Restaurants*: King's Arms, High Street,
Cookham; Complete Angler, Marlow; Angel on the Bridge,
Henley.

Accommodation
Hotels: South Lawn, Bisham, Marlow SL7 1RP (0628-43348); Olde Bell, Hurley SL6 5LX (0628-825881); Red Lion Hotel, Thames-side, Henley RG9 2AR (0491-572161). *Guest houses and small hotels*: Mrs S. Bendall, 5 Pound Lane, Marlow SL7 2AE (0628-42649); New Lodge, Henley Park, Henley RG9 6HU (0491-576350). *Camping*: Harleyford Estate, Henley Road, Marlow SL7 2DX (0628-471361); Hurley Caravan and Camping Site, Hurley SL6 5NE (0628-823501); Swiss Farm International Camping, Marlow Road, Henley RG1 2HY (0491-573419).

Admission
Stanley Spencer Gallery, Cookham, Easter to October daily, and November to Easter Saturdays and Sundays.

Stage 5 **Cookham to Henley** 12.3 miles (19.7 km)

Cookham Bridge is a wrought-iron structure of 1867 which has been preserved for light traffic. The stretch of water above it has been the setting for many regattas and also for the first-ever river concert. It took place in 1887, and Patricia Burstall has described the scene (18, page 126). On the adjacent bank Cookham Common and then Cock Marsh provide a fine sweep of natural meadow.

Bourne End railway bridge is an iron and steel structure of 1895 with three river spans. This branch line once linked Maidenhead and Wycombe: the Bourne End-Wycombe section is now closed but the Marlow spur remains open. On the stretch between the railway bridge and the new road bridge 2½ miles upstream, the left bank has the Marlow rail spur as a close companion, though the trains only run once each hour, and not on Sundays. Box hedges divide the riverside dwellings from their waterfronts, on either side of a yacht club and a marina. The towpath switched from right bank to left at the former Spade Oak Ferry, where the housing ends.

Winter Hill, which runs along the right bank of this stretch, has a north-facing scarp slope which accounts for its name. Where we first see it, it is grassy and bushy, and a little away from the river: the flat ground in between is called Cock Marsh, and on it are four barrows, or burial mounds, which have been identified as Bronze Age. Winter Hill then becomes wooded, though housing spoils the effect of the great beeches on the steep incline. On the far side of the hill is Cookham Dean, where Kenneth Grahame, an official at the Bank of England, once lived. To amuse his small son, Mouse, he wrote a fantasy called *The Wind in the Willows*, and its scenes must be imagined along this reach of the Thames, with Quarry Wood on Winter Hill featuring as the Wild Wood (19, page 129). Rat (a water-rat or, more correctly a water-vole) personifies the river folk who were then crowding into Cookham and Marlow and building their unfortunate bungalows. Mole, whose timidity is linked to that of young Mouse, represents the vague apprehension of the middle-class inhabitants of Cookham Dean at the conurbations of Maidenhead and Slough, whose smoke could be detected from the slopes of Winter Hill. Neither of these two would have cared much for walking: for any inclinations towards pedestrianism we would have to turn to the determined figure of Badger, for the fourth archetypal character, Toad, is completely car-crazed.

After the soulless bypass bridge, with its pre-stressed concrete beams and its post-tensioned steel cables, we arrive at *Marlow* (a name whose meaning is unclear), passing the new housing by the former mill to where the weir cuts sideways across the stream in sight of the suspension bridge and church spire. At the far end of the High Street is West Street, where Shelley once lived, writing 'The Revolt of Islam' while his wife Mary was writing *Frankenstein*. Like most of the poets of the Romantic Movement he was an energetic walker, sometimes walking the 32 miles from here to London in a day. All Saints church is not very distinguished, but the tower and spire provide a fine vertical against the horizontal river. The bridge, by contrast, is most distinguished. Built at about the same time as the body of the church, in the 1830s, it was designed by William Tierney Clark, whose greatest monument is the suspension bridge across the Danube between Buda and Pest (destroyed in 1945 but since rebuilt). Marlow Bridge is a scaled-down model of his former bridge at Hammersmith. The stone towers are formed as classical archways, and the white suspension chains are slender and elegant, though actually they are now of steel, replacing the original iron, for the bridge was reconstructed in 1965. It is our only suspension bridge and, as such, the only one that is better seen lengthways than sideways, so a stroll on to it is recommended. From the centre, looking upstream, we should imagine ourselves one warm summer evening in 1884 when Charles Footit, proprietor of the Compleat Angler, laid on the first Venetian fête seen on the Thames. A procession of about fifty boats, illuminated by Chinese lanterns, bucket lamps and fairy lights, passed slowly under the bridge. In later years the displays became more elaborate and included such exciting features as a fire-spitting dragon, a sea serpent, an iceberg, a polar bear and a naval fighting ship.

For most of the way up to Temple we are in sight of two buildings

on the far bank, Bisham church and then Bisham Abbey. The
Abbey at *Bisham* (Bissel's settlement) has had a curious history.
Originating as a preceptory of the order of the Templars, it
graduated to a priory of the Augustinians and then an abbey of the
Benedictines. Then it became a country house, originally for Anne
of Cleves, the divorced wife of Henry VIII, and then for the families
of Hoby and Vansittart. Now it houses the Central Council of
Physical Recreation, and is surrounded by a sports centre with
every conceivable facility. So its function has shifted from one
extreme to the other, though its continuity remains in some arches
and stone walls. The future Queen Elizabeth I when a girl was sent
here for three years to be guarded by the Hobys, whose tombs are
in the church (All Saints): its tower is twelfth century.

Just before *Temple* a plaque set in a large stone reminds us that
Marlow, too, has its regatta: here also there occurred a major river
accident when the steamer *Empress of India* crashed into another
boat, the *Bona Fide*. The Templars' water-mill continued to grind
corn, until it was used for a brass foundry and then a paper mill.
Now it has been cleverly developed for housing, the complex of
dark brick walls and glass windows giving the suggestion of a
huddled village such as one might find where rock formations
restrict the use of space.

For a mile and a half above Temple the Thames is over-run by
marinas and extensive boat-moorings, and our bank is given over to
caravan sites and car-access points. Certainly, these have been
tidied and controlled to an extent, but we can readily appreciate the
horror felt by our fellow-walker Martin Briggs when he came by
nearly forty years ago (20, page 132).

Set amid this is the seclusion of Hurley Lock and the tree-shaded
islands beside it, mercifully protected from development. Hurley
Lock is thought to be the 'Plashwater Weir-Mill Lock' in Dickens's
Our Mutual Friend, scene of a fight between two angry men who,
grappling together in a death struggle, both fall into the lock and are
drowned. Immediately above Hurley Lock is the last surviving weir
winch, by which boats were pulled up through the flash locks: it
must accordingly date from before 1773, when the first pound lock
was built here.

Where we recross from the island to the right bank, a narrow path leads into *Hurley* (corner glade). The partly Norman church of St Mary is in fact the chapel of another monastery, the Benedictine Hurley Priory, and the house beside it was the refectory range: there is also a dovecote and a barn. Of the Tudor house owned by Lord Lovelace, who here plotted against James II (21, page 132), nothing remains.

On the further bank are three other large houses. Harleyford Manor is just below Hurley Lock, a red-brick mansion designed by Robert Taylor. Next comes Danesfield, built at the turn of the century, very prominent on its bluff and now part of an RAF station. Then, after the houses at Frogmill, we see Medmenham, yet another former religious house. Of the old Cistercian abbey nothing remains, and what appear to be ruins are really decorative devices. It is famous for its association with the notorious Sir Francis Dashwood, the leading spirit in a group of high-living rakes, some of whom held important public positions. His house was at West Wycombe, ten miles off, but he took a lease of Medmenham mainly for the purpose of turning it into a high-class brothel. This would have been unexceptional had not he and his friends conceived the fancy of dressing up as monks and calling themselves the Franciscans of Medmenham. Their enemies spread rumours of unimaginable orgies, sacrilegious and obscene, so that the group, who had been dubbed the Hellfire Club, quickly disbanded, and Medmenham was restored to its accustomed repose.

In the garden at Culham Court we see, both up and down, a skilful juxtaposition of house, garden, river and landscape. Culham Court, built in 1770, is one of the very few large houses by the Thames still in private occupation. At *Aston* (east settlement) the Flower Pot Inn announces on its walls that it caters for boating parties but will look after walkers also.

At Hambleden Lock a footbridge crosses the weir and although off our course it is worth going over to look at the tumbling water and the white weatherboarded mill house. The original pound lock here was one of eight built in the 1770s, and Caleb Gould, its keeper from 1777 to 1822, was another of the legendary Thames characters. He lived to the age of ninety-two and ascribed his health to his

invariable supper of a dish of onion porridge. He supplemented his
meagre wage of five shillings a week by selling to the bargees bread
made by his wife in a large oven behind his cottage. His son Joseph
was lock-keeper after him, until 1855.

Above *Hambleden* the towpath is smooth and easy. As we round
the bend we pass Greenlands, a large white building surrounded by
cedars and framed by the beeches of the Chilterns. Now a training
and conference centre, it was built for W. H. Smith, a Victorian
self-made man who founded the stationers and was at one time First
Lord of the Admiralty (satirized in Gilbert and Sullivan's *HMS
Pinafore* – 'I polished those buttons so successfully, that now I am
the ruler of the Queen's Navee'). During the Civil War a former
house at Greenlands was a stronghold for the Royalists. Next comes
Temple Island, luxuriant with trees and with a willow partly
disguising the little 'temple' at the upper end, really a decorative
cupola atop a cottage designed by James Wyatt.

The straight 1½-mile stretch of river with Henley at the far end is
an unusual feature on the twisting Thames, and drew the early
rowing enthusiasts here to organize their races. The regular Henley
Royal Regatta has been held since 1839 and is the premier regatta in
Britain. The course, which starts on the far side of Temple Island,
is 1 mile 550 yds (2.1 km) long and is protected from other boats by
wooden booms to give a width of 24 m. The eights enter for the
Grand Challenge Cup and also for the Ladies Plate and Princess
Elizabeth Cup, which is for schools and colleges; the fours for the
Wyfold, Visitors or Stewards Cups; the pairs for the Silver Goblets;
and the scullers for the Diamond Sculls. The fastest recorded time
for the course was 6 minutes 10 seconds (Leander, 1984), around
thirteen miles an hour.

On our side is the little hamlet of *Remenham* (settlement beside
the bank), with St Nicholas' church: it has a Norman-style
semicircular apse, and in the churchyard is the grave of Caleb
Gould. Glimpsed on the other side down a long avenue of poplars is
Fawley Court, a fine eighteenth-century mansion notable for its
plasterwork within. Passing by riverside houses of the sort hired by

Hambleden Weir

eights for the regatta, we come to the area of the grandstands and the Stewards' Enclosure, with Phyllis Court providing more viewing stands opposite. In Henley Week (late June or early July) they are filled with crowds of the smartly dressed, for sartorial standards are strictly observed. Smartest of all is to wear caps, ties and boating jackets or blazers which proclaim the wearer's rowing prowess, of however long ago. Some of them may be pink, the colour of the Leander Club whose boathouse is immediately before the bridge. The scene has not changed appreciably since Jingle Junior of the Jaunt described it a century ago (22, page 133), except that the flower-decked houseboats have all gone, as have the 'nigger minstrels' with their banjos and the carriages which lined the bridge (the original course ended just below it). Throughout the year thousands of merry folk in small boats – the smaller the merrier – come shooting under the bridge, as they do in John Betjeman's poem 'Henley-on-Thames':

> When shall I see the Thames again?
> The prow-promoted gems again,
>> As beefy ATS
>> Without their hats
> Come shooting through the bridge?
>> And 'cheerioh' and 'cheeri-bye'
>> Across the waste of waters die,
>> And low the mists of evening lie
> And lightly skims the midge.

ANTHOLOGY
(18) River concerts at Cookham: from Patricia Burstall's *The Golden Age of the Thames*, 1981.

River concerts originated at Cookham, apparently in 1887. As twilight thickened, the moon rose above the trees, and over the million twinkling lights on river and river bank the dome of night

Henley Regatta

was jewelled with starshine, so a hush fell on the audience gathered on lawns and towpath or in boats slightly swaying to the motion of the current. A few tinkling notes, magnified by the water, sounded from the piano aboard the large ferry-punt moored in mid-stream which served as a concert platform, and then clear voices rang out into the darkness. Songs included Tosti's 'Beauty's Eyes' and his 'Venetian Boat Song', 'Alice Where Art Thou?', 'The Lost Chord', 'I'll Sing Thee Songs of Araby', 'O Dry Those Tears', the 'Bedouin Love Song', 'Excelsior' and 'For Thee My Love', this last always sung by Colonel F. C. Ricardo, a well-known local figure. Sometimes tenor and baritone or tenor and soprano sang in duet, weaving patterns of harmony, as in 'O that We Two were Maying', or Benedict's 'The Moon Hath Raised her Lamp Above' from *The Lily of Killarney*. Gilbert and Sullivan was sung, and sometimes there were whistling solos. Patriotic songs were heard too – 'The Lads in Red' and 'Yes, Let Me like a Soldier Fall', the last accompanied by cornet obbligato.

Comic songs were popular. The audience heard about the 'Three Little Niggers', the 'Putney 'Bus' and 'Muddled Maxims'; they were informed that by misfortune 'The Vlies be on the Turmeyguts', but were cheered to know that 'His 'art was true to 'is Poll'. The favourite was 'Razors', which was taken up by the audience. In 1891 river concerts were temporarily abandoned at Cookham because what had previously been a small local occasion had by then come to attract thousands of spectators from further away, and attempts of singers to make themselves heard were 'baulked and rendered nugatory by crackers, steam whistles, and the varied diversions of a tightly-packed crowd'. However, 'Razors' broke through, in response to insistent calls for melody, and the chorus was taken up by the various groups of spectators, each choosing its own key, words and style. These occasions were brought to an end by 'Auld Lang Syne' and the National Anthem, led from the ferry-punt which was brightly illuminated by electricity, taking its current from the electric launch *Loosestrife*.

(19) The River and the Wild Wood: from Kenneth Grahame's *The Wind in the Willows*, 1908.

'I beg your pardon,' said the Mole, pulling himself together with an effort. 'You must think me very rude; but all this is so new to me. So – this – is – a – river!'

'*The* River,' corrected the Rat.

'And you really live by the river? What a jolly life!'

'By it and with it and on it and in it,' said the Rat. 'It's brother and sister to me, and aunts, and company, and food and drink, and (naturally) washing. It's my world, and I don't want any other. What it hasn't got is not worth having, and what it doesn't know is not worth knowing. Lord! the times we've had together! Whether in winter or summer, spring or autumn, it's always got its fun and its excitements. When the floods are on in February, and my cellars and basement are brimming with drink that's no good to me, and the brown water runs by my best bedroom window; or again when it all drops away and shows patches of mud that smells like plum-cake, and the rushes and weed clog the channels, and I can potter about dry-shod over most of the bed of it and find fresh food to eat, and things careless people have dropped out of boats!'

'But isn't it a bit dull at times?' the Mole ventured to ask. 'Just you and the river, and no one else to pass a word with?'

'No one else to – well, I mustn't be hard on you,' said the Rat with forbearance. 'You're new to it, and of course you don't know. The bank is so crowded nowadays that many people are moving away altogether. O no, it isn't what it used to be, at all. Otters, kingfishers, dabchicks, moorhens, all of them about all day long and always wanting you to *do* something – as if a fellow had no business of his own to attend to!'

'What lies over *there*?' asked the Mole, waving a paw towards a background of woodland that darkly framed the water-meadows one side of the river.

'That? O, that's just the Wild Wood,' said the Rat shortly. 'We don't go there very much, we river-bankers.'

'Aren't they – aren't they very *nice* people in there?' said the Mole a trifle nervously.

'W-e-ll,' replied the Rat, 'let me see. The squirrels are all right. *And* the rabbits – some of 'em, but rabbits are a mixed lot. And then there's Badger, of course. He lives right in the heart of it; wouldn't live anywhere else, either, if you paid him to do it. Dear old Badger! Nobody interferes with *him*. They'd better not,' he added significantly.

'Why, who *should* interfere with him?' asked the Mole.

'Well, of course – there – are others,' explained the Rat in a hesitating sort of way. 'Weasels – and stoats – and foxes – and so on. They're all right in a way – I'm very good friends when we meet, and all that – but they break out sometimes, there's no denying it, and then – well, you can't really trust them, and that's the fact.'

The Mole knew well that it is against animal-etiquette to dwell on possible trouble ahead, or even to allude to it; so he dropped the subject.

'And beyond the Wild Wood again?' he asked: 'where it's all blue and dim, and one sees what may be hills or perhaps they mayn't, and something like the smoke of towns, or is it only cloud-drift?'

'Beyond the Wild Wood comes the Wide World,' said the Rat. 'And that's something that doesn't matter, either to you or me. I've never been there, and I'm never going, nor you either, if you've got any sense at all. Don't ever refer to it again, please. Now then! Here's our backwater at last, where we're going to lunch.'

Leaving the main stream, they now passed into what seemed at first sight like a little landlocked lake. Green turf sloped down to either edge, brown snaky tree-roots gleamed below the surface of the quiet water, while ahead of them the silvery shoulder and foamy tumble of a weir, arm-in-arm with a restless dripping water-wheel, that held up in its turn a grey-gabled mill-house, filled the air with little clear voices speaking up cheerfully out of it at intervals. It was so very beautiful that the Mole could only hold up both fore-paws and gasp, 'Oh my! O my! O my!'

Temple Island, at the end of Henley reach

(20) A Thames Path walker receives some nasty shocks at Hurley: from Martin Briggs' *Down the Thames*, 1949.

As I emerged on to an enormous meadow, my gaze was first attracted by a colossal white modern house, Danesfield, standing high on a wooded bluff above Marlow; and next to it another great mansion, brick and neo-Georgian, built a few years ago by the late Lord Davenport. My first thought was that these two opulent dwellings must enjoy a magnificent view of the rich flat valley below them; but that hasty impression was soon dispelled as I crossed the meadow, for beyond it lay a specimen of uncontrolled human settlement that even Peacehaven could hardly rival. The whole landscape was littered with Cockney caravanners and the air was humming with transatlantic crooning from countless radio-sets and gramaphones. In one field alone I counted more than sixty shacks and caravans. Four of them were provided with Anderson shelters as privies; for the rest – well, one wondered! Yet I was now on the outskirts of one of the most celebrated beauty-spots on the Thames, the village of Hurley, to wit: described in the CPRE Report of less than twenty years ago as 'a completely unspoilt village'. Intensely depressed, I repaired for a drink to its famous old inn, the 'Bell', which externally preserves all the charm of the past, but no longer exists to provide village yokels with half a pint and a seat by the inglenook. The name of an Italian manager over the lintel of the ancient doorway was a sinister presage of change, and on entering I found that this was no place for a humble pedestrian with a knapsack. White-coated bar-tenders mixed lasciviously named cocktails in a gleaming bar; and across the passage, lunch was awaiting the advent of expensive motorists. Shrinking out with my glass into the garden behind the inn, I found a prospect of real loveliness, with great pine trees closing the vista . . .

(21) Lord Lovelace of Hurley Priory plots against James II: from Macaulay's *History of England*, 1861.

His mansion, built by his ancestors out of the spoils of Spanish galleons from the Indies, rose on the ruins of a house of Our Lady in that beautiful valley through which the Thames, not yet defiled by the precincts of a great capital, nor rising and falling with the flow and ebb of the sea, rolls under woods of beech round the gentle hills of Berkshire. Beneath the stately saloon, adorned by Italian pencils, was a subterraneous vault, in which the bones of ancient monks had sometimes been found. In this dark chamber some zealous and daring opponents of the government had held many midnight conferences during that anxious time when England was impatiently expecting the Protestant wind.

(22) Henley Regatta, by Jingle Junior of the Jaunt:
from *Punch*, 1885.

All right – here we are – quite the waterman – jolly – young – white flannels – straw hat – canvas shoes – umbrella – mackintosh – provide against a rainy day! Finest reach for rowing in England – best regatta in the Eastern hemisphere – finest picnics in the world! Gorgeous barges – palatial houseboats – superb steam-launches – skiffs – randans – punts – wherries – sailing-boats – dinghies – canoes! Red Lion crammed from cellar to garret – not a bed to be had in the town – comfortable trees all booked a fortnight in advance – well-aired meadows at a premium! Lion Gardens crammed with gay toilettes – Grand Stand like a flower-show – band inspiriting – church-bells distracting – sober grey old bridge crammed with carriages – towing-path blocked up with spectators – meadows alive with picnic parties – flags flying everywhere – music – singers – niggers – conjurers – fortune-tellers! Brilliant liveries of rowing-clubs – red – blue – yellow – green – purple – black – white all jumbled up together – rainbow gone mad – kaleidoscope with delirium tremens. Henley hospitality proverbial – invitation to sixteen luncheons – accept 'em all – go to none! Find myself at luncheon where I have not been asked – good plan – others in reserve! Wet or fine – rain or shine must be at Henley! If fine, row about all day – pretty girls – bright dresses – gay sunshades. If wet, drop in at hospitable houseboat just for a call – delightful damsels –

mackintoshes – umbrellas! Houseboat like Ark – all in couples – Joan of Ark in corner with Darby – who is she? Don't Noah – pun effect of cup. Luncheons going on all day – cups various continuing circulating – fine view – lots of fun – delightful, very! People roaring rowists howling along bank – lots of young men with red oars in boat over-exerting themselves – lot more in boat with blue oars, also over-exerting themselves – bravo! – pick her up! – let her have it! – well pulled – everybody gone raving mad! Bang! young men leave off over-exerting themselves – somebody says somebody has won something. Seems to have been a race about something – why can't they row quietly? Pass the claret-cup, please – Why do they want to interupt our luncheon? – Eh?

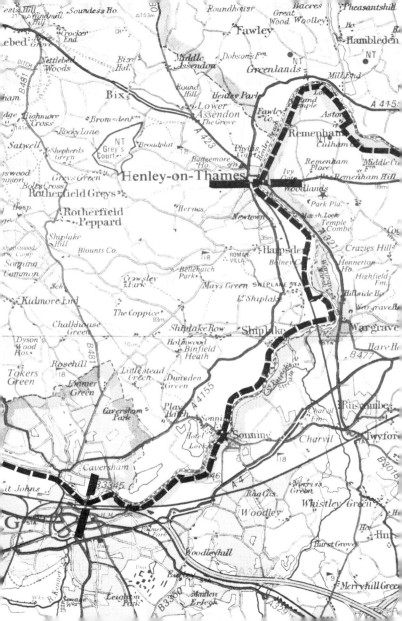

Stage 6 **Henley to Reading** 9.6 miles (15.5 km)

SPECIFICS

Stage 6 is attractive and rural except for the last 2 miles, where it comes to the industrial edge of Reading; though even here it is secluded between bushes and the river. There is also a mile of suburban scenery in Lower Shiplake. The going is all easy, most of it on grass and earth, although the section between Lower Shiplake and Shiplake Locks can be a little rough. Half a mile is on small roads.

Path Upstream: see also Strip Chart
Marsh Lock to Shiplake Lock
   After 0.5 miles the route leaves the river and takes an enclosed path beside a drive, then a surfaced road ahead, bearing left at a fork. 450 m on, bear right on to an enclosed path as far as a railway. *Then left beside the line: over the level-crossing and along Shiplake Station (either through the car park or along the platform) to a path beside the line, then left under the viaduct and ahead across a field to regain the river by Ferry Cottage, and so along the bank. Shortly after the railway bridge go behind houses via Mill Lane to gain Shiplake Lock.*
   The alternative route to this section (2.0 miles, 3.3 km) is as follows: the same as above to railway; then cross it on to a track. At a road, by the Baskerville Arms, go ahead on to Mill Road for 0.5 miles. Left into a driveway; 100 m on, right on a path across a field and along the side of others to Mill Lane, then right and immediately left to Shiplake Lock.

Path Downstream: see also Strip Chart
Shiplake Lock to Marsh Lock
   Go behind houses via Mill Lane to regain the river. Then along the bank, under the railway bridge, for 1.1 miles. At Ferry Cottage bear left across a field and under a railway viaduct; then right beside the railway and through Shiplake Station (car park or platform). Over the level crossing to continue along another path beside the railway. Bear right on an enclosed path, then left along a road and follow it

round to the right to an enclosed path beside a drive which leads to a field and back to the river, and so down to Marsh Lock.

The alternative route (2.0 miles, 3.3 km) is as follows: at Mill Lane, right, and immediately left on to a path along the edge of fields, later veering left to gain a drive, and left to a road. Right along Mill Road to its end by the Baskerville Arms at Lower Shiplake, then ahead on to a track to cross the railway. Then as described above.

Approach by car
At start: Henley is in Oxfordshire, 8 miles north of Reading, at the junction of the A423 and the A4155; car-park off Market Place. *At end*: Reading is in Berkshire, and is approached from the M4 exits 10, 11 or 12; Station car-park. *Also*: at Lower Shiplake, 2 miles south of Henley on the A4155, park in lane near the lock; and at Sonning, off the A4 west of Reading, park in side streets near the bridge.

Approach by other transport
Train: British Rail stations at Henley, Shiplake and Reading. *Bus*: from London, Oxford City Link to Henley and London Link to Reading. *Boat*: summer service at Henley and Reading. *Taxi*: Henley, AK Cabs (0491-572422); Reading, 1A Cabs (0734-874444).

Refreshment
Pubs: Little White Hart, Riverside, Henley; Bull, Sonning; Caversham Bridge Hotel, Reading. *Restaurants*: Angel on the Bridge, Henley; White Hart Hotel, Sonning.

Accommodation
Hotels: Red Lion Hotel, Thames-side, Henley on Thames RG9 2AR (0491-572161); George Hotel, King Street, Reading RG1 2HE (0734-53445). *Guest houses and small hotels*: New Lodge, Henley Park, Henley RG9 6HU (0491-576350); Holly House, Lower Shiplake, Henley on Thames RG9 3JP (0735-223182); Thames House, 18 Thames-side, Reading RG1 8DR (0734-507860).

Camping: Swiss Farm International Camping, Marlow Road, Henley RG1 2HY (0491-573419).

Stage 6 **Henley to Reading** 9.6 miles (15.5 km)

DESCRIPTION

In the days of the stage coaches *Henley* (high glade) was an important halfway point between London and Oxford. Descending the new cutting down Remenham Hill, the four-in-hands crossed the river by the magnificent new bridge (1786 and still going strong), with its five arches of Headington stone and its sculpted heads of Thames and Isis on the keystones of the central arch. They would then stop at the Red Lion or the Angel while the horses were changed and the passengers took refreshments. These two inns still grace the entrance to Henley, and the Red Lion still names its bedrooms after famous people who spent the night there – Charles I, General Blücher, the Duke of Marlborough, Dr Johnson and the Prince Regent. There is also Prince Rupert's room, recalling that Henley was a border town in the Civil War, when it suffered severely from the garrisoning of troops and factional hatred. Behind the Red Lion the chequer-pattern walls of St Mary's church bar the vista into Hart Street, but from them soars the sixteenth-century tower, made even taller by four battlemented pinnacles dominating town and river. In Hart Street are several Georgian houses and a few sixteenth-century buildings, including the Old White Hart Inn and the house of William Lenthall, who was Speaker of the House of Commons when Charles I entered the chamber and personally arrested five members.

Upstream from Henley Bridge Victorian housing fronts the river and looks down at the boats for hire. This is succeeded by a municipal waterside park in which is a stone obelisk which once acted as the plinth for the Henley town pump.

At Marsh Lock we go by a long towpath bridge across the mainstream to the lock island, and then back to shore by another footbridge, a splendid opportunity to survey the turbulent waters below the weir and admire the charm of the setting, with the old keeper's cottage and the hanging woods of Mill Bank, and to imagine scenes in the lock as described by G. D. Leslie (23, page

Henley Bridge

147). Had we been here in the early 1770s we would have observed a gentleman supervising the construction of the original lock and might well have supposed he was the engineer, especially when we learnt that he had also superintended the new road-cutting up Remenham Hill, for which he had invented a system of rail trolleys. But in fact Humphrey Gainsborough was minister of the Independent Chapel in South Street, Henley; unlike his famous brother Thomas, he was unable to exploit his skills fully, being merely a gifted amateur rather than a professional.

The meadow which follows is made even more delightful by the steep chalk hills on the further bank, covered in foliage and with a combe (known as Happy Valley) dividing them. They are on the estate of Park Place, a great house built in the French Renaissance style in the 1870s. It is not visible from the river, and is now a school. It is on the site of an earlier house whose grounds were laid out by James 'Athenian' Stuart and then further extended by the owner, Henry Conway, a well-connected man who became a field marshal. Among the focal points were an amphitheatre and temple in the classical Roman style and built from stones from the ruins of Reading Abbey, and a prehistoric stone circle brought from Jersey where Conway had been Governor.

In our meadow is a line of iron studs near the bank. These were placed in 1903 to mark a 4-m width of towpath, and it is disturbing to see how far the bank has been eroded since then. The towpath used to change banks by the former Bolney Ferry at the far end of the meadow, which is why the Thames Path now has to take a rather unsatisfactory route away from the river for the next mile. We pass a series of up-market houses, walking for some time beneath an avenue of pollarded chestnuts, and thus arrive at the centre of *Lower Shiplake* (sheep-wash stream) which unlike Shiplake itself is of recent origin.

Beyond Lower Shiplake the riverbank loops around a semicircle of meadow, with *Wargrave* (weir grove, or grave) on the far side, to a bridge carrying the branch railway line to Henley. This bridge dates from 1897, a wrought-iron affair with two spans supported by

Towpath bridge at Marsh Lock

a pair of cast-iron cylinders filled with concrete. Just after it the Lodden enters the Thames, immediately below where the Thames itself re-unites from its division between Shiplake Lock and Weir. A small flow of water, known as the St Patrick's Stream, bypasses this lock and weir into the Lodden.

The three miles of path between the locks at Shiplake and Sonning are quite superb, with nothing to jar the eye and only the hum of passing cruisers to offend the ear. A stretch of parkland is succeeded by a wood as we go beneath the grounds of a school and past the college boathouse. Also up in the wood is the parish church of Shiplake, St Peter and St Paul's. Its great glory is its stained-glass windows, which are fifteenth-century French from St Omer in Artois: they had miraculously survived the French Revolution by being buried and an enterprising vicar acquired them for Shiplake. Tennyson was married here in 1850. The river now twists and turns around two sizeable islands, the Lynch and Hallsmead Eyot, and soon flows by the smaller Buck Eyot and Long Eyot. Earlier we passed Phillimore Island just above Shiplake Lock, so I reckon that Buck Eyot was probably the mooring-place where Harris and Montmorency were so happily asleep when rudely awoken by their tipsy companions who had walked some five miles from Henley (24, page 148).

Suddenly we come upon *Sonning* (Sunna's people) and the red-brick humped bridge spanning the lock channel, framed by willows and gardens. This bridge was built in the eighteenth century, together with the causeway which carries the road across two islands. The two weir streams are spanned by modern bridges, but at least part of the causeway and all the main bridge were saved by early conservationists led by Edwin Lutyens and William Holman Hunt. For Sonning has long been a recognized beauty spot, and we can be thankful that we reach it on foot, for apart from the usual problems of parking, the traffic queues at the bridge are often interminable. At the entrance stands the White Hart Hotel, with medieval elements, and beyond it are narrow streets of cottages, some thatched and timber-framed. The Deanery, a larger house in Thames Street, was designed by Lutyens and has gardens by Gertrude Jekyll, who once lived at Wargrave. Its name recalls the fact that Sonning was once owned by the bishops of Salisbury, and fragments of their palace are to be found in the churchyard wall. The tower of St Andrew's church (whose large chancel also recalls episcopal influence) dates from around 1530, just before the Reformation. But though the Tudors shortly afterwards forced the bishop to relinquish his pleasant property at Sonning, the bishop had the last laugh: for the upkeep of the rotting wooden bridge, which went with the property, was so onerous that the Crown soon sold out in its turn. The new squires of Sonning took up residence at Holme Park to the south of the village, on a bluff overlooking the river, and their mansion is now occupied by the Reading Bluecoat School.

Below the bluff lies Sonning Lock. There was a weir here certainly from the fourteenth century, and then came the pound lock of 1773, the furthest upstream of a series of five built at that time. The lock was kept for forty years from 1845 by James Sadler, followed by his son Michael for twenty-six years more. The intermittent nature of his work provided James with a good opportunity for pursuing his two hobbies, bee-keeping and poetry: there is a certain rustic charm in this, especially if one realizes that the correct pronunciation for Sonning is 'Sunning':

> Is there a spot more lovely than the rest,
> By art improved, by nature truly blest?
> A noble river at its base is running,
> It is a little village known as Sonning.

Another Sonning family also maintained a continuity of river employment. John Treacher, a local carpenter, builder and decorator who was appointed Surveyor to the Thames Commissioners in 1770 and supervised the construction of many Thames locks and bridges, was succeeded by his son John and his grandson George, who continued till 1863. John Treacher's very first work was to construct the towpath above Sonning Bridge known as Thames Parade.

Within a mile of Sonning Lock the scene changes abruptly, as we walk within sight and sound of industrial *Reading*, with gravel pits

beyond the far bank. And yet it is not oppressive since the depots and factories lie away from our route, which is on rough pasture and then a recreation area. In this way we come alongside the main railway line, where it bridges the Kennet. In contrast to the solid brick of the railway bridge, the wooden towpath bridge is a curious affair in the form of a horseshoe-shaped ramp: below it are the longboats preparing to enter the Kennet and Avon Canal. Finally we emerge on to the municipal tidiness of King's Meadow and come up to Caversham Lock and Reading Bridge.

ANTHOLOGY
(23) Marsh Lock on a Henley Regatta morning: from George Leslie's *Our River*, 1888.

Marsh Lock is a terrible place to pass through on a regatta morning. I shall never forget coming through from Wargrave on one of these occasions. The gates could hardly open on account of the jam of boats against them, everybody wanting as usual to get in first, the ladies being far the most eager and energetic in their endeavours. The whole mass of boats shaped itself into the form of a huge arrow-head, and right down into the middle of the pack came slowly but surely a large tug-barge, called the *Spitfire* (since blown-up and wrecked at Sonning), with a crowd of Reading folks aboard at a shilling a head. As the gates at last opened, the wedge tightened up, and I was glad to remember that my punt's sides were inch stuff, and the oak treads very strong, for I felt and heard the sides of other boats giving way like baskets, with many an ominous creak; outriggers and rowlocks got jammed and broken, and amidst cries of vituperation of every sort, the lock gradually filled. I had no idea how many boats a lock would really hold till then. The excitement reached its peak when the gun at Henley was heard announcing the start of the first race, and the instant the lower gates could be opened the whole crowd of boats rushed out, splash, dash, and away, like boys out of school.

Reading gasometers

(24) Finding the boat in the dark near Shiplake: from Jerome K. Jerome's *Three Men in a Boat*, 1889.

It was a dismal night, coldish, with a thin rain falling; and as we trudged through the dark, silent fields, talking low to each other, and wondering if we were going right or not, we thought of the cosy boat, with the bright light streaming through the tight-drawn canvas; of Harris and Montmorency, and the whiskey, and wished we were there.

We conjured up the picture of ourselves inside, tired and a little hungry; of the gloomy river and the shapeless trees; and, like a giant glow-worm underneath them, our dear old boat, so snug and warm and cheerful. We could see ourselves at supper there, pecking away at cold meat, and passing each other chunks of bread; we could hear the cheery clatter of our knives, the laughing voices, filling all the space, and overflowing through the opening out into the night. And we hurried on to realize the vision.

We struck the two-path at length, and that made us happy; because prior to this we had not been sure whether we were walking towards the river or away from it, and when you are tired and want to go to bed uncertainties like that worry you. We passed Shiplake as the clock was striking the quarter to twelve; and then George said thoughtfully:

'You don't happen to remember which of the islands it was, do you?'

'No,' I replied, beginning to grow thoughtful too, 'I don't. How many are there?'

'Only four,' answered George. 'It will be all right, if he's awake.'

'And if not?' I queried; but we dismissed that train of thought.

We shouted when we came opposite the first island, but there was no response; so we went to the second, and tried there, and obtained the same result.

'Oh! I remember now,' said George; 'it was the third one.'

And we ran on hopefully to the third one, and hallooed.

No answer!

The case was becoming serious. It was now past midnight. The hotels at Shiplake and Henley would be crammed; and we could not go round, knocking up cottagers and householders in the middle of the night, to know if they let apartments! George suggested walking back to Henley and assaulting a policeman, and so getting a night's lodging in the station-house. But then there was the thought, 'Suppose he only hits us back and refuses to lock us up!'

We could not pass the whole night fighting policemen. Besides, we did not want to overdo the thing and get six months.

We despairingly tried what seemed in the darkness to be the fourth island, but met with no better success. The rain was coming down fast now, and evidently meant to last. We were wet to the skin, and cold and miserable. We began to wonder whether there were only four islands or more, or whether we were near the islands at all, or whether we were anywhere within a mile of where we ought to be, or in the wrong part of the river altogether; everything looked so strange and different in the darkness. We began to understand the sufferings of the Babes in the Wood.

Just when we had given up all hope – yes! I know that is always the time that things do happen in novels and tales; but I can't help it. I resolved when I began to write this book, that I would be strictly truthful in all things; and so I will be, even if I have to employ hackneyed phrases for the purpose.

It *was* just when we had given up all hope, and I must therefore say so. Just when we had given up all hope, then, I suddenly caught sight, a little way below us, of a strange, weird sort of glimmer flickering among the trees on the opposite bank. For an instant I thought of ghosts: it was such a shadowy, mysterious light. The next moment it flashed across me that it was our boat, and I sent up such a yell across the water that made the night seem to shake in its bed.

We waited breathless for a minute, and then – oh! divinest music of the darkness! – we heard the answering bark of Montmorency. We shouted back loud enough to wake the Seven Sleepers – I never could understand myself why it should take more noise to wake seven sleepers than one – and, after what seemed an hour, but what was really, I suppose, about five minutes, we saw the lighted boat creeping slowly over the darkness, and heard Harris's sleepy voice asking where we were.

There was an unaccountable strangeness about Harris. It was

something more than ordinary tiredness. He pulled the boat against a part of the bank from which it was quite impossible for us to get into it, and immediately went to sleep. It took us an immense amount of screaming and roaring to wake him up again, and put some sense into him; but we succeeded at last, and got safely on board.

Stage 7 **Reading to Goring** 10.9 miles (17.5 km)

SPECIFICS

As far as Mapledurham this Stage is affected by Reading and the extensive housing in Caversham, Tilehurst and Purley. But thereafter it is of high quality as it approaches the Goring Gap where the Thames runs between hills, and it features the only stretch of hillside trail in the entire Thames Path. We pass two sets of twin villages, all of character. The going is easy, though of very mixed variety – gravel, asphalt, concrete, earth, grass and chalk.

Path Upstream: see also Strip Chart
Caversham Bridge to Mapledurham Lock
    After 2.8 miles turn left up to a footbridge over the railway. By the Roebuck turn right along the A329. *Within 100 m find to the right a path ahead through woods to Skerrit Way. Along Skerrit Way to Marshall Close and along a path to Hazel Road: then by a path beside the railway, and under it through a tunnel and ahead to pass Purley Church. Along Thames Reach and Waterside Drive, then right by a path to regain the river, and up the bank to Mapledurham.*
    The alternative route (4.0 miles, 6.4 km) is as follows: same as above to A329. Along A329 for 0.7 miles; right into New Hill, over the railway, and then ahead along a track (Mapledurham Drive) to regain the river by Mapledurham Lock.

Whitchurch Bridge to Basildon railway bridge
    Immediately after Whitchurch Bridge turn left along a drive, then right by an enclosed path into the churchyard. Beyond, turn right along a drive to regain the road, and so up through Whitchurch. 100 m after a road junction, turn left on to a bridleway track. 0.8 miles on, where the track turns left, the bridleway continues ahead, at first across a valley and then through a wood, gradually descending and emerging as a broad track. Before Gatehampton Farm turn left by a path across a field to gain the river bank by a cottage, and so up to the railway bridge.

Path Downstream: see also Strip Chart
Basildon railway bridge to Whitchurch Bridge

   0.3 miles beyond the railway bridge turn left by a cottage away from the river by a path across a field to a bridleway track. Turn right along this and gradually up into woods, later emerging across a valley to join a driveway; then ahead to the B471. Turn right on to the road, and down through Whitchurch, turning right into a drive just before the church, to go through the churchyard, and beyond by an enclosed path and a drive to regain the road immediately before the bridge.

Mapledurham Lock to Caversham Bridge

   After 0.5 miles turn right along an enclosed path into Purley. Left into Waterside Drive and Thames Reach, passing Purley Church. Ahead by a path leading to a tunnel under the railway, then left up a path beside the railway to Hazel Road. By a path to Marshall Close, then left into Skerrit Way. Ahead by a path through woods to gain the A329. By the Roebuck, turn left by a footbridge over the railway to regain the river, then along the bank to Caversham Bridge.

   The alternative route (4.0 miles, 6.4 km) is as follows: by Mapledurham Lock turn right away from the river along Mapledurham Drive. At a road junction go ahead up New Hill and over the railway. Turn left along the A329 for 0.7 miles as far as the Roebuck. Then as described above.

Approach by car
At start: Reading is in Berkshire, and is approached from the M4 exits 10, 11 or 12; Station car-park. *At end:* Goring (by Streatley Bridge) is in Oxfordshire, between Reading and Wantage off the A329; car-park. *Also:* at Pangbourne (by Whitchurch Bridge) at the junction of the A329 and the A340 4 miles west of Reading; car-park in Station Road.

Approach by other transport
Train: British Rail stations at Reading, Tilehurst, Pangbourne and Goring. *Bus:* From London, London Link to Reading. *Boat:*

summer service at Reading. *Taxi:* Reading, 1A Cabs (0734-874444).

Refreshment
Pubs: Caversham Bridge Hotel, Reading; Roebuck, Tilehurst;
Ferryboat, Whitchurch; Miller of Mansfield, Goring. *Restaurants:*
Swan Hotel, Pangbourne.

Accommodation
Hotels: George Hotel, King Street, Reading RG1 2HE
(0734-53445); Copper Inn, Church Road, Pangbourne RG8 7AR
(0735-72244); Swan Hotel, Streatley RG8 9HR (0491-873737).
Guest houses and small hotels: John Barleycorn, Manor Road,
Goring on Thames RG8 9DP (0491-872509). *Youth hostel*: Hill
House, Reading Road, Streatley RG8 9JJ (0491-872278).

Admission
Mapledurham House, Easter to September, Saturday and Sunday
afternoons; Childe Beale Wildlife Trust, April to September, daily
except Fridays; Basildon Park, April to October Wednesday and
Saturday afternoons.

Stage 7 **Reading to Goring** 10.9 miles (17.5 km)

DESCRIPTION

The old centre of *Reading* (the people of Reada) is separated from
the Thames by the main railway line, and the InterCity trains
rushing through the station somehow symbolize the story of the
town. For Reading has always been a place of transit and
transiency, a halting-place on the mainline of history, often
appearing in terms of a return ticket. In the ninth century the
Danes, who navigated the Thames in their long-boats, established a
base here for a while before being driven back by the Saxons. In the
seventeenth century the town was taken in turn by Royalists and
Parliamentarians. Transient visitations in the legal system have
included the evacuation to Reading of the Law Courts of London to
escape the plague in 1625, and the sojourn here of Reading Gaol's
most famous prisoner, Oscar Wilde, 1896–7. But the Latin
admonition *sic transit gloria mundi* is most clearly seen in the utter
destruction of the great Benedictine Abbey of Reading. For not
only was its spiritual life extinguished but, since virtually all the
buildings in it were torn down (save only the gatehouse and some
other fragments), the town was left without any major historical
monument or focal point.

   The very first building we pass after Reading Bridge is Nugent
House, headquarters of the Thames Water Authority. One of the
achievements of Thames Water has been the great reduction in
water pollution. Every day Thames Water treats nearly 4.5 billion
litres of sewage in a process which is necessarily clinical and so
rather uninspiring to describe. First the large objects are screened
off, then the detritus and sludge is separated, after which the liquid
is put through secondary treatment plants where special microbes
feed on all remaining waste matter and destroy it, themselves being
separated in final sedimentation tanks before the clean water goes
into the river. Industrial effluent is also strictly controlled by
monitoring and sampling. These processes all improve the oxygen
content of the water, thus providing life-giving force to water
animals and plants. How different this is to the filthy conditions of
the past, such as might have been found on the Thames and Kennet

here at Reading, and satirized in a passage which shows all too
clearly how literature, like journalism, thrives on dirt and horror
(25, page 165).

From Reading Bridge to Caversham Bridge is only half a mile:
between them lies a neat island, now called Fry's but once de
Montfort from a duel fought on it by Robert de Montfort and Henry
of Essex in 1157. Though the first bridge appears to be of iron and
the second of stone, they are both largely of concrete, powerful
structures of the 1920s. They differ in history, however, for there
has been no bridge where the former stands, whereas Caversham
Bridge is on the site of two earlier bridges, of which the first lasted
for hundreds of years. Constructed in the Middle Ages, it was made
of timber and on the central pier was a chapel dedicated to St Anne,
housing important relics such as 'the blessed knife that killed St
Edward' and 'a piece of the halter Judas hanged himself with'.
During the Civil War the central spans were cut by the
Parliamentarian defenders of Reading.

Thames Side Promenade is a linear park of grass and trees facing
across to housing on Caversham (Cafhere's settlement) heights:
several clear instances of shore erosion from power-boat wash can
be seen. After the slipways of the Reading Marine Services
Boatyard we are back by the main railway line. The dark brick
embankment along the side of Tilehurst Hill is high above us, but
there are good views to the alluvial flats and the hills beyond. There
follows an unfortunate deviation through a housing estate. This is
no recent fracture of the towpath but one which goes back over 200
years, for in 1778 it was recorded that the path was to go behind
Purley Church 'so as to avoid Mr Waldridge's orchard and yard'. To
achieve this two ferry crossings were needed for a towpath section
of only 500 m on the far bank.

Once back on the towpath we come round the bend into sight of
the beautiful ensemble at *Mapledurham* (settlement by the stream
and the maples). This comprises a large brick Tudor manor house, a
fifteenth-century church, a mill, and a secluded hamlet which
includes Jacobean almshouses. The house is the ancestral home of
the Blount family: an early Blount was the Sir Walter who appears
in Shakespeare's *Henry IV*. Throughout the Reformation they

remained obstinately Roman Catholic, braving restrictive laws and sometimes persecution, so the house boasts a priest's hole and a secret passage, and the church (St Margaret's) though Anglican, possesses a Roman Catholic chapel containing the tombs of the Blounts. The sisters Martha and Teresa Blount were the recipients of long letters from Alexander Pope, also a Roman Catholic. With their sympathy for the Stuarts and their toasts to 'the king over the water', they would have been astonished and indeed dismayed to know that a century later the Anglican vicar of Mapledurham would be none other than the illegitimate son of the Hanoverian King William IV by his mistress Mrs Jordan, who went by the splendid name of the Reverend Lord Augustus Fitzclarence. The old mill is now working again for its original purpose, the grinding of corn, producing fine wholemeal flour in the time-honoured fashion.

Sadly we cannot cross to Mapledurham, and this absence of a crossing was likewise an inconvenience for the characters in Galsworthy's *The Forsyte Saga* who lived in a house there. When Fleur, the daughter of the house, comes down from London with her lover Jon, they get out at Reading and enjoy a final walk along the towpath before he returns to London while she speeds on towards the ferry, only to be intercepted by the thick-skinned Michael Mont, who rows her across in his skiff. Some weeks later Fleur, having rowed Jon's sister back across the Thames, pauses to absorb the peaceful summer scene (26, page 165).

From Mapledurham to Whitchurch we walk in unadulterated beauty, the grassy path giving views of a sweep of river framed by the encircling hills and with pastures and vineyards in the valley. Not surprisingly it attracted the Victorian houseboats, as described by G. D. Leslie (27, page 166). Leslie was an artist, a Royal Academician, and also a fanatical river-punter. He tells us with pride: 'In the summer of 1871 two events happened to me of some importance, namely, I got married, and I bought a new punt.' This punt was called the *Strawberry Pottle*, and he used it for several long-distance excursions, demonstrating a proper disdain for the sybaritic river-folk who took no exercise.

Canoe championship race at Thames Side Promenade

Seen down an avenue is Hardwick House. Like its close neighbour Mapledurham House, Hardwick is Tudor, red-brick with stone mullions, sturdy chimneystacks and steep roofs. Both can claim that 'Queen Elizabeth slept here'. Hardwick belonged to the Lybbe family till sold to Sir Charles Rose, who put much money into its upkeep while carefully preserving its character: he died, as a memorial in Mapledurham Church tells us, on 'April 20th 1913 from the effects of an aeroplane flight'.

Pangbourne (its parish church is Victorian, though with an eighteenth-century tower, and is dedicated to St James the Less) is an ancient village, now much expanded. Kenneth Grahame came to live here, in Church Cottage, towards the end of his life. On the Thames frontage of Pangbourne above the lock the Swan Hotel still flourishes, scene of the ignominious termination of the boat trip of the Three Men and their Dog (28, page 167).

The bridge linking Pangbourne (the stream of Paega's people) to *Whitchurch* is, together with Swinford Bridge, one of only two still charging tolls – for vehicles, not for pedestrians. Nowadays it seems just an amusing quirk that a bridge should charge a toll, but the whole principle of highway and bridge tolls was once a burning issue in the politics of local government, and it was not only private owners who charged but also corporations and councils who had inherited the bridges from landowners or the church. Frequently they were content to rake in an annual income which only partly went towards the bridge repair. Legal action, or the threat of it, was needed in the case of nearly all the scores of bridges over the Thames before they were freed of tolls. That the tolls could be heavy is proved by peeping ahead to our next bridge, at Streatley: in 1837 they were '1½d for every foot passenger, 3d for a dog drawing a cart, 1s for a carriage with four wheels and 2s per wheel for any vehicle moved or propelled by other than animal power'. On the question of bridge tolls for pedestrians, practices varied. At the worst, all were charged, in which case many rolled up their clothes and forded the river, or took the cheaper ferries. At the best, no pedestrians were charged. Rickman Godlee, a resident of

The Thames between Mapledurham and Whitchurch

Whitchurch, once undertook research into the local parish records on the incidence of marriages between the young people of Whitchurch and Pangbourne in the years before and after the original timber bridge of 1793. He could find no increase in cross-river romance; maybe toll deterrence had something to do with it.

Despite Rickman Godlee's findings, there must always have been an intimate relationship between twin communities across the Thames, and this Stage contains three such pairs – Reading and Caversham, Pangbourne and Whitchurch, and Streatley and Goring. This is no accident, but the simple result of geography: for in this Stage more than any other the Thames flows between appreciable hills as it penetrates the gap between the Chilterns and the Berkshire Downs. Houses here could be built close to the river on both banks without fear of flooding. Thus Whitchurch church (St Mary's, and not white, despite the name) is close by the lock island, and the village street progresses gradually uphill past several Georgian houses and old brick walls.

Now begins our only hillside section in the entire length of the Thames Path, although in truth we are less than 50 m above the level of the river. But it is satisfactory to plant one's feet on a slope and briefly enjoy a vertiginous thrill. After Combe Park Farm and its little combe we enter Hartslock Wood. The path here is in places on the exposed white chalk, which adds a special quality with its bright colour and crunchy texture. Where we stand, the Thames and its antecedents have worn a path through the chalk and have carried back into the ocean the sediments once slowly deposited in earlier oceans a hundred million years ago. On the thin acidic topsoil, or renzina, we will find flowers such as scabious, marjoram, St John's Wort and harebells, and above us are beeches and yews cling to the steep hillside. On the far side of the valley is Basildon Park, an eighteenth-century mansion designed by John Carr. In the valley is the Childe Beale Wildlife Trust where, on the site of an osier farm, an extensive sanctuary has been created for a vast range of exotic birds, as well as rare breeds of sheep and cattle.

In Hartslock Wood

Immediately below us is the Thames, and on it a small eyot with
bushes trailing; Hartslock wood, is named after a weir that once
straddled the river here.

As well as any other this charming setting fits Robert Bridges'
poem 'There is a hill beside the silver Thames', though the poet
purposely disguises the actual site. Still, since he once lived close by
here at Yattendon, it is to this reach that I shall award his lines: I
quote merely the second verse of what to me is one of the very best
Thames poems:

> A rushy island guards the sacred bower,
> And hides it from the meadow, where in peace
> The lazy cows wrench many a scented flower,
> Robbing the golden market of the bees:
>   And laden barges float
>   By banks of myosote;
> And scented flag and golden flower-de-lys
>   Delay the loitering boat.

The poem even describes an aged walker passing through the wood
beside the river 'with tottering care upon a staff propping his weary
knees'. In better nick than this we will by now have left Hartslock
Wood towards Gatehampton Farm and then regained the river.
Here the main railway line, sweeping towards us from the isolated
buildings by Church Farm, Lower Basildon, leaps the river for the
second time on its route from Paddington. Although the spans are
only half as wide as at Maidenhead and the arches slightly less flat,
Basildon Bridge, built in 1839 and doubled in width in 1892, bears
the imaginative stamp of its great designer, Brunel. What is more
we see it in a pastoral setting, as when it was originally built (though
it was at first whitewashed). From here we come round to Streatley
Bridge. Shortly before it is the former ferry cottage in which Oscar
Wilde lived in the summer of 1893. In his ensuing play, *An Ideal
Husband*, the characters include Viscount Goring, the Earl of
Caversham, the Countess of Basildon and Sir Robert Chiltern.

(25) Father Thames' filthy friends: from *Household Words*, 1851.

'How very thick the water is hereabouts, Father Thames; and, pray, may I enquire what that black, sluggish stream may be which I see pouring into you from a wide, bricked archway, yonder?'

'Oh, that's one of my sewers,' replied the Father of Rivers.

'But what are those smaller mouths that send forth strange parti-coloured currents to mingle with your waters?'

'That one belongs to a soap-boiler – a particular friend of mine; the next to it, is from a slaughter-house, kept by a very estimable friend indeed, who wouldn't allow a particle of the refuse and drainage of his yards to run anywhere else, on any account. Those other agreeable little outlets you are looking at, or will shortly see, on both sides of my banks, are from gas-factories, brewhouses, shot-factories, coal-wharfs, cow-houses, tan-pits, gut-spinners, fish-markets, and other cheerful and odiferous tributaries; while the inky flood yonder which your eyes are now fixed upon is from a very populous grave-yard, which produces so large a quantity of liquid every four-and-twenty hours, that it has to be drained off by regular arrangement, and made to flow into my convenient, all-embracing bosom.'

(26) Day-dreams near Mapledurham: from John Galsworthy's *The Forsyte Saga*, 1922.

After taking her elderly cousin across, Fleur did not land at once, but pulled in among the reeds, into the sunshine. The peaceful beauty of the afternoon seduced for a little one not much given to the vague and poetic. In the field beyond the bank where her skiff lay up, a machine drawn by a grey horse was turning an early field of hay. She watched the grass cascading over and behind the light wheels with fascination – it looked so green and fresh. The click and swish blended with the rustle of the willows and the poplars, and the cooing of a wood-pigeon, in a true river song. Alongside, in the grey-green water, weeds like yellow snakes were writhing and nosing with the current; pied cattle on the farther side stood in the shade lazily swishing their tails. It was an afternoon to dream.

(27) Houseboats above Mapledurham: from George Leslie's *Our River*, 1888.

Just above the lock a friendly row of trees casts an agreeable shade across the river and tow-path; here a small island is reached, a favourite resting-place for camping parties. The attractions of Maple Durham also induce possessors of house-boats to anchor there. I am glad to say they generally have the taste to moor above the lock, so as not to interfere with the beauty of the scene below. In all my river experiences I have never tried one of these boats, but they have their charms, no doubt, and much fine, independent pleasure may be got out of them. They look inviting and snug with their little windows and curtains, their bird cages and pots of flowers, the smoke curling up from the kitchen chimney and the cooking and washing up going on inside; but I cannot help thinking it must be a little tedious, and I have observed that if not employed on some active business, such as cleaning or cooking, the occupants very often wear rather a blasé expression. There is rather a significant thing about these boats, which is that after one year's trial they are frequently abandoned, great numbers being often seen at anchor quite tenantless.

Of course there are house-boats and house-boats. Some of the great saloon barges, varnished and gilt, and furnished with profuse magnificence, refrigerators, pianos, etc., with kitchen in a separate boat and a host of attendant servants, appear sadly out of place on the river, and make one suspect that the proprietors are gentlemen with a penchant for yachting, but deterred from the marine indulgence of their hobby by a dread of sea-sickness. In a moderately-sized house-boat an artist or anyone fond of the river ought to be pretty happy, especially if he is not above doing a lot of things for himself, as it is precisely the novelty of such work which gives the whole charm to this mode of life; and in any case house-boats are in no sense open to the objections of the steam launch.

(28) Abandoning ship at Pangbourne: from Jerome K. Jerome's *Three Men in a Boat*, 1889.

The second day was exactly like the first. The rain continued to pour down, and we sat, wrapped up in our mackintoshes, underneath the canvas, and drifted slowly down.

One of us – I forget which one now, but I rather think it was myself – made a few feeble attempts during the course of the morning to work up the old gipsy foolishness about being children of nature and enjoying the wet; but it did not go down well at all. That was so painfully evident, as expressing the sentiments of each of us, that to sing it seemed unnecessary.

On one point we were all agreed, and that was that, come what might, we would go through with this job to the bitter end. We had come out for a fortnight's enjoyment on the river, and a fortnight's enjoyment on the river we meant to have. If it killed us! well, that would be a sad thing for our friends and relations, but it could not be helped. We felt that to give in to the weather in a climate such as ours would be a most disastrous precedent.

'It's only two days more,' said Harris, 'and we are young and strong. We may get over it all right, after all.'

At about four o'clock we began to discuss our arrangements for the evening. We were a little past Goring then, and we decided to paddle on to Pangbourne, and put up there for the night.

'Another jolly evening!' murmured George.

We sat and mused on the prospect. We should be in Pangbourne by five. We should finish dinner at, say, half-past six. After that we could walk about the village in the pouring rain until bed-time; or we could sit in a dimly-lit bar-parlour and read the almanac.

'Why, the Alhambra would be almost as lively,' said Harris, venturing his head outside the cover for a moment and taking a survey of the sky.

'With a little supper at the – to follow,' I added, half unconsciously.

'Yes, it's almost a pity we've made up our minds to stick to this boat,' answered Harris; and then there was silence for a while.

'If we *hadn't* made up our minds to contract our certain deaths in this bally old coffin,' observed George, casting a glance of intense malevolence over the boat, 'it might be worth while to mention that there's a train leaves Pangbourne, I know, soon after five, which would just land us in town in comfortable time to get a chop, and then go on to the place you mentioned afterwards.'

Nobody spoke. We looked at one another, and each one seemed to see his own mean and guilty thoughts reflected in the faces of the others. In silence, we dragged out and overhauled the Gladstone. We looked up the river and down the river; not a soul in sight!

Twenty minutes later, three figures, followed by a shamed-looking dog, might have been seen creeping stealthily from the boat-house at the 'Swan' towards the railway station . . .

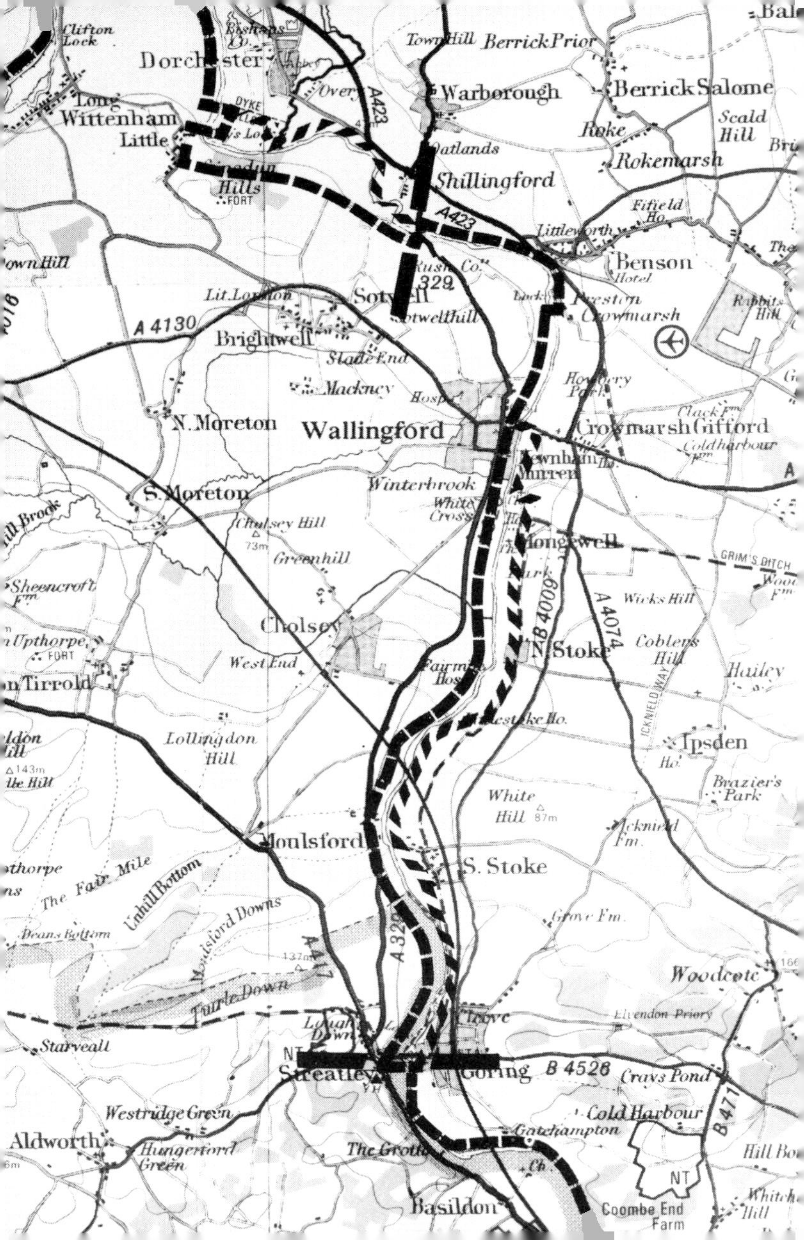
Clifton Lock
Dorchester
Long Wittenham
Little Wittenham
Sinodun Hills
FORT
DYKE
Overy
Town Hill
Berrick Prior
Warborough
Berrick Salome
Scald Hill
Roke
Rokemarsh
Oatlands
Shillingford
A423
Fifield Ho.
Littleworth
Benson
Hotel
Rush Ct.
329
Lit. London
Sotwell
Sotwellhill
Lock
Preston Crowmarsh
Rabbits Hill
A 4130
Brightwell
Slade End
Mackney
Howbery Park
Hosp.
Clack Fm.
N. Moreton
Wallingford
Crowmarsh Gifford
Coldharbour Fm.
Newnham Murren
Winterbrook
White Cross
S. Moreton
Chulsey Hill
73m
Mongewell
Greenhill
GRIM'S DITCH
Sheencroft Fm.
B 4009
A 4074
Wicks Hill
Cholsey
Upthorpe
FORT
N. Stoke
Coblers Hill
West End
Fairmile Hosp.
Hailey
Tirrold
ICKNIELD WAY
Westoke Ho.
Lollingdon Hill
Ipsden Ho.
143m
White Hill
87m
Braziers Park
Icknield Fm.
Moulsford
S. Stoke
The Fair Mile
Unhill Bottom
Moulsford Downs
Grove Fm.
Deans Bottom
A 417
137m
A 329
Woodcote
Lough Down
Elvendon Priory
Cleeve
Starveall
NT
Streatley
Goring
B 4526
Crays Pond
YH
Westridge Green
Cold Harbour
B 471
Gatehampton
Aldworth
Hungerford Green
The Grotto
Ch.
Hill Bottom
NT
Basildon
Coombe End Farm
Whitchurch Hill

Stage 8 **Goring to Shillingford** 9.2 miles (14.8 km)

SPECIFICS

Except for half a mile along the main road at Moulsford, Stage 8 has many fine ingredients – views of rural scenes on both banks, panoramas of distant hills, and distinguished housing at Streatley, Wallingford and Benson. There may be a rough patch upstream of the railway bridge, and perhaps between Wallingford and Benson, but otherwise the route is easy, mostly on earth and grass.

Path Upstream: see also Strip Chart
Cleeve Lock to Wallingford Bridge
   After 1.2 miles, at the Beetle and Wedge, turn left up a lane to the A329. Right through Moulsford for 0.7 miles to Offlands Farm. *Then turn right, down a farm track, to the edge of a copse; then ahead on a path to regain the river just below the railway bridge. Then on up the bank for 0.6 miles to a former ferry point.* Later, after 2.3 miles of towpath and after going through a boatyard at Wallingford, at Lower Wharf take a passage between terraced houses into an enclosed path into St Leonard's Lane, and thence by St Peter's Street to Thames Street and Wallingford Bridge.
   The alternative route to this section (6.7 miles, 10.8 km), is as follows: as described above to Offlands Farm, then ahead along the A329 for a further 0.8 miles, then left down the lane past Fair Mile Hospital to regain the river: then up the right bank as described above.

Wallingford Bridge to Benson Lock: alternative route 1.9 miles (3.1 km)
   Until Benson Lock crossing is opened, it is necessary to cross Wallingford Bridge to Crowmarsh Gifford, then left by local roads to Preston Crowmarsh and Benson.

Path Downstream: see also Strip Chart
Benson Lock to Wallingford Bridge: alternative route 1.9 miles (3.1 km)
   Until Benson Lock crossing is opened, it is necessary to go by

local roads to Preston Crowmarsh and Crowmarsh Gifford, then right to Wallingford Bridge.

Wallingford Bridge to Cleeve Lock

Go up Thames Street, then immediately left into St Peter's Street and ahead into St Leonard's Lane. Take an enclosed path to the left of St Leonard's church to emerge to Lower Wharf Road: then ahead by an enclosed path through a boatyard, and so on down the right bank. 2.7 miles after Wallingford Bridge, at the site of a former ferry, *continue along the bank to the railway bridge. Beyond the railway bridge find the designated path leading to a farm track, and so up to the A329.* Left along this through Moulsford for 0.7 miles, then left along a lane to the Beetle and Wedge to regain the river, then down the bank to Cleeve Lock.

The alternative route (6.7 miles, 10.8 km) to this section is as follows: initially as described above. 2.7 miles from Wallingford Bridge take the lane leading right up to and past the Fair Mile Hospital. Then left along the A329 for 0.8 miles to Offlands Farm. Then as described above.

Approach by car
At start: Goring (by Streatley Bridge) is in Oxfordshire, between Reading and Wantage off the A329; car-park. *At end*: Shillingford is in Oxfordshire, 3 miles beyond Wallingford on the A423 towards Oxford; park in village near the bridge. *Also*: at Wallingford, off the A423 between Henley and Oxford; car-park by the bridge.

Approach by other transport
Train: British Rail stations at Goring and Didcot (5 miles from Wallingford). *Bus*: from London, Oxford City Link to Wallingford and Shillingford. *Taxi*: Wallingford, Hills Taxis (0491-37022); Didcot, David's Taxis (0235-818582).

Refreshment
Pubs: Miller of Mansfield, Goring; Town Arms, Wallingford. *Restaurants*: Beetle and Wedge, Moulsford; Nautical Wheel, Wallingford.

Accommodation
Hotels: Swan Hotel, Streatley RG8 9HR (0491-873737); George
Hotel, High Street, Wallingford OX10 0BS (0491-36665);
Shillingford Bridge Hotel, Wallingford OX10 8LZ (0867-328567).
Guest houses and small hotels: John Barleycorn, Manor Road,
Goring on Thames RG8 9DP (0491-36665); *Youth hostel*: Hill
House, Reading Road, Streatley RG8 9JJ (0491-872278). *Camping*:
Benson Cruisers, Benson OX9 8SJ (0491-38304).

Admission
Wallingford Castle Grounds, March to October daily.

Stage 8 **Goring to Shillingford** 9.2 miles (14.8 km)

Of all the Thames crossing-places, the passage between Streatley and Goring must have been the earliest and most important in those unknown centuries before the dawn of history some 2,000 years ago in Britain. For this is where the ancient ridgeway track, the Icknield Way, which for the early pastoralists provided a dry and open route between south-west and north-east, negotiated its ford across the river. Although the hills grip the Thames at this its geographical epicentre, they still allow it to broaden into two channels. So here we may imagine huge flocks of sheep and goats and herds of cattle being driven through the shallow water with much bleating and bellowing at the brink in closely packed masses. Up on the chalk ridgeway there were several parallel paths, but here at the ford all concentrated into one; so predators lurked around, with plenty of cover from the thorns and brambles on the lower hill slopes. Just as the ridgeway antedated the Thames as a long-distance route for prehistoric man, our modern Ridgeway Path has seniority over the Thames Path, and backpackers along it crossing Streatley Bridge may also feel that the high road is better than the low road, though we should know by now that this 'ain't necessarily so'.

Streatley Bridge, though of concrete, looks like an old wooden trestle bridge. Its predecessor, built in 1837, was one such: the local vicar was so keen to be the first over that he placed planks across the unfinished section and slowly rode his grey pony over them. Before this, when the mail arrived at Streatley, they used to raise a flag for the Goring people – white for mail, black for no mail. Leaning on the ornamental wooden parapet we see the weir and lock, the sycamore-clad island, the Oxford College barge by the Swan and the brow of Lough Down. Before the era of photography, when so many leisured people were keen to sketch and paint, this was one of their favourite subjects, and on summer weekends straw-hatted figures equipped with stools and easels were to be seen at every corner.

Magdalen College Barge at Streatley

Goring (Gara's people), now just behind us, clusters around the church of St Thomas of Canterbury, its perpendicular tower housing medieval bells. It was once the chapel of a nunnery, with other monastic buildings where now are gardens. Ahead is *Streatley* (the glade by the Roman road), the Swan Hotel fronting the river upstream and the mill-site downstream. Streatley a hundred years ago was, like other Thames-side villages, still largely a self-contained community, socially dominated by the local landowner, Mrs Morrell. Besides the farmers, there was a grocer, a baker, a miller, a tailor, a draper, a blacksmith, a carpenter, a plasterer and a cobbler – all for a community of less than a thousand people. The church (of St Mary), to which most of them went to worship on Sunday, with Mrs Morrell preceded by a footman carrying her prayer-book, was restored in 1864, but many ancient elements remain, including the heavily buttressed tower.

In 1674 some forty people were drowned at Goring (29, page 182): in reading the contemporary account it must be noted that in those days a 'lock' meant a weir. In January 1892, the river being completely bound by ice a foot thick, a whole sheep was roasted on a brazier on it just upstream of the lock island, and hundreds gathered to eat.

On a backwater on the far bank at Cleeve Lock, Cleeve Mill is now used for generating electricity. A little upstream of it, in a brick well beside the Old Leatherne Bottel, is the Cleeve spring. This consists of two very weak springs which bubble out of the whiteish soil. In the past this water was considered just the thing for ulcers or fluxes or whatever (John Taylor in 1632 lists twenty such ailments for which it was thought to be curative, including 'Mange, Murrians, Meazles, Melancoly dumps'), but now no one bothers to collect it.

The stretch between the locks at Goring and Cleeve was hardly more than half a mile, the shortest on the river. In compensation, the stretch from Cleeve to Benson Lock is the longest – six and a half miles. This has made it a good place for serious rowing, a training-ground for the Oxford University crews. Some three-quarters of a mile above Cleeve Lock we pass from Berkshire to Oxfordshire; though, until it was cut back in 1974, Berkshire's boundary extended up the right bank of the Thames all the way to Lechlade.

We arrive at the Beetle and Wedge Inn (a beetle is a large, heavy mallet used to drive a wedge into wood) and turn away from the river at the former ferry point. H. G. Wells stayed at the Beetle and Wedge when writing *The History of Mr Polly* and it inspired his description of the Potwell Inn (30, page 183), though it would be hard to recognize it as such today. *Moulsford* (Mul's ford) is uninspiring, and we are condemned to a road through it, but it does contain the small fourteenth-century church of St John the Baptist, restored by Gilbert Scott. And at the far end of it is the Moulsford railway bridge, another Brunel masterpiece (1839). It is similar to his Basildon Bridge but much more exciting because its arches are dramatically oblique, their brick courses dizzily twisted, and because the 1892 widening to four tracks was achieved by a separate upstream twin bridge, divided from the original by 2 m. The effect of approaching it on foot is extraordinary because the perspective is misleading due to the angle of the arches; and the effect of looking up to it from below has been likened to the fantastical architectural drawings of Piranese. As a good example of John Pitt's 'Descriptive Poem' on the Thames, here is his reference to the GWR bridges on his downward course from Wallingford Bridge:

Three miles below the bridge, which was rebuilt in 1809,
The Thames is crossed again by main Great Western Railway
    Line;
Which, starting from its London Terminus, proceeds through
    Slough,
And crosses Thames at Maidenhead, at Basildon, and now . . .

The towpath resumes in our side at another former ferry point by Littlestoke. The large mental hospital up to our left, though never a private residence, will serve for the subject of P. G. Wodehouse's Walsingford Hall (31, page 184), and the sight of it may well cause us to trip up as it did the oarsmen to catch crabs. The path to Wallingford runs past meadows and a wood and paddocks. On the farther bank is *North Stoke* (Stoke means a cattle-farm) whose church, St Mary's, has many medieval features though the brick tower is eighteenth-century. Clara Butt, a leading contralto of Edwardian days, lived at Brook Lodge, North Stoke, until her death. Next on the far bank comes Carmel College, built around the nucleus of Mongewell House. Of the Georgian mansion previously on this site, Boydell in 1794 reveals something of those leisurely pre-Tractarian days of the established church when he unctuously records of Mongewell House that: 'It is the seat of the Honourable Shute Barrington, bishop of Durham, where he sometimes retires from the toil of prelatic dignity to enjoy the repose of polished life'.

Just upstream from *Mongewell* (the spring of the Mundingas) a prehistoric boundary earthwork, known to the Saxons as Grim's Ditch, leads from the far bank straight to the top of the Chilterns near Nuffield. The modern Ridgeway Path comes up from Streatley Bridge by a route close to the left bank and then goes along Grim's Ditch, a dog-leg that would never have been taken by the original users of the Icknield Way. All the same, we encounter Edward Thomas nosing around by the river in his pedestrian researches into the Icknield Way earlier this century, giving us an acute description of the left bank from Wallingford to Littlestoke Ferry (32, page 186). He was much concerned with the inter-relationship of the ridge path and the underhill lane which lay below the chalk scarp and where many early settlements were sited, attracted by the springs of water; the Stokes and Mongewell fell into this category, as did Ewelme to the north and Cholsey to the west.

Approaching *Wallingford* (the ford of Wealh's people) the towpath leads through a succession of gardens. One of the houses is on stilts: rather alarmingly, it is the property of Thames Water – they must know something we don't! On the river just at this point there was once a lock and weir. However it was only used at times of low water, usually in summer, and at all other times was left open. Deemed superfluous, it was removed in 1883, and its disappearance occasioned an amusing scene in *Three Men in a Boat* when in the twilight they became quite disorientated from constantly expecting to see it when they had in fact long passed it.

Moulsford railway bridge

Then, in one of those intimate and intriguing short urban sections of our path, we slip under an arch between terraced houses and over a stream into the churchyard of St Leonard's and thence along Thames Street to Wallingford High Street, just by St Peter's with its unusual open-work spire. Old houses in the High Street include Caneva House, a fine mansion of red and blue brick right beside us, and further up the George Hotel with its overhanging gables. Out of sight is the Market Place, dominated by the Town Hall (1670) and St Mary's Church.

Wallingford is now only a small market town, but once it was one of the most important towns in England. The original Saxon bridge was probably the first across the Thames at any point. After his victory at Hastings William I came by way of Wallingford towards London, and it was then certainly the largest town in Berkshire. It became a main stronghold for the forces of the Empress Matilda and her son Henry II, who rewarded it with special privileges. But Wallingford then declined in favour of Abingdon and Oxford, though in the Civil War it was a Royalist stronghold and the last to surrender to Parliament, in July 1646. For this defiance Cromwell ordered its fortifications to be destroyed, or 'slighted'; and so thoroughly was this done that scarcely any of its castle masonry remains: though there is a hint of former grandeur in the names of the two fields between the castle and the river – Queen's Arbour and King's Meadow. But the bridge is still in part medieval, for although new and wider river arches were constructed in 1809 and the whole thing widened, a few of the pointed thirteenth-century arches may still be seen on the downstream side of the causeway towards Crowmarsh Gifford. Some of the other arches are brick: these are ones which had been demolished by Colonel Blagge, the Royalist commander.

Benson Lock and Weir are emphatically fortified by the concrete gun emplacements of 1940 in the adjacent field. But the military fortification of *Benson* is as nothing compared to the obstructions made against peaceful pedestrians, who for too long have been prevented from crossing here. Benson used to be called Bensington

Wallingford Bridge

(the settlement of the Benesingas) until recently. In the pre-railway age it was a staging-post between Henley and Oxford, and the Old Castle Inn and White Hart once saw grander days. The church (of St Helen) is largely Victorian, and contains an amusing epitaph.

The final section of towpath in this Stage was created in 1788, together with the original Benson Lock, and the bank clearance cost five shillings for each 160 willows and ash trees taken away. A caravan park now stands where these trees were, and just beyond the road is the end of the runway of RAF Transport Command's base at Benson. Finally, we come to a truly splendid line of Lombardy poplars in the reach towards Shillingford Bridge.

ANTHOLOGY
(29) Ferry tragedy at Goring weir: from a pamphlet of 1674.

This being on age, and this year especially a year of wonders, and if not everywhere prodigious, yet in no part not remarkable in some eminent example of Providence or other: not to speak now of Wars and Battels or Christians unnaturally welt'ring in Christian Goa, now in most parts of Europe, what prodigious inundations Snow and cold have molested our climate, what losses by Sea, what mischiefs by land have in several parts afflicted us – In a word have we not been daily alarmed with an infinite variety of unwonted Accidents that God seems resolved to chastise our delight in false and Romantick news, etc., and therefore giving you first in charge that evangelical rule that you should never think persons falling under any disaster to be the greater sinners, upon this Christian stipulation I shall give you a punctual account of a most true and unparalleled Disaster which happened at Goring Lock, going to Stately on Monday the 6th of this instant July 1674 about 7 aclock at night where about 50 or 60 persons, of Men, Women, and Children, with one Mare crossing the water together in a boat from Oxfordsheir to Barksheir by the waterman's imprudently rowing too neer the shore of the Lock they were by the force of the water drawn down the Lock, where their boat being presently overwhelmed they were all turned into the Pool except fourteen or fifteen (who had been all then at the feast at Goring) were all unfortunately drowned, and to show how vain all humane aid is when Destiny interposes, this happened in the view of hundreds of people, then met at the same feast, near this fatal Lock, who found the exercise of their pastime disturbed and their Jollity dashed by this mournful Disaster of which they were helpless – but not I hope fruitless – spectators.

(30) A portly walker arrives at the Beetle and Wedge, Moulsford: from H. G. Wells's *The History of Mr Polly*, 1910.

It was about two o'clock in the afternoon, one hot day in May, when Mr Polly, unhurrying and serene, came upon that broad bend of the river to which the little lawn and garden of the Potwell Inn ran down. He stopped at the sight of the place and surveyed its deep tiled roof, nestling under big trees – you never get a decently big, decently shaped tree by the seaside – its sign towards the roadway, its sun-blistered green bench and tables, its shapely white windows and its row of upshooting hollyhock plants in the garden. A hedge separated the premises from a buttercup-yellow meadow, and beyond stood three poplars in a group against the sky, three exceptionally tall, graceful, and harmonious poplars. It is hard to say what there was about them that made them so beautiful to Mr Polly, but they seemed to touch a pleasant scene with a distinction almost divine. He stood admiring them quietly for a long time.

At last the need for coarser aesthetic satisfactions arose in him.

'Provinder,' he whispered, drawing near to the inn. 'Cold sirloin for choice. And nutbrown brew and wheaten bread.'

The nearer he came to the place the more he liked it. The windows on the ground floor were long and low, and they had pleasing red blinds. The green tables outside were agreeably ringed with memories of former drinks, and an extensive grape vine spread level branches across the whole front of the place. Against the wall was a broken oar, two boat-hooks, and the stained and faded red cushions of a pleasure-boat. One went up three steps to the glass-panelled door and peeped into a broad, low room with a bar and a beer-engine, behind which were many bright and helpful-looking bottles against mirrors, and great and little pewter measures, and bottles fastened in brass wire upside down, with their corks replaced by taps, and a white china cask labelled 'Shrub', and cigar boxes, and boxes of cigarettes, and a couple of toby jugs and a beautifully coloured hunting scene framed and glazed, showing the most elegant people taking Piper's Cherry Brandy, and cards as the law requires about the dilution of spirits and the illegality of bringing children into bars, and satirical verses about swearing and asking for credit, and three very bright, red-cheeked wax apples, and a round-shaped clock.

(31) A Victorian monstrosity: from P. G. Wodehouse's *Summer Moonshine*, 1938.

Walsingford Hall had not always presented the stupefying spectacle which it did today. Built in the time of Queen Elizabeth on an eminence overlooking the silver Thames, it must, for two centuries and more, have been a lovely place. The fact that it now caused sensitive oarsmen, rounding the bend of the river and seeing it suddenly, to wince and catch crabs was due to the unfortunate circumstance of the big fire, which, sooner or later, seems to come to all English country houses, postponing its arrival until midway through the reign of Queen Victoria, thus giving the task of rebuilding it from the foundations up to Sir Wellington Abbott, at that time its proprietor.

  Whatever may be said in favour of the Victorians it is pretty generally admitted that few of them were to be trusted within reach of a trowel and a pile of bricks. Sir Wellington least of any. He was as virulent an amateur architect as ever grew a whisker. Watching the holocaust in his nightshirt, for he had to nip rather smartly out of a burning bedroom, he forgot the cold wind blowing about his ankles in the thought that here was his chance to do a big job and do

The towpath near Benson

it well. He embarked upon it at the earliest possible moment, regardless of expense.

What Sir Buckstone was now looking at, accordingly, was a vast edifice constructed of glazed red brick, in some respects resembling a French chateau, but, on the whole, perhaps, having more the appearance of one of those model dwellings in which a certain number of working-class families are assured of a certain number of cubic feet of air. It had a huge leaden roof, tapering to a point and topped by a weathervane, and from one side of it, like some unpleasant growth, there protruded a large conservatory. There were also a dome and some minarets.

Victorian villagers gazing up at it had named it Abbott's Folly, and they had been about right.

(32) A naturalist examines the left bank on foot, from Wallingford to Stoke Ferry: from Edward Thomas's *The Icknield Way*, 1913.

I went past the little towerless and spireless church of Newnham Murren, which had a number of crooked, ivy-covered tombstones, and was itself covered with ivy, which travellers' joy was beginning to climb. Then over Grim's Ditch, a mile and a half west of the Icknield Way crossing, I came to Mongewell park, and my path was along a line of huge elms and sweet limes. On my left, the main road and its telegraph wires ran bordered with sharlock along the top of a low ridge above these meadows. From North Stoke there was a good road. I turned aside to the church, but found what was better, a big range of tiled, thatched sheds and barns extending on either side of my path, with a cattle-yard in the midst full of dazzling straw and richly-stinking cow dung, and a big black sow lying on it like a recumbent statue on a huge pedestal. Swifts were shrieking above and chickens clucking in the corners. From the road the tiled church and the thatched barn fell into line, and seemed one, especially as the farm pigeons were perched on the ridges of both. On a corn rick behind I saw the figure of a sheep on a weather-vane. This road went alongside hedgeless barley on the left, over which I could see the bare, low hills between me and the Icknield Way, and far beyond them the wooded fields around Nuffield and Nettlebed; on the right there was hay to the river; there was succory on the roadside, scabious, knapweed, rest-harrow, and long grass.

To reach the ferry at Little Stoke I turned off to the right under elm trees and was rowed across.

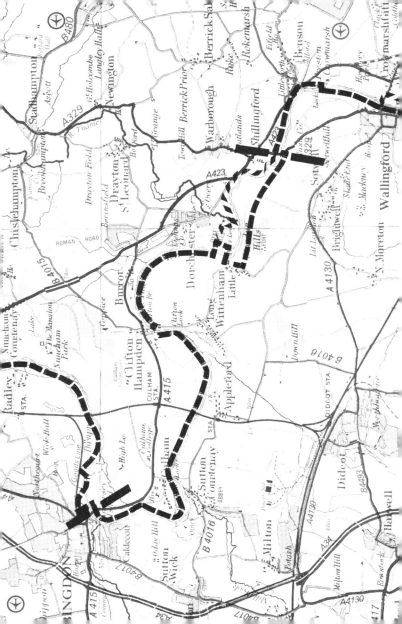

Stage 9 **Shillingford to Abingdon** 9.9 miles (16 km)

SPECIFICS

Another lovely stage along the Middle Thames, enhanced by a 2-mile
section away from the river bank between Shillingford and Little
Wittenham. Clifton Hampden provides a perfect midway point
and Abingdon a perfect destination; and Dorchester, the Sinodun
Hills and Sutton Courtenay are three delightful places fractionally
off course. Easy throughout, virtually all on earth or grass.

Path Upstream: see also Strip Chart
Shillingford Bridge to Little Wittenham footbridge
　　Up the right bank for 0.3 miles, then left to gain a bridleway track
parallel to the river. Ahead along this, past North Farm and
through fields and then through Little Wittenham Wood. Then go
half right across a field to Little Wittenham Church, and by a lane
down to the river.

Little Wittenham footbridge to Clifton Hampden Bridge:
alternative route 3.7 miles (6 km)
　　Until the crossing at Day's Lock is opened, take the road up
through Little Wittenham, then right to Long Wittenham and
Clifton Hampden Bridge.

Path Downstream: see also Strip Chart
Clifton Hampden Bridge to Little Wittenham footbridge:
alternative route 3.7 miles (6 km)
　　Until the crossing at Day's Lock is opened, take the road to Long
Wittenham, then left to Little Wittenham, and down to the
footbridge.

Little Wittenham footbridge to Shillingford Bridge
　　Up the lane to Little Wittenham Church. Left on to a bridleway
across a field, heading for the top far corner. The bridleway then
leads straight through Little Wittenham Wood and fields beyond, to
North Farm. 0.3 miles on, turn left to regain the river bank, and go
along it to Shillingford Bridge.

Approach by car
At start: Shillingford is in Oxfordshire, 3 miles beyond Wallingford on the A423 towards Oxford; park in village near the bridge. *At end*: Abingdon is in Oxfordshire, 5 miles south of Oxford on the A34; car-park by the bridge. *Also*: at Clifton Hampden, 3 miles east of Abingdon on the A415; car-park on the farther side of the bridge.

Approach by other transport
Train: British Rail station at Didcot (4 miles from Clifton Hampden and 6 miles from Abingdon). *Bus*: from London, Oxford City Link to Shillingford, Dorchester and Abingdon. *Taxi*: Didcot, David's Taxis (0235-818582); Abingdon, Auto Taxis (0235-27711).

Refreshment
Pubs: Fleur de Lys, Dorchester; Barley Mow, Clifton Hampden; Nags Head, Abingdon. *Restaurants*: Abingdon Bridge Restaurant.

Accommodation
Hotels: Shillingford Bridge Hotel, Wallingford OX10 8LZ (0867-328567); White Hart Hotel, Dorchester on Thames OX9 8HN (0865-340074); Upper Reaches, Thames Street, Abingdon OX14 3JA (0235-22311). *Guest houses and small hotels*: Barley Mow, Clifton Hampden, Abingdon OX14 3EH (0867-307847).

Admission
Abingdon County Hall, afternoons except Mondays.

Stage 9 **Shillingford at Abingdon** 9.9 miles (16 km)

Shillingford Bridge, with its three semicircular arches and its decorative balustrade, is one of the finest Thames bridges. It was built in 1827 (partly rebuilt in 1906) in conjunction with a new turnpike road to Reading. This is why it is not actually at the village of *Shillingford* (the ford of the Scillingas), which we see within a few minutes after starting this Stage. The village street leads down to where there was once a wharf for a brewery, and the large house at the water's edge was built early this century for a prosperous tailor. From the mud of the river near here a ceremonial Saxon sword, the tip of its blade broken, has recently been recovered. Three-quarters of a mile upstream is where the Roman Road leading from Silchester (near Reading) to Alchester (near Bicester) via Dorchester crossed the Thames at a point known as Old Street Ford.

On the right bank is Little Wittenham Wood, now a nature reserve, with plenty of mammals such as foxes, rabbits, stoats and weasels, and birds such as magpies, jays, wood pigeons and pheasants. Behind and above the wood are two hillocks: these are the Sinodun Hills, or Berkshire Bubs; and the trees on them are known as the Wittenham Clumps. The one less well seen by us is called Castle Hill, and massive earthworks demonstrate that it was once a formidable Iron Age fort, with banks and ditches more than twice their present size, with wooden palisades and fortified entrance gate. Indeed, it is no exaggeration to say that in Iron Age times this fort was the strategic centre of Southern England, and there was probably more fighting around here than anywhere else on our Path, as for instance between the Atrebati and the Catuvellauni who respectively controlled the land north and south of the Thames immediately before Roman rule.

On the left bank the Thame flows into the Thames just opposite the lower end of Little Wittenham Wood. This is confusing, even though the Thames is like 'hems' and the Thame like 'name'. The medieval scholars of Oxford, of the sort that spent their time calculating how many angels could sit on the tip of a needle,

pondered this and came up with a solution. Because Julius Caesar had refered to *Thamesis* that must mean the junction of the Thame and the 'Isis' – an entirely bogus name that has stuck to the Thames above the Thame. Not only that, but the tiny Thame thus acquired a sort of seniority, and when Michael Drayton in Elizabethan times wrote of their union, Isis was the bride and Thame the bridegroom.

At *Little Wittenham* (Witta's dry ground) a small group of houses nestles around the church of St Peter, protected by a chestnut and a Wellingtonia. The tower is fifteenth-century, the rest 1863. On the footbridge we see the pool described by C. J. Cornish when so unusually low after a dry autumn (33, page 199). The footbridge gives on to an area of land bounded on two sides by the Thames and on a third by the Thame. The Iron Age chiefs made use of this geographical advantage to secure the landward side by an immense double line of banks with intervening ditch, known as the Dyke Hills. This enclosed an area of 46 hectares, which would have been used for the protection of the tribe and its livestock in times of danger. Just outside the line of the Dyke Hills is Dorchester.

The story of *Dorchester on Thames* begins with the Romans who, rejecting the old hill fort on Castle Hill, built their own fort (Dorcina Castra) on the line of their new road. Trade then followed the flag (or rather, the eagles) and it grew into a commercial centre. But by the fifth century AD the legions had left; and the English (or Saxon) tribesmen were building their huts amid the Roman ruins; in time they founded their own town of Dorchester. It was here that St Birinus came and in 635 baptized Cynegils, the Saxon King of Wessex (34, page 201). The ceremony probably took place in the Thame, with the King and his warriors, stripped of their ornaments, passing through the stream in total submersion before being blessed by the Saint under the approving eye of the visiting King of Northumbria. This momentous event greatly helped the spread of Christianity in England, and Dorchester became a religious centre comparable to Canterbury. But in the eleventh century the bishop moved to Lincoln, and the great Augustinian abbey-church of St Peter and St Paul, which we now see, replaced the Saxon cathedral.

Wittenham Clump

Day's Lock is the main gauging station for measuring the flow of water in the Upper Thames. From it we walk two and a half miles around the curve to Clifton Hampden, all the way on fields and meadows in a rural setting only slightly marred by some housing on the Burcot Bank (John Masefield lived in one of these). Approaching Clifton Hampden we came to the only place in its entire course where the Thames flows over a bed of hard sandstone and not on alluvial sediment. This feature always made it dangerous for boats and is why the first Royal Commission on the Thames had Burcot at the lower end of its remit. But it still continued to be a hazard, and the Lord Mayor of London's barge, in its progression downstream in 1826, was 'detained at Clifton a considerable length of time', even though it drew hardly two feet of water. The mirth and jollity of the local peasantry, so patronizingly described by Lord Mayor Venables' chaplain, Mr Dillon, in his official account of this joy-ride (35, page 201), may at this juncture have been at the expense of the mayoral party, and even Mr Alderman Atkins may have tired of hurling out largesse. At any rate, *The Lord Mayor's Visit to Oxford* was in London received with hilarity and Venables became something of a laughing-stock, neatly hoist by his own petard.

As we see it, *Clifton Hampden* (the settlement on the river buff, belonging to the Hampdens), is in large measure the creation of an enlightened landowner, Henry Gibbs, who purchased the estate in 1842. He it was who restored the church (St Michael and All Angels) and built the large gabled rectory on the river bluff, now occupied by his descendant who has placed two splendid old statues, of Marlborough and Prince Eugene, on the terrace. More important for us, Gibbs also ordered the building of the bridge, which was badly needed after the dredging to deepen the Burcot shallows. The design (first sketched by Giles Gilbert Scott on his starched shirt-cuff) is Norman Gothic and includes pedestrian refuges above all the cutwaters, still very necessary. It is made of local bricks, and was opened in 1867. Of course, it was financed by tolls like all the other bridges, and at some period the following

Marlborough about to attack Clifton Hampden Bridge

notice had been erected by it: 'For every horse, or other beast drawing any Coach, Stage Coach, Omnibus, Van, Caravan, Sociable, Berlin, Landau, Chariot, Vis-a-Vis, Barouche, Phaeton, Waggonet, Chaise, Marina, Caleche, Curricle, Chair, Gig, Dog-Cart, Irish-Car, Whiskey-Hearse, Litter, or any like Carriage, Sixpence'. The pub on the right bank is the Barley Mow: though badly damaged by fire in 1975, it was rebuilt with a thatched roof to harmonize with those parts which date from 1350.

Lying up in his boat just here above the bridge we find Robert Gibbings (36, page 202), author of *Sweet Thames Run Softly* and *Till I End My Song*, two books which evoked the spirit of the Thames to a past generation. He lived at Footbridge Cottage, Long Wittenham, but was often on the river and once sailed down from Lechlade to Kingston in a specially built flat-bottomed boat called *The Willow*, announcing his approach with blasts blown through a conch shell. As the quotation shows, he understood women as much as he did all forms of natural life, and had great success with them, for he was a tall, handsome man with aquiline features. Besides boating he also made use of the towpath and describes a walk along the stretch above Clifton Hampden in a light fall of snow in December beside the dark running water, and noting how the snipe had arrived from Norway and the sandpipers had departed for Africa.

Our route goes successively alongside two long lock cuts – the Clifton Cut and later the Culham Cut. Each bypasses a meander of the river, the first at Long Wittenham and the second at Sutton Courtenay. Between the cuts is the Appleford railway bridge, with steel bowstring girders of lattice construction, built in 1929. Sutton Bridge, though much restored, dates from 1807 and pre-dates by a few years the Culham Cut, for which a separate bridge had to be built in the long stone causeway. *Sutton Courtenay* (the south settlement, belonging to the Courtenays) is half a mile off our course, either by the mainstream bridge or by a later footbridge over the cut. It features a charming village green, two water-mills, a Norman hall, a Tudor manor house, a medieval grange known as The Abbey, and a fourteenth-century church (of All Saints), in whose churchyard H. H. Asquith (Prime Minister 1908–16) and

Eric Blair (George Orwell) are buried.

After Culham Lock, to our right, is the village of *Culham* (Cula's dry ground) including the manor house, mainly Jacobean and with parts of a medieval grange. At the turn of the river we head north beside a broad reach, good for sailing, and at its end come to a footbridge over a backwater with a good view of a lovely old brick bridge just above it. This backwater is supposed to have been the original mainstream of the Thames, but the Saxon Abbots of Abingdon found it worth while to divert as much water as they could to the side streams which ran past their abbey, and the present river is the result of their dredging. The Swift Ditch, as the former mainstream was now called, still attracted a certain flow of water, besides being three-quarters of a mile shorter. So it is not surprising that the Oxford-Burcot Commissioners should have decided to build a pound lock in the Swift Ditch in the 1630s. This pound lock was the lowest of the original three as described more than 300 years ago with admirable clarity by Dr Plot (37, page 204). It remained the navigational channel till 1790 when a new lock was constructed at Abingdon and the Swift Ditch was dammed by an overspill weir.

As to the brick bridge across the Swift Ditch, it is part of a substantial engineering project by the merchants of Abingdon in the fifteenth century. Their problem was that the rival Wallingford was thriving on the commerce that passed over its Thames bridge, especially the pack-trains of mules carrying wool from the Cotswolds towards London. Their solution was to finance and build their own bridge. But because of the split streams this meant bridges over both and a long causeway over the low Andersey Island. So through their guild, the Fraternity of the Holy Cross, they purchased the land from the Abbot, obtained a charter from Henry V, and laid the first stone on 17 June 1416: the whole thing was completed in 1422.

The causeway is still walkable, since the modern road goes alongside it, but our route is by the river through the meadows till the spire of St Helen's affirms our approach to *Abingdon*. Just before the church the little Ock joins the Thames under an iron bridge: at one time the Wiltshire and Berkshire Canal also entered here.

I conclude with a restrospective glance down Stage 9 in the
doggerel verse of John Taylor who voyaged down the Thames from
Oxford in 1632. He was, after all, a famous pedestrian, once
walking the 400 miles from London to Edinburgh for a bet, though
when it came to water he was very much at home in a boat, being at
one time a professional London Waterman:

> At Abingdon the shoals are worse and worse,
> That Swift Ditch seems to be the better course,
> Below which town near Sutton there are left
> Piles that almost our barge's bottom cleft;
> Then Sutton locks are great impediments,
> The waters fall with such great violence,
> Thence down to Culham, stream runs quick and quicker,
> Yet we rubbed twice aground for want of liquour.
> The weir of carpenter's sans fault I think,
> But yet near Wittenham town a tree did sink,
> Whereas by fortune we our barge did hit,
> And by misfortune there a board was split;
> At Clifton there are rocks, and sands, and flats,
> Which made us wade, and wet like drownéd rats,
> The passage bare, the water often gone,
> And rocks smooth worn, do pave it like free stone.
> From Clifton down to Wallingford we fleet,
> Where (for annoyance) piles are placed unmeet . . .

ANTHOLOGY
(33) The pool below Day's Lock after the dry autumn of 1893: from
Charles Cornish's *The Naturalist on the Thames*, 1902.

'Thee've got no water in 'ee, and if 'ee don't fill'ee avore New Year,
'ee 'll be no more good for a stree-um'! Thus briefly, to Father
Thames, the shepherd of Sinodun Hill. He had pitched his float into
the pool below the weir – the pool which lies on the broad, flat

The spire of St Helen's, Abingdon

fields, with scarce a house in sight but the lockman's cottage – and for the first time on a Saturday's fishing he saw his bait go clear to the bottom instead of being lost to view instantly in the boiling water of the weir-pool. He could even see the broken piles and masses of concrete which the river in its days of strength had torn up and scattered on the bottom, and among them the shoals of fat river fish eyeing his worm as critically as his master would sample of most inferior oats. Yet the pool was beautiful to look upon. Where the water had sunk the rushes had grown taller than ever, and covered the little sandbanks left by the ebbing river with a forest of green and of red gold, where the frost had laid its finger on them. In the back eddies and shallows the dying lily leaves covered the surface with scales of red and copper, and all along the banks teazles and frogbits, and brown and green reeds, and sedges of bronze and russet, made a screen, through which the black and white moorhens popped in and out, while the water-rats, now almost losing the aquatic habit, and becoming pedestrian, sat peeling rushes with their teeth, and eyeing the shepherd on the weir. Even the birds seemed to have voted that the river was never going to fill again, for a colony of sandpipers, instead of continuing their migration to the coast, had taken up their quarters on the little spits of mud and shingle now fringing the weir-pool, and were flitting from point to point, and making believe it was a bit of Pagham Harbour or Porchester Creek. On every sunny morning monster spiders ran out from the holes and angles of the weir-frame, and spun webs across and across the straddling iron legs below the footbridge, right down to the lowered surface of the water, which had so sunk that each spider had at least four feet more of web than he could have reckoned upon before and waxed fat on the produce of the added superficies of enmeshed and immolated flies. So things went on almost till New Year's Eve.

(34) The conversion of the West Saxons at Dorchester in 635:
from Bede's *Anglo-Saxon Chronicle*, eighth century (translation
J. A. Giles).

At that time, the West Saxons, formerly called Gewissae, in the
reign of Cynegils, embraced the faith of Christ, at the preaching of
Bishop Birinus, who came into Britain by the advice of Pope
Honorius; having promised in his presence that he would sow the
seed of the holy faith in the inner parts beyond the dominions of the
English, where no other teachers had been before him. Hereupon
he received episcopal consecration from Asterius, bishop of Genoa;
but on his arrival in Britain, he first entered the nation of the
Gewissae, and finding all there most confirmed pagans, he thought
it better to preach the word of God here, then to proceed further to
seek for others to preach to.
   Now, as he preached in the aforesaid province, it happened that
the king himself, having been catechized, was baptized together
with his people, and Oswold, the most holy and victorious king of
the Northumbrians, being present, received him as he came forth
from baptism, and by an alliance most pleasing and acceptable to
God, first adopted him, thus regenerated, for his son, and then took
his daughter in marriage. The two kings gave to the bishop the city
called Dorcic, there to settle his episcopal see; where, having built
and consecrated churches, and by his labour called many to the
Lord, he departed this life, and was buried in the same city . . .

(35) Largesse scattered to the peasantry: from Robert Dillon's *The
Lord Mayor's visit to Oxford*, 1826.

The crowds of people, – men, women, and children, – who had
accompanied the barge from Oxford, were continually succeeded
by fresh reinforcements from every town and village that is skirted
by the river. Distant shouts of acclamation perpetually re-echoed
from field to field, as the various rustic parties, with their fresh and
blooming faces, were seen hurrying forth from their cottages and
gardens; climbing trees, struggling through copses, and traversing

thickets, to make their shortest way to the waterside. Handfuls of halfpence were scattered to the children as they kept pace in running along the banks with the City Barge; and Mr Alderman Atkins, who assisted the Lord Mayor in the distribution, seemed to enter, with more than common pleasure, into the enjoyment of the little children. It was gratifying to see the absence of selfish feeling manifested by some of the elder boys, who, forgetful of themselves, collected for the younger girls.

There is, unquestionably, something genuine and affectionate in the cheerfulness of the common people, when it springs from the bounty and familiarity of those above them: the warm glow of gratitude spreads over their mirth; and a kind word, or look, or a little pleasantry, frankly said or done, – and which calls in no degree for any sacrifice of personal dignity, – always gladdens the heart of a dependant a thousand times more than oil and wine. It is wonderful, too, how much life and joy even one intelligent and good-humoured member of a pleasure-party will diffuse around him. The fountain of indwelling delight, which animates his own bosom, overflows to others; and every thing around quickly freshens into smiles.

(36) An invitation to come aboard near Clifton Hampden: from Robert Gibbings' *Sweet Thames Run Softly*, 1940.

I happened to be tied up at the mouth of a backwater, and I suppose my craft was inconspicuous. Anyway, just as I lifted the corner of the canopy to glimpse if there was a break in the sky, what should I see on the opposite bank but a girl, running fast and upstream, and she with nothing on. It was still raining so hard that I could not see clearly, but instead of the delicate pink which I am led to believe is the usual colour of naked damsels, this naiad was shining all over with the rain, so that she might have been clothed in silver sequins.

Now, said I to myself, is this nature, or am I a gentleman? But before I had reached a conclusion my head touched one of the main

supports of the canopy, and a sluice of water into the stern of the boat abruptly changed the subject of my thoughts.

The shower passed as quickly as it had come on. A few minutes later the sun was shining, and I was rolling up the canvas hood in readiness for breakfast. Suddenly in mid-stream I saw the head of my sprite, her black hair encrusted with pearls of rain. She was swimming down-stream, and she looked in my direction, just as I caught sight of her.

'Hallo,' she said, 'where did you come from?'

'Been here all night,' I replied. 'Have you come far yourself?'

'From below the bend,' she said.

I had a sort of idea that I knew her face, and she seemed to know who I was.

'Got much drawing done?' she asked.

'Come aboard and I'll show you,' I said, looking as innocent as a lamb.

'I couldn't do that,' she replied.

'Why not?' said I.

'I'm not dressed for the occasion.'

'That won't embarrass me,' I ventured.

'It might *me*, though.'

'Look here,' said I, 'I've been watching birds, fish, frogs, cows, horses, and rabbits for the past month, and not one of them has worn as much as a pair of pants or a brassière.' The poor girl was obviously getting cold, and I was sorry for her. 'Come on,' I said, 'the kettle is boiling over, and I'll make you a cup of tea.'

(37) An early description of the three original Thames pound locks ('turnpikes') and their improvements over the flash locks ('locks'): from Dr R. Plot's *The Natural History of Oxfordshire*, 1677.

Hither also belong the Locks and Turn-pikes made upon the River Isis, the 21 of King James, when it was made navigable from Oxford to Bercot, which are absolutely necessary for that purpose, on shallow rivers that have also great falls, to keep up the water, and give the vessels an easie descent. For the first whereof, provided the

fall of the water be not great, a Lock will suffice, which is made up
only of bars of wood called Rimers, set perpendicularly to the
bottom of the passage (which are more or less according to its
breadth) and Lock-gates put down between every two of them, or
boards put athwart them, which will keep a head of water as well as
the Turn-pike for the passage of a Barge, but must be pulled up at
its arrival, and the water let go till there is an abatement of the fall,
before the boat may pass either down or upwards; which, with the
stream, is not without violent precipitation; and against it, at many
places, not without the help of a Captain at land; and sometimes
neither of them without imminent danger.

But where the declivity of the Channel, and fall of water is so
great, that few barges could live in the passage of them, there we
have turn-pikes, whereof there are three between Oxford and
Bercot; one at Ifley, another at Sanford, and a third at Culham in
the Swift-ditch, which was cut at that time when the river was made
navigable; and all are thus contrived. First, there are placed a great
pair of Folding doors, or Flood-gates of timber cross the river, that
open against the stream and shut with it, not so as to come even in a
straight line, but in an obtuse angle, the better to resist and bear the
weight of the water, which by how much the greater it is, by so
much the closer the gates are pressed; in each of which Flood-gates
there is a sluce to let the water through at pleasure, without opening
the gates themselves. Within these, there is a large square taken out
of the river, built up at each end with Free-stone, big enough to
receive the largest barge afloat; and at the other end another pair of
Flood-gates, opening, and shutting, and having sluces like the
former. Which is the whole fabric of a Turn-pike.

At the uppermost pair of these gates the water is stopt, which
raises it in the river above, and gives the Vessels passage over the
shallows, which when come to the Turn-pikes, the sluces are first
opened, and the water let in to the square or inclosed space between
the two pair of gates, where it must necessarily rise (the lower gates
being shut) till at length it comes to be level with the surface of the
river above: when this is done, the upper stream then making no
such pressure on the gates as before, they are easily opened by two
or three men, and the Vessels let in one at a time; which done, they

shut these upper gates and sluces as before: then they open the sluces of the gates at the other end of the Turn-pike, and let the water by degrees out of the enclosed square till it is sunk down, and the Vessel with it, level with the river below, and then open the gates themselves, and let the Vessel out; the upper gates all the while being drove too, and kept so fast by the water above, that little of it can follow. And thus the boats go downstream.

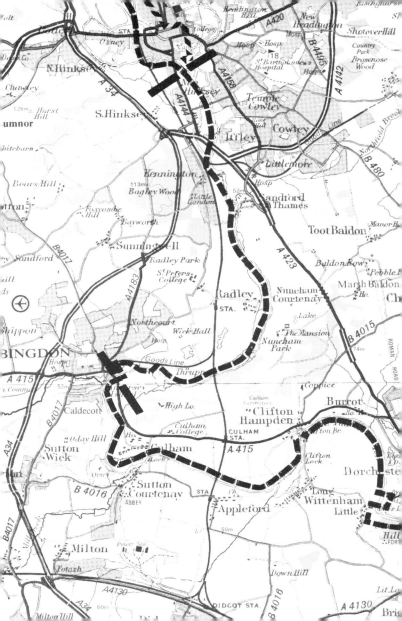

Stage 10 **Abingdon to Oxford** 8.3 miles (13.3 km)

SPECIFICS

As far as Sandford this Stage leads from the fine old centre of
Abingdon through an entirely rural sweep of the Thames past the
high bank of Nuneham. Beyond Sandford we are in the orbit of
Oxford, though set between parks and gardens, and we come right
up to the glorious buildings of the ancient colleges. Between
Abingdon and Sandford it is nearly all earth or grass; between
Sandford and Oxford mainly gravel or metal. The going is easy
throughout.

Path Upstream and Downstream: see Strip Charts

Approach by car
At start: Abingdon is in Oxfordshire, 5 miles south of Oxford on the
A34; car-park by the bridge. *At end*: Oxford (for Folly Bridge, St
Aldate's) is 55 miles from London by the A40/M40; St Ebbe's
car-park. *Also*: at Sandford on Thames, 1 mile south of the Oxford
ring road off the A423; park in the village street.

Approach by other transport
Train: British Rail station at Oxford. *Bus*: from London, Oxford
City Link to Abingdon and Oxford. *Boat*: summer service at
Abingdon and Oxford. *Taxi*: Abingdon, Auto Taxis (0235-27711);
Oxford, ABC Taxis (0865-770681).

Refreshment
Pubs: Nags Head, Abingdon; King's Arms, Sandford; Isis, Iffley
Lock; Head of the River, Folly Bridge, Oxford. *Restaurants*:
Abingdon Bridge Restaurant, Abingdon; Restaurant Elizabeth, St
Aldate's, Oxford.

Accommodation
Hotels: Upper Reaches, Thames Street, Abingdon OX14 3JA
(0235-22311); Randolph Hotel, Beaumont Street, Oxford

OX1 2LN (0865-247481). *Guest houses and small hotels*: Bassimer, Church Road, Sandford on Thames OX4 4XZ (0865-779324); Tree Hotel, Iffley, Oxford OX4 4EY (0865-775974); Newton House, 82 Abingdon Road, Oxford OX1 4PL (0865-240561). *Youth hostel*: Jack Straw's Lane, Oxford OX3 ODW (0865-62997). *Camping*: Oxford Camping International, 426 Abingdon Road, Oxford OX1 4XN (0865-246551).

Admission
Abingdon County Hall, afternoons except Mondays; Oxford colleges' admissions for visits vary and fluctuate, but generally they are open most afternoons.

Stage 10 **Abingdon to Oxford** 8.3 miles (13.3 km)

For walkers along the Thames the most attractive riverside towns are those with unspoilt river frontages and historic centres close behind, where one can imagine oneself in the past and feast on ancient architecture. In this respect Abingdon is outstanding and possesses more important buildings than either Henley or Wallingford despite the thorough destruction of its great abbey. *Abingdon* (Aebba's hill) was the county town of Berkshire, and to this we owe its central monument, the County Hall, which dominates the Market Place, site of the great Abingdon fairs of the past. From behind the County Hall East St Helen Street, with nice old houses, leads to Abingdon's principal church, St Helen's, right beside the river. Here the wealth of the burghers of Abingdon is richly displayed, for much of the church was financed by the same Fraternity of the Holy Cross who built the original bridge and causeway. Outside the church and below the soaring spire are three sets of almshouses, the oldest Long Alley (1446), built by the Fraternity.

Abingdon Bridge, which crosses the little Nags Head Island, was entirely rebuilt in 1929 but with great care to preserve the appearance of the bridge of 1790. The former county boundary ran along the river and is one reason why the town never spread over to the left bank, so preserving a fine open space and enhancing the quality of life at Abingdon which must more than compensate for civic disappointments of the past such as the absorption into Oxfordshire and the closure of the MG car factory.

Once over lock and weir we tread briefly on Abbey Meadow and then cross the Abbey mill-stream by the first two new footbridges which secure our route through yet another missing link in the old tow-path. The entrance to the Swift Ditch is to be seen on the far bank near where we rejoin the river.

Nuneham railway bridge dates also from 1929. It is the second Thames crossing of the line between Didcot and Oxford. Unlike the original main line to Bristol, this line was not graced with beautiful brick bridges. Money was tighter, and Brunel was anxious to open

the line quickly, so he built only wooden viaducts, later succeeded by iron and then steel bridges.

Once under it we look ahead to a conifer-covered hillside along the far bank. This is Lock Wood, so named from the weir (or 'lock') that once blocked the river at the little island half a mile on. A rustic bridge once linked this island to the far bank, where stood a picturesque cottage. This is where Wellington Wack had his brush with the old lady (38, page 220). She was evidently under orders to keep people away, for this had become a favourite spot for Victorian excursionists; but it was a poor reception for a couple of Anglophilic Yankees in their canoe the *Fuzzy-Wuzzy*, which Wellington describes as 'a light, tippy, fifteen-foot canoe, prettily ribbed with ash and cedar, and decked-in fourteen inches from stern and bow. She was a rakish little craft, promising sport and mishap.'

Nuneham (new settlement) Park now opens up and the first thing we see is a stone monument atop a hillock. This is the Carfax Conduit: that is to say, it is the decorative cistern that once stood at Carfax in the centre of Oxford, from which could be drawn the water that was supplied to the city from a reservoir by means of lead pipes and hollow elm trunks. It contained a primary cistern reserved for university people, and an overflow cistern for the townspeople. Anyway, this system eventually was superseded, and the Conduit Head was relegated to Nuneham Park. Seen close up, it is an elaborate piece of sculpture dating from 1616 and carved with mermaids, dragons and unicorns.

Nuneham House, for which this park was formed, is a Palladian mansion built for the Harcourt family. It became famous for the magnificent setting, used to brilliant effect by 'Capability' Brown, who so arranged the grass rides and clumps of trees that a series of separate vistas, most of them towards the Thames, could be seen from the house. As William Whitehead, a poet of those times, wrote of Brown's work at Nuneham:

Who thinn'd, and who group'd, and who scatter'd those trees,
Who bade the slopes fall with that delicate ease,

The Carfax Conduit at Nuneham

Who cast them in shade, and who plac'd them in light,
Who bade them divide, and who bade them unite?

This landscaping called for the razing of an entire village near the
house and the building of a new model village along the main road
nearly a mile off. This drastic action, though not unique, divided
opinion between those who thought that everyone had benefited,
including the cottagers in their new houses, and those who deplored
the depopulation of the countryside, as expressed in Goldsmith's
The Deserted Village. Nuneham was also well known because the
Harcourts were leading figures in society and many famous people
visited them here.

One has to bear all this in mind to appreciate fully the scene of the
bestowal of prizes for industry and merit as described by Boydell
(39, page 222). There are lovely similarities with scenes in *The
Marriage of Figaro* and *Albert Herring*; and, of course, one can either
admire the social paternalism of Lord and Lady Harcourt or despise
their atrocious condescension. Incidentally, the church to which they
all repaired is the domed structure (All Saints), disguised as a
classical temple. The house has since been extended and the park
partly ploughed and forested, and neither looks as good as it once did.

Soon after Nuneham Boathouse on the far bank we come to
Radley College boathouse on ours. Radley (the College is a mile
and a half off) has a rowing tradition second only to Eton's and an
even better stretch of river for rowing on. Moored in front of the
boathouse when not in use is a training raft on which the coach
stands like a slave-driver while the oarsmen perform like
galley-slaves.

Alders, which have predominated all the way from Abingdon,
now line our route up to *Sandford*. These small trees look most
effective during winter because, although all the leaves have blown
away, they remain covered with purplish-brown club-shaped buds,
set alternately along dark brown twigs, as well as spent cones and
drooping catkins; and they are to be welcomed also for
strengthening the bank against erosion.

Sandford Lock

Sandford Lock (1973) has the deepest fall on the Thames – 2.7 m. It is on the site of one of the three original Thames locks or 'turnpikes', as described by Dr Plot (37, page 204): Iffley and Sandford were both working by 1632 and the Culham Lock in the Swift Ditch soon after, and then no more were built for a century and a half. We approach it by a footbridge over a large weir stream towards the housing on the site of the old paper mill. The millstream is now blocked, and beyond it and the lock is the excellent King's Arms.

After Sandford Lock we enter the orbit of the university, an area where Oxford men (and now women) have for long come on foot or by water; a guidebook of 1823 refers to 'cutting down swiftly, amid light breezes and pleasant sunshine, to Sandford, quaffing a cup of Mrs Davies' Anno Domini'. They also came to bathe in the lasher pool just below the weir which is audible to our left. Through a protective railing we can see on the weir a stone memorial to five undergraduates of Christ Church who, over the years, lost their lives here: one was Michael Llewelyn Davies, one of the brothers who inspired James Barrie's *Peter Pan*.

Just opposite, on the far bank, is an old stone building slightly set back. Parts of it are medieval and are the remains of a former preceptory of the Knights Templar, who were given land here in 1240, though their tenure was short indeed for in 1312 the Order was dissolved and savagely suppressed.

Our route up to Iffley is pleasant although we are aware of high-tension wires, railways and extensive housing all close by. The only house by us is on Rose Island at the sharp bend, and it looks charming but definitely floodable. The Kennington railway bridge is an unlovely affair of 1923: it is used only for freight traffic to the Cowley Works. Immediately beyond it is our nice wooden bridge over the Hinksey Stream, which here returns to the Thames the waters drawn from it at various points upstream. And then, after a grove of poplars, we go under the 1962 ring-road bridge, which, like others of its type, is so disproportionately broad and wide and so plain, flat and utilitarian, that we can hardly admire it even though it does keep the traffic out of our way. Once under it, we come to *Iffley* (plover glade).

The tower of St Mary's, Iffley stands high on the far bank just below the lock. This is arguably the finest, and certainly the most complete, Norman church in England; an entity of elaborate sculpture fashioned around deeply recessed doors and windows. Beside it is the original rectory, available from the Landmark Trust on short leases. These, and other surrounding houses and walls, are all of stone, for we have by now crossed an important boundary in terms of architecture. Until now brick has been the basic material: from now on, as we come closer to the quarries of the Cotswolds, stone predominates. In and around Oxford the grander and older buildings are of pure limestone ashlar, whilst most of the more ordinary and modern ones are of a honey-coloured rubble stone known as coral rag.

Iffley Lock is most attractively situated with rollers on one side and on the other a covered wooden footbridge over a former mill stream (the mill burnt down in 1908), providing a crossing to Iffley. At the upper end of the rollers is a balustraded bridge, and from it steps lead down to a waterside platform where a plaque with a bronze bull's head records that the ubiquitous Lord Desborough donated it to mark the official starting point of the bumping races.

These developed purely spontaneously. Back in the early nineteenth century, eights, who had rowed down to Mrs Davies at Sandford of a summer evening, on returning through Iffley Lock (before the rollers were laid) four at a time, took to racing out of it and trying to bump the one in front. Soon this became the main inter-college rowing contest. The Summer Eights take place in late May or early June, and the Torpids in late March or early April, each over four days and split into divisions. The eights are stationed 40 m apart and at the sound of the gun all start rowing furiously to try and hit the boat ahead. The next day the successful eights start at a higher position and the unsuccessful at a lower. The ultimate aim is to end the final day as 'head of the river'. The reach up to Folly Bridge is strong in association with these races. The towpath is broad and well laid, suitable for the bicycles of the coaches and the crowds of supporters. After a road bridge comes the Gut, about half way up the course at a bend. Then, once over the Hinksey Millstream and past Harris's Boathouse, the river broadens and

excitement quickens as we reach the *Oxford* University Boathouse opposite the entrance of the Cherwell. A row of college boathouses lines the far bank, but formerly this is where the ceremonial barges were moored, all the way up to Folly Bridge. These barges (of which one at least – that of Jesus College – has been brought back and repaired to its glory by the College Barge Preservation Society) were the setting for the mass-suicide scene in *Zuleika Dobson* (40, page 224). This elaborate fantasy, written in 1911, bore an awful prescience, for shortly afterwards a whole generation of young men were dying on the Western Front in mass self-sacrifice.

Beyond where the boathouses are (and barges were) is Christ Church Meadow. Looking at it, I always recall a line from G. M. Hopkins's poem about Oxford: 'Cuckoo-echoing, bell-swarmèd, lark-charmèd, rook-racked, river-rounded'. The meadow has for centuries been a place for taking brisk walks, or 'constitutionals' as they used to be called, long recognized as good for mind and body. Through the trees we can see some of the dreaming spires. The central group comprises the spires of the Cathedral of St Frideswide and the Church of St Mary, the dome of the Radcliffe Camera, and the tower of Merton. Obscured to the left of them is the octagonal Tom Tower, whose bell is tolled 101 times at five past nine each evening. And to the right of them is Magdalen, from the top of whose graceful tower the choir annually sings its May morning hymn.

At a lower level the college buildings back against the meadow, including the Victorian Meadow Buildings of Christ Church, from one of whose windows Anthony Blanche, in Evelyn Waugh's *Brideshead Revisited*, through a megaphone 'in languishing, sobbing tones recited passages from "The Waste Land" to the sweatered and muffled throng that was on its way to the river'.

By Folly Bridge the stream divides around an island with Salters Boatyard on it. Salters was established in 1858 and soon became the leading Oxford builder of all sorts of boats. At the height of its fame, the firm insituted long-distance steamboat journeys in 1888. The voyage down to Kingston took two days, overnighting at

Punting at Oxford

Henley, and by 1892 this became a daily service in summer. Famous steamers such as *Kingston*, *Cliveden*, *Windsor* and *Henley*, were built for Salters by Clark's of Brinscombe, and the boat which inaugurated the service, *Alaska*, is at present being restored.

Across on the left bank is the Head of the River pub, whose water frontage was once an important wharf. Just beside it is the tiny Trill Mill Stream, one of Oxford's many branches of the Thames, which passes through a long tunnel, a subterranean passage very tempting to intrepid canoeists ever since Ronald Knox first explored it and emerged triumphantly beside Christ Church meadow. Though for sheer guts Ronald Knox's eccentric achievement is as nothing compared to that of Lord Newry who, at 3 a.m. on 15 August 1822, together with five hired men, embarked here in a clinker boat and rowed all the hundred miles to London, reaching Godfrey and Searle's wharf at 9 p.m.: all the locks were by special arrangement ready to receive the boat, and the oarsmen kept up their energy with small rolls of bread dipped in brandy.

ANTHOLOGY
(38) Armed encounter near Nuneham between an old lady and a couple of Yankees: from Henry Wellington Wack's *In Thamesland*, 1906.

Just below Nuneham Park a very picturesque island is well worth exploration, provided the old lady who lives in the straw-thatched cottage near the rustic bridge which joins the island to the park will permit a landing. This old dame – perhaps a pensioner of the manor – would not permit us to approach her shore in order to photograph the island and the moss-grown bridge, which appears more like a well-designed stage setting than a structure in a man's service.

In passing through that arm of the stream which washes the banks of Nuneham Park we disturbed the old dame's ducks with our audible admiration of the scene's loveliness. It may have been Russell's red face or my white hat, the refreshments tucked in the

The Thames at Nuneham

boat on both sides of Russell's round body; or it may have been due
to the old lady's bad liver – a common complaint in the malaria of
the Thames valley. At any rate, this irate dame took her stand on
the duck-landing with a broom in her fist and a look on her unkindly
face that portended assassination. As the nose of the canoe touched
the beach, Russell leaned forward to step out. Suddenly a shower of
gravel and water poured upon us from the enemy's vigorously
wielded broom; a shove and a kick and we were literally swept out
to sea, followed by the anathema of this rebellious shrew. There
was no arguing the matter with her for either brotherly love or the
king's coin. Her obstructive zeal evidently amounted to a passion,
and the kodaker from the fastnesses of New York seems to be the
special *bête noire* of this beaver-tailed dame of the banks of
Nuneham. However, once out of reach of her sand-spitting broom,
we photographed her cottage and the bridge. Then, waving back
our qualified respects, we emerged into the broader reach of the
river.

(39) Prizes for industry and merit awarded by Lord and Lady
Harcourt at Nuneham: from Boydell's *History of the Thames*, 1794.

About twenty years since, Lord and Lady Harcourt formed a design
to encourage industry among the women of their parish, by giving
annual prizes to a certain number of the best spinners of thread. An
idea afterwards suggested itself, that to the *prizes of industry* might
be added *prizes of merit*; so that, at length, the importance of the
annual festival being increased by the addition of its object and
influence, it has gradually risen into an institution, which, besides its
moral interest, is a most delightful spectacle, considered merely in
the character of village festivity. An history of the day in which it is
celebrated, will best explain the object and effect of this admirable
establishment. It must, however, be premised, that the persons of
either sex deserving the prizes of merit are named some time
previous to the festival, by an assembly of those villagers who have
already obtained it. The prizes of industry are contended for on the
day, and on the spot, when and where they are distributed. The

morning is appropriated to the prizes of merit; the noon to the village banquet; the afternoon to the contest for the prizes of industry; an early portion of the evening to the distribution of these prizes; and the subsequent part to the festivity of all.

The villagers, who have obtained the prize of merit in former years, followed the rector of the parish to the church through the garden; the rest of them repaired thither by the common approach: and such as had already been successful competitors for the prize of industry wore them on the occasion. These consist of useful articles of dress, with some small peculiarity of form, or trifling decoration, just sufficient to render the distinction conspicuous. The family attended in the tribune; and the morning service was celebrated with proper psalms and lessons, selected for the occasion. The service was succeeded by a discourse from the pulpit, in the close of which, the persons who had been chosen to receive the prize of merit for the year, and who were conspicuously seated in the centre of the church, were separately addressed by name, with a particular specification of those meritorious actions, and that virtuous conduct, for which they were elected to receive their present distinction. At the conclusion of the service, Lord Harcourt descended from the tribune, and presented the usual prize for the men to the clergyman, who transferred it to the attending claimants. It consists of a hat, whose only distinction is the buckle that fastens the band; which has the name of the person to whom it is destined, with the date of the year, and the words 'prize of merit' engraved upon it. The prizes for the women were presented by Lady Harcourt in the same manner; and consist of straw hats decorated with scarlet riband. The names of the happy and distinguished villagers were then hung up in the church, under the date of the year, among those who at former periods had been found to deserve the honour.

The three groups of stately elms that range in the park front of the house, have already been mentioned in the description of it, and seem to have been placed there to serve the purposes of this festival. Beneath the shade of the central group, dinner was served at two separate tables. The upper table was occupied by those who had at different periods obtained the prize of merit; the lower one was set apart for the several candidates for the prize of industry: both of them were most plentifully, as well as suitably spread; and the happy guests arrived in procession, preceded by a village band of music, to partake of the banquet prepared for them. At proper intervals the healths of their lord and lady, and excellent rector, were drank, who repaid those attentions with similar returns. All the domestic servants attended with eager assiduity upon the village guests; and that they might not be interrupted in the duties of the feast, the family partook of a cold repast. Nor is this all; for these good people not only appeared to be happy, but at their ease; and were rather enlivened into cheerfulness, than restrained into solemnity, by the well-ordered presence of the noble persons to whom they were endebted for the felicity of the day.

(40) Mass suicide at Eights Week: from Max Beerbohm's *Zuleika Dobson*, 1911.

From the towing-path – no more din there now, but great single cries of 'Zuleika!' – leapt figures innumerable through rain to river. The arrested boats of the other crews drifted zigzag hither and thither. The dropped oars rocked and clashed, sank and rebounded, as the men plunged across them into the swirling stream.

And over all this confusion and concussion of men and man-made things crashed the vaster discord of the heavens; and the waters of the heavens fell ever denser and denser, as though to the aid of waters that could not in themselves envelop so many hundreds of struggling human forms.

All along the soaked towing-path lay strewn the horns, the rattles, the motor-hooters, that the youths had flung aside before they leapt. Here and there among these relics stood dazed elder men, staring through the storm. There was one of them – a grey-beard – who stripped off his blazer, plunged, grabbed at some live man, grappled him, was dragged under. He came up again further along stream, swam choking to the bank, clung to the grasses. He whimpered as he sought foot-hold in the slime. It was ill to be down in that abominable sink of death.

Abominable, yes, to them who discerned there death only; but sacramental and sweet enough to the men who were dying there for love. Any face that rose was smiling.

The thunder receded; the rain was less vehement; the boats and oars had drifted against the banks. And always the patient river bore its awful burden towards Iffley.

As on the towing-path, so on the youth-bereft rafts of the barges, yonder, stood many stupefied elders, staring at the river, staring back from the river into one another's faces.

Dispeopled now were the roofs of the barges. Under the first drops of the rain most of the women had come huddling down for shelter inside; panic had presently driven down the rest. Yet on one roof one woman still was. A strange, drenched figure, she stood bright-eyed in the dimness; alone, as it was well she should be in her great hour; draining the lees of such homage as had come to no woman in history recorded.

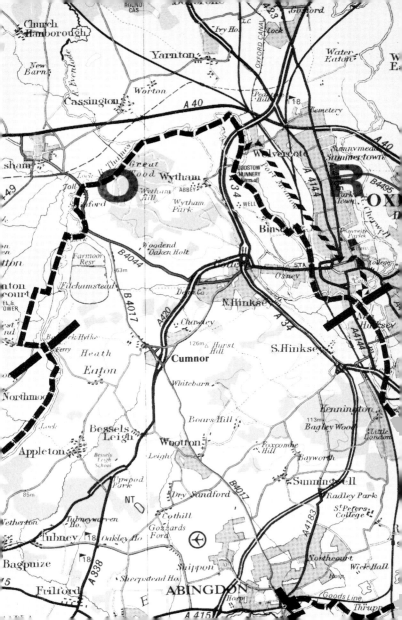

Stage 11 **Oxford to Northmoor** 10.8 miles (17.5 km)

SPECIFICS

The first mile of this Stage is through residential Oxford, followed by a fine open stretch beside Port Meadow. After Godstow we leave the orbit of Oxford and walk in an entirely rural setting, the last 2 miles being away from the river through fields. To Godstow the route is mostly gravel; from Godstow to Pinkhill mostly grass, with some rough passages by Wytham Great Wood; from Pinkhill to Bablock Hythe the route across the fields can be wet and rough.

Path Upstream: see also Strip Chart
Pinkhill Lock to Bablock Hythe
    The path cuts the loop of the Thames across a field, then continues beside or close by the river. 0.5 miles from the weir, and 200 m beyond a riverside enclosure, head for the far corner of a field. After crossing an embankment and footbridge, continue in the same direction across and along other fields to a corner. Turn right on to an enclosed surfaced track for 250 m. Then left along a bridleway beside a hedgeline for 0.8 miles. At end, turn left on to a small road; where this bears right, go left on to an access road to Bablock Hythe.

Path Downstream: see also Strip Chart.
Bablock Hythe to Pinkhill Lock
    At Bablock Hythe leave the left bank by an access road; then, at a junction, ahead along a small road for 300 m. Here turn right on to a bridleway along a hedgeline for 0.8 miles. At an enclosed track turn right for 250 m to its end. Turn left on a path along a field and to the far corner of another. After crossing a footbridge and embankment, continue in the same direction to regain the river bank. The path now leads beside or close by the river for 0.5 miles, finally cutting a loop to arrive at Pinkhill Weir and Lock.

Approach by car
At start: Oxford (for Folly Bridge, St Aldate's) is 55 miles from

London by the A40/M40; St Ebbe's car-park. *At end*: Northmoor is
a small village in Oxfordshire off the B4449 between Eynsham and
Kingston Bagpuize, and Bablock Hythe (1 mile from Northmoor)
must be approached via the very small lane between Stanton
Harcourt and Northmoor; park at the end of the lane near the river.
Also: at Godstow, approached from the Wolvercote junction of the
A40 and the Oxford Woodstock Road, car-park on Port Meadow;
and at Swinford Bridge, approached on the B4044 between Oxford
and Eynsham, park near the bridge.

Approach by other transport
Train: British Rail station at Oxford. *Bus*: from London, Oxford
City Link to Oxford; also local buses from Oxford to Eynsham.
Taxi: Oxford, ABC Taxis (0865-770681); Stanton Harcourt,
Eynsham Taxis (0865-881912).

Refreshment
Pubs: Head of the River, Folly Bridge, Oxford; Perch, Binsey;
Talbot, Eynsham. *Restaurant*: Restaurant Elizabeth, St Aldate's,
Oxford; Trout Inn, Godstow.

Accommodation
Hotels: Randolph Hotel, Beaumont Street, Oxford OX1 2LN
(0865-247481); Harcourt Arms, Stanton Harcourt OX8 1RJ
(0865-881931). *Guest houses and small hotels*: Newton House, 82
Abingdon Road, Oxford OX1 4PL (0865-240561); Wayside, 49
Witney Road, Eynsham OX8 1PL (0865-880245); Saddle Stones,
Linch Hill, Stanton Harcourt OX8 1BB (0865-882256). *Youth
hostel*: Jack Straw's Lane, Oxford OX3 ODW (0865-62997).
Camping: Oxford Camping International, 426 Abingdon Road,
Oxford OX1 4XN (0865-246551); Cassington Mill Caravan Site,
Eynsham Road, Cassington, Oxford OX8 1DB (0865-881081).

Admission
Oxford colleges' admissions for visits vary and fluctuate, but
generally they are open most afternoons; Stanton Harcourt Manor,
alternate Thursday and Sunday afternoons, April to September.

DESCRIPTION

Folly Bridge gets its name from a building that once stood at the *Oxford* end of it. Originally a drawbridge gateway, it was used by Francis Bacon, a Franciscan friar, as a study and observatory. Later a further storey was added and it was known as a Folly; it was demolished in 1779. Hence the bridge has been Friar's Bridge, then Folly Bridge, though its true name was Grandpont: the present stone bridge was built in 1857. On the island is a house which makes a good substitute as a folly, castellated, with decorative brickwork and a balcony, and sporting a number of white statues in niches.

The first mile lies through what was once a grimy locality of shunting steam-engines and gasometers and run-down housing with all the ingredients of early industrialisation. Although W. H. Auden in the 1920s declared that this riverside wasteland was the most beautiful place in Oxford, few walkers of the Thames Path would have found it so. But a pleasant surprise now awaits us, for the passage of the Thames through this area has been entirely transformed by excellent new housing and a thorough clean-up, and nowhere do we find anything sleazy or ugly. The traditional terraced houses on our bank contrast pleasingly with the new dark-brick steep-pitched frontages on the far bank.

We pass under two bridges now converted to pedestrian use. The first, with two spans of double-lattice wrought-iron girders, was built in 1886 to link parts of the Oxford Gas Light and Coke Company plant where rolling-stock and carts could pass, and had five large gas mains slung underneath it. The second, also of iron and 1886, carried the railway coal wagons to the plant: it now acts as a sort of piazza for the housing, and looks bright and cheerful with its central pier painted red and green. Reality then follows fancy under the low-slung working railway bridge (1850), dark and purposeful and the last railway bridge on our route.

Meanwhile a bewildering maze of streams intermingle around here, giving an almost Venetian effect. Just upstream of the gas railway bridge is the Old Navigation: all boats once took this route, which goes through the town by the old castle mound, and where we

go was once the weir stream. Then, just upstream of the working railway bridge, is the Bulstake Stream; opposite it, a mill stream; and by Osney Lock, a weir stream. All these are the products of conflicting interests in water use, one of the interested parties being the powerful Abbey of Osney (Osa's island), now entirely vanished. The abbey was built on low-lying land under the watchful eye of Oxford Castle: somewhere across these streams and marshes, in a December white-out, Matilda made her escape to Wallingford (41, page 238).

A collection of barges, canal boats and cruisers are moored below Osney Lock. Several will go no further, for the clearance of Osney Bridge is only 2.3 m at standard summer level and beyond is the Upper Thames, where things are on a smaller scale. Osney Bridge was built in 1888 and is linked to a long causeway over the low ground to *Botley*. After it we are outside the town again, past allotments and garden walls and more interweaving streams (one the entrance to the Oxford Canal) and, though the railway is still close, insulated by trees and bushes and a parallel stream. At Medley there was once a weir, and where we cross the high bridge we find Bossom's Boatyard: the family of this name for long held the toll rights at the Thames locks around Oxford, finally relinquishing control of their boatyard in 1960.

For virtually the only occasion on the Thames Path, we now enjoy the sight of unenclosed land. On the far bank is Port Meadow, a large area of common land (in all, 178 hectares) which from time immemorial has been held by the freemen of Oxford. Scores of horses and ponies graze on it, and flocks of Canada Geese peck at it. Beyond are the towers and spires of Oxford, though not those of the older colleges but the Victorian parish churches and the Observatory and Science Laboratories. And in front are the bright sails of dinghies.

On our side is *Binsey* (Byni's island) and a sign for the Perch pub; and half a mile beyond the Perch is the small medieval church of St Margaret. Beside it is a well which was highly regarded for its curative effect for the eyes, for it was well known that St Margaret

Folly Bridge, Oxford

had here restored to sight the man who had been blinded because of his lust for St Frideswide, the religious patroness of Oxford. Before Godstow the towpath passes some fine Lombardy poplars. Somewhere here we must imagine the scene on 4 July 1862 (42, page 238) with the two clerical gentlemen and the three little girls eating their picnic. Although this was certainly the setting for the creation of *Alice in Wonderland* it is sad that the author did not bring any Thames scenes or river stories into his book.

In a field by Godstow Lock are undulations thought to be relics of a medieval field-strip system; and then comes even more emphatic evidence of the Middle Ages, for the ruin that we see is a relic of Godstow Nunnery. Of all the monastic foundations along our route, Godstow (God's place, i.e. the nunnery) was undoubtedly the most aristocratic. It was heavily endowed by some of the leading Norman lords whose widows and unmarried womenfolk found here a pleasant and comfortable cloister from the rough hurly-burly of baronial life. Among them lived Rosamund Clifford, the mistress of Henry II, when by pressure of his Queen Eleanor he was persuaded to part with her. She died here in 1176 and her shrine soon rather scandalously became a place of pilgrimage, until the bishop put a stop to such profanity. In the fifteenth century things became rather lax, as the records of the episcopal visitations show (43, page 239).

The lock at *Godstow* was first constructed in 1788, and that is the date of the little road bridge spanning the navigation channel. But the bridge over the weir stream is even older, one of its arches (the pointed one) being medieval. The Trout Inn is famous and has peacocks in its garden and ivy on its walls and shoals of chub in the unfished weir stream beside it. It is the counterpart to the King's Arms at Sandford in Stage 10, each being the termination of an established university riverside walk. In fact, the limit of the Oxford city orbit, recorded by an iron marker, is brutally affirmed by the roaring ring road which we now go under, rather as if through a gateway in a walled town. Somewhere just here, before this road was built, Lionel Rolt tied up his boat and has left us his moving account of his midnight swim and his sensation of complete

Cattle by Godstow Lock

identification with Father Thames (44, page 240).

Several river loops precede King's Lock, a recent addition to the
lock system (1928): its weir stream only rejoins the river below
Godstow Lock, and it also has a cut across to the Oxford Canal.
From here the character of our river path changes. First of all, our
route turns west and then south. Second, the Thames is detectably
smaller, and also quieter with fewer motor-cruisers. And third, the
country looks more rural and the towpath less frequented. Soon we
pass a weir where water falls into the Seacourt (or Wytham)
Stream, returning its water to the Thames at Oxford. It was here,
before the weir was placed, that Fred Thacker had a curious
nocturnal experience in his small rowing-boat (45, page 241), with
the water behaving as if it were tidal. His account of the things that
go bump in the night is entirely appropriate for our approach to the
wilder Thames and a reminder that the countryside can still exercise
its mysterious spell, especially in darkness. Thacker was a
remarkable enthusiast whose love was the Thames. *The Stripling
Thames* is an evocative description of the upper river, and he
succeeded it with his *Thames Highway*, published at his own
expense. It is still a standard source document: for instance, of this
reach he writes, 'Clay Weir is mentioned between Eynsham and
King's in 1796. I have no further history. It charged 1s per boat for
shutting.'

In the days when grass was cut by men with long scythes, the
mowing of the fields around here used to be arranged in the
traditional way. It was divided by markers into large strips and each
strip was balloted for; the ballots were balls of cherry-wood, each
painted with a name. The mowers then set to work in steady,
sweeping strokes, and an image of them has been preserved by
Matthew Arnold, who writes of the haymakers in these fields above
Godstow that 'many a scythe in sunshine flames' in the 'wide fields
of breezy grass'.

On the far bank the Evenlode enters the Thames, and in the
distance are the tower of Yarnton (Eandred's settlement) and the
spire of Cassington (water-cress settlement); on our bank the side of
Wytham Great Wood comes down to the river. This wood covers
the slopes of Wytham Hill, round which this Stage revolves in a

stately semicircle. Wytham Hill is a formation of hard corallian rock or rag from which Oxford Clay has worn away, and its highest points are capped with Lower Greensand. The wood is part of the Wytham (river-bed settlement) Estate, donated to the University under a covenant which was particularly strict against housing development, fortunately; though, unfortunately, pedestrian access is also strictly controlled.

After Eynsham Lock and the adjacent water works we come to Swinford bridge, as handsome as any over the Thames and gaining over its contenders (such as Maidenhead and Henley) from the rural charm of its setting. The arches are set in rusticated stones, giving the illusion that cyclopean builders had set to work; but the elegant balustrade over the three semicircular river arches affirms the civilized tastes of the Age of Reason. The approach walls and towpath arches are plainer, thus rightly emphasizing the central section and avoiding the sweeping effect of most modern bridges. Like Shillingford Bridge, Swinford (swine ford) Bridge was built for a road turnpike project, and in both cases the prime mover was an ambitious lawyer, William Blackstone. He saw it as an opportunity of improving the shaky finances of his patron, Willoughby Bertie, Earl of Abingdon, and duly negotiated the necessary Act through Parliament in 1767. But the scheme was not a success. The turnpike cost more than expected, and the Shillingford Ferry had to be bought out for a very large sum. But the Act had secured for the Earl and his successors the rights for tolls in perpetuity and free of tax, which is why Swinford is one of the only two remaining toll bridges on the river. This privilege has a catch in it, however, for the charge has to remain at its original level of an old penny a wheel, so it is now only 2p per vehicle: pedestrians have gone free since 1853.

Before the bridge was built a curious annual ceremony was performed on the ferry. The parish of *Cumnor* (on our side) extended into some water-meadows on the far side. So, as part of 'beating the bounds', the vicar of Cumnor would be formally received by the Swinford ferryman with a bowl of water and an offering of 6s 8d and then be transported to the far bank where he symbolically clutched at the reeds.

Rather more than half a mile on across the bridge is *Eynsham*.

Here stood yet another Benedictine abbey, though all that remains of it is a tall stone shaft in the market place, part of a preaching-cross where monks spoke on feast days and special occasions. St Leonard's church is mostly thirteenth-century, with a big south aisle separated from the nave by arches with elegant columns.

With a backward glance at Swinford Bridge, perhaps picturing Emily Cook's ruminating yokel gazing down at us (46, page 242), we progress towards Pinkhill, cutting loops as necessary. After the diversion behind the cruiser station we arrive at the lock and tree-shaded island. The long grass bank just here is the embankment of the vast Farmoor Reservoir, which has a total capacity of 13.8 million litres. It supplies to much of Oxfordshire water which it extracts from the Thames; and it is also used to recharge water into the river during times of very low flow. Trout-fishers, dinghy-sailors and bird-watchers make use of its 153-hectare surface.

The remainder of the Stage moves away from the river through fields. At the point where we turn off the enclosed farm track we are less than a mile from *Stanton* (stony settlement) *Harcourt*, and in winter can see the grand old buildings across the fields. These consist of a cruciform and largely Perpendicular church (of St Michael), a medieval kitchen and Pope's tower. They are all associated with the Harcourts, whose ancestral seat this was till, as we have seen, they moved to Nuneham Courtenay. The kitchen and the tower are the remains of their house. The tower is named after Alexander Pope, who spent two summers here transcribing a translation of Homer's *Iliad* into heroic couplets. The two lovers struck by lightning provided him with good material for letters (47, page 243) and an epitaph in the church, which also contains some fine Harcourt monuments, including a plaque purporting to trace their ancestry back to a certain Bernard the Dane in the ninth century.

Swinford Bridge

ANTHOLOGY
(41) Matilda's escape from Oxford Castle in 1142: from Roger of
Wendover, fourteenth century (translation J. A. Giles).

At this time king Stephen, hearing that the empress was at Oxford
Castle with a small retinue, collected a numerous army, and,
marching thither after Michaelmas, besieged that fortress until
Advent. The empress, seeing that for so long a time none of her
friends came to her assistance, played off a woman's trick upon king
Stephen, and escaped by night over the river Thames, which was
frozen, dressed in white, and attended by a few companions, and so
escaped, for the enemy could not see her on account of the dazzling
of the snow, and the similarity of colour between it and her clothes.
She therefore fled to the castle of Wallingford, and committed
herself to the charge of Brian FitzEarl. In this manner the castle of
Oxford was given up to the king.

(42) The origin of *Alice in Wonderland*: from Florence Lennon's
Lewis Carroll, 1947.

The path to the Isis from Tom Quad passed the smelly Trill Mill
stream. Dean Liddell had a new and more appetizing path dug;
meanwhile, stepping gingerly, the girls in their big shade hats clung
to the hands of the two young men who were simultaneously
juggling the luncheon basket. Arrived at the river, young Mr
Dogson would select the safest, roomiest, and most comfortable
boat, stock it with cushions, and bestow his guests and the luncheon
baskets with accurate balance. He rowed stroke and Mr Duckworth
rowed bow; an extra pair of oars was added for the girls' rowing
lessons. One of them might hold the tiller rope, and if the boat wove
a crooked course, it was all in the name of education.

Dogson celebrated the occasion by doffing his new clericals, and
appearing in white flannel trousers and a hard straw hat, with black
shoes, of course, since tennis shoes has not been invented. These
were the most festive times of his life – he was only thirty on July 4,
1862, when all rays converge. His life was before him and his

powers were at their height. Drifting on the slow river that flows into the Thames, in his slow voice with its 'curious stutter' he wove a dream story for three lovely young ladies and a don. Duckworth asked if it was purely extemporaneous, and he truthfully answered 'Yes'. Germination acts that way – one moment there is a brown bud; next moment it is cracked, and a green shoot pushes out. The preparation had been going on in the dark.

They rowed up to Godstow, had tea beside a haystack, and rowed back again, returning by about eight-thirty. Stories had been told and songs had been sung, and at the deanery door ten-year-old Alice said, 'Oh, Mr Dodgson, I wish you would write out Alice's adventures for me'.

(43) Scandals at Godstow as found in the episcopal visitations: from the *Victoria History of the County of Oxford*, 1907.

The first visitation of which we have record was in 1357. The bishop orders that the nuns shall not absent themselves from the monastery for more than three weeks, and then only for reasonable and necessary cause; and that inasmuch as secular people living in the abbey have greatly disturbed the service of God, no secular woman is to be an inmate, except the necessary servants and such persons as have corrodies. However, in 1363, his successor, at the earnest prayers of Alice, wife of Alan of Ayote, granted permission that she might stay for two years at Godstow at her own expense. In 1384, the abbey being vacant, the bishop warns the prioress that nuns should not be permitted out of the convent, cases of scandal having arisen; and in 1392 the abbess is ordered to forbid the visits of John de Kirkeby, chaplain of Wolvercot. In 1432 the discipline of the house was lax; the bishop ordered that the porter was to take an oath not to admit strangers; certain women, who were evil examples by their extravagant dress, were to be excluded; the bailiff was to have no more secret talk with any nun, 'foreasmuch as he says that there is no good woman in the monastery'; there is to be no drinking (*potationes*) after compline, but all were to go to the dormitory; if any nuns admit secular men to feasts in their rooms they are to be excommunicated, 'for the scholars of Oxford say that they can have all kinds of good cheer (*omnimodas solaciones*) with the nuns to their heart's desire'; nuns are not to go into Oxford, not to talk with secular persons in the nave of the church, or in the chapels, but only in the hall of the abbess, and in the hearing of another nun; the porter is not to convey letters or presents or tokens to any scholar at Oxford or any other secular person. One nun had broken the vow of chastity.

At the visitation by Bishop Alnwick in 1445, the house consisted of the abbess and sixteen nuns, and returned its income at £200. The abbess complained that the scholars of Oxford had common access to the monastery and the cloisters, and that she could not stop it; that secular people had access to the nuns in the choir during divine service, and also in the refectory at meal-time; the prioress complained that nuns went often to Oxford; several, however, of the nuns said 'omnia bene'. The bishop's injunctions were much as before concerning the exclusion of secular people; the abbess was herself to sleep often in the dormitory, and was to rise to mattins with the sisters 'at least on all double feasts'. No seculars were to sojourn in the abbey unless it be children, and in that case, if boys, they must be not more than nine years old; if girls, not more than twelve.

(44) The effects of a midnight bathe at Godstow: from Lionel Rolt's *The Thames*, 1951.

If we search through the stores of memory, it will become apparent to many of us, I think, that the most memorable moments of our lives are not necessarily the occasion of important events or of meetings with people and places whose significance only becomes apparent later. Often when time has blurred our recollection of many things which seemed memorable, the mind will yet retain most vividly the image of the experience of some brief and fortuitous moment. Who can say why this should be so? Unless it be that there are rare occasions when our cabined faculties are for an instant liberated and privileged to apprehend the eternal in the temporal. So it was that an experience during our stay at Godstow, which seems of little account in the telling, will, I know, remain with me most vividly when all other recollections of the Thames have faded. The occasion was merely a bathe in the river at midnight. The last of the patrons of the nearby 'Trout' inn had long ago departed on his noisy way, and the night was not only silent but breathlessly still and very warm. It was also very dark, for the sky was completely overcast. Only in the far west over the river there appeared an occasional swift flicker of imminent storm but its pale echo reflected momentarily between cloud and water. This light, whose source was neither moon nor star nor sun, seemed to possess an apocalyptic quality; it suggested that the dark horizon it revealed in such sudden and fleeting chiaroscuro might be no part of our familiar earth, but the rim of some strange world towards which our course was set. And as I swam through the cool water, making as little noise as possible, I experienced a curious feeling, exalting yet at the same time humbling, of becoming for a moment a part of this great river, ever changing yet always the same, eternally dying in the sea because it is eternally renewed.

(45) A strange experience on the Seacourt Stream: from Fred Thacker's *The Stripling Thames*, 1909.

After lights are out sounds grow loud which in the day time pass unnoticed. A leaping fish will fall back into the water with a crack like a pistol; leaves drop with a hard and sudden rap; the night breeze sets the boat creeping to and fro a short length against the grass and rushes on the bank; a rat or so will scuff its claws along the top of the canvas and plop into the water off the end (I never saw one in the craft); a shower may swell from tiny needle taps to an almost deafening fusillade; there will be sudden foaming rushes through the water, perhaps of an otter after his prey; and creatures of the dark steal and rustle over the dry leaves and underwood ashore. I woke once above King's weir and lay listening to slow hoofs and slow heavy breathing close at hand, and peering under the canvas could just discern in the white dense mist of an August night a ghostly grey old horse moving about at pasture, and stopping now and then to stare uncannily at me. At Bablock Hythe I was entertained several mornings soon after dawn by a score of skittish young bullocks, whose youthful inquisitive nosings of my hamper and gear on the meadow-side were very amusing. And I had a curious experience once at Eynsham. I had moored one night in a little stream six feet deep that runs out of the Thames and rejoins him lower down. There was a string of barges to pass down the River, and as the weir was flashed to float them over my current reversed itself, and we sank lower into the channel until we almost touched bottom. About ten o'clock they had done; and as the paddles were replaced in the weir the current resumed its ordinary direction, and my boat began to rise again with the rising water, and we had to sit with lighted candles and watch the vertical bank, as in a lock, lest the boat should catch and overturn. A bereaved cow will mourn the whole night through; and once a great company of ducks had a terrible scare from a rat, and talked about it until daylight.

(46) Rustic indifference on Swinford Bridge: from Emily Cook's *From a Holiday Journal*, 1904.

But the Oxfordshire rustic, on the rare occasions when you do come across him (apart from bridges), in no wise interferes with your solitude. He distracts you no more than the ruminating oxen who gaze on you so plaintively as you glide past them. He has become incorporated with his surroundings – 'rolled round', so to speak, 'in earth's diurnal force' – and it has crushed all power of expression out of him. All the 'joy of life' he knows is either boozing at the 'Pig and Whistle' or enjoying a short clay pipe on a bridge. On one occasion above Eynsham one of these rustics was as usual on the bridge, when an upset occurred in a boat passing underneath it. The youthful scullers had been changing places in mid-stream – always a rash thing to do, and especially so when the boat is outrigged. The stream happened to be deep at this particular place, and enclosed between high mud-banks, sparsely covered by day weeds. These reeds snapped when grasped like tinder, and it accordingly took the submerged ones some time to extricate themselves from their difficulties. But the man on the bridge did not budge an inch. When at last one of the sufferers, impelled thereto by an imperative desire for dry clothes, went up and accosted him, he slowly removed his pipe:—

'There was a young man,' he said, 'drowned in this very place six weeks ago today, and they ain't found 'is body yet.'

(47) Lovers killed by lightning at Stanton Harcourt: from Alexander Pope's letter to Lady Mary Wortley Montagu, 1 September 1718.

I have in mind to fill the rest of this paper with an incident that happened just under my eyes, and has made a great impression on me. I have passed part of this summer at an old romantic seat of my Lord Harcourt's, which he has lent me; it overlooks a common field, where, under the shade of a haycock, sat two lovers, as constant as were ever found in romance, beneath a spreading beech. John was a wellset man, about five-and-twenty; Sarah a brown woman of eighteen. Their love was the talk, but not the scandal of the neighbourhood, for all they aimed at was the blameless possession of each other in marriage. It was but this very morning that he obtained her parents' consent, and it was but till the next week that they were to wait to be happy. Perhaps this very day, in the invervals of their work, they were talking of their wedding clothes, and John was now matching several kinds of poppies and field-flowers to her complexion, to make her a present of knots for the day. While they were thus employed (it was on the last day of July), a terrible storm of thunder and lightning arose, and drove the labourers to what shelter the trees and hedges afforded. Sarah, frightened and out of breath, sank on a haycock, and John (who never separated from her) sat by her side, having raked two or three heaps together to secure her. Immediately there was heard so loud a crack as if heaven had burst asunder. The labourers, all solicitous for each other's safety, called to one another; those who were nearest our lovers, hearing no answer, stepped to the place where they lay. They saw first a little smoke, and after, this faithful pair – John with one arm about his Sarah's neck, and the other held over his face, as if to screen her from the lightning. They were dead. There was no mark or discolouring on their bodies, only that Sarah's eyebrow was a little singed, and a small spot between her breasts. They were buried the next day in one grave, in the parish of Stanton Harcourt, in Oxfordshire, where my Lord Harcourt, at my request, has erected a monument over them.

Stanton Harcourt

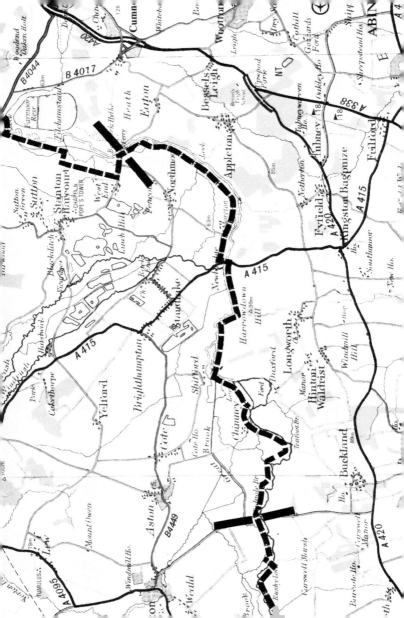

Stage 12 **Northmoor to Bampton** 9.4 miles (15.1 km)

SPECIFICS

Stage 12 is the first in which substantial sections are rough and untrodden (until they become cleared for the Thames Path), especially between Shifford Lock and Tadpole Bridge. But it is also the only Stage where not even any villages are encountered, and where the river flows entirely through pastoral solitude. Newbridge provides an excellent halfway point.

Path Upstream: see also Strip Chart
Proposed footbridge by Shifford Lock to Tenfoot footbridge: alternative route 2.0 miles (3.2 km)
   Until the new footbridge is opened it is necessary to keep to the right bank after passing Shifford Lock, and battle with the 'towpath', now entirely overgrown. At Duxford ford leave the river along a path and track, then follow a small road to the right to its extremity at Duxford Farm. Then ahead on a bridleway to the right of a hedgeline. At its end, go into the next field, skirting round it; and then, on the opposite side, at a gap in a hedge, double back to the right. Then left for 200 m; then right on to a path to Tenfoot footbridge and cross to the left bank.

Path Downstream: see also Strip Chart.
Tenfoot footbridge to proposed footbridge by Shifford Lock: alternative route 2.0 miles (3.2 km)
   Until the new footbridge by Shifford Lock is opened, it is necessary to cross to the right bank at Tenfoot footbridge. A footpath leads from the river to a bridleway, at which turn left for 200 m; then turn right to the right of a hedge. At a gap in the hedge, turn left and skirt around a field to the opposite side. Then left through a hedge and ahead, to the left of a hedgeline, to reach Duxford Farm. Follow the small road 0.4 miles; then, where it turns right by a cottage, take a track to the left which reduces to a path to arrive at Duxford ford. From here it is necessary to battle with the 'towpath', now entirely overgrown, to where the Shifford Lock Cut joins the river on the far bank by the site of the proposed footbridge.

Approach by car
At start: Northmoor is a small village in Oxfordshire off the B4449
between Eynsham and Kingston Bagpuize, and Bablock Hythe (1
mile from Northmoor) must be approached via the very small lane
between Stanton Harcourt and Northmoor; park at the end of the
lane near the river. *At end*: Bampton is in Oxfordshire, on the
A4095 between Witney and Faringdon, and Tadpole Bridge (2
miles from Bampton) may be approached on the road between
Bampton and Buckland; park near the bridge. *Also*: at Newbridge,
on the A415 between Witney and Kingston Bagpuize; park near the
bridge.

Approach by other transport
No satisfactory public transport, but there are local bus services at
Kingston Bagpuize and Bampton. *Taxi*: Standlake, Standlake Taxis
(0867-31236); Witney, Hunts Cars (0993-5136).

Refreshment
Pubs: Red Lion, Northmoor; Maybush Inn, Newbridge; Trout Inn,
Tadpole Bridge.
Restaurants: Rose Revived, Newbridge.

Accommodation
Hotels: Fallowfields, Southmoor, Kingston Bagpuize OX13 5BH
(0865-820416).
Camping: Lincoln Farm, High Street, Standlake OX8 7RH
(0867-31239).

Admission
Kingston House, Kingston Bagpuize, Wednesday and Sunday
afternoons, May to June and September.

Stage 12 **Northmoor to Bampton** 9.4 miles (15.1km)

DESCRIPTION

A ferry operated at *Bablock Hythe* (the landing-place by Babba's stream) for at least a thousand years, but now is no more. At one time it was quite a large affair, with a fixed chain, and could transport vehicles. When the ferry closed a few years ago, the Ferry Inn closed also. Commercial activity has now switched to a large camping and caravan park around the former inn.

Bablock Hythe has a special place in English literature because of a verse in Matthew Arnold's 'The Scholar Gipsy'. The scholar gipsy is a sort of drop-out who lives an alternative existence around these parts. Although given to some energetic night walking, he is usually to be found loitering around the place, always planning to do something but never doing anything. But he does possess an excellent appreciation of nature, as expressed by Arnold in scores of evocative phrases. Verse 8 reads:

> For most, I know, thou lov'st retired ground.
>   Thee, at the ferry, Oxford riders blithe,
>   Returning home on summer nights, have met
>   Crossing the stripling Thames at Bablock-hithe,
>   Trailing in the cool stream thy fingers wet,
>   As the slow punt swings round:
>   And leaning backwards in a pensive dream,
>   And fostering in thy lap a heap of flowers
>   Pluck'd in shy fields and distant Wychwood bowers,
>   And thine eyes resting on the moonlit stream;

It is by the action of lifting the Bablock Hythe ferry chain that William Morris introduces his lyrical passages about the scenery of this Stage (48, page 257), rather as if he had squeezed through the fence into an enchanted garden. And, despite occasional cruisers and parallel pylons, the scene today is largely unchanged. As far as Newbridge the poplar-lined far bank rises gently back to low hills. On our side are grass fields, bordered by thick untended hedgerows. In clumps or long straggled stretches, tall wild flowers line our turfy

path. Prominent are two pea-flowers, the loosestrife and the willowherb: both have purplish pink flowers, the loosestrife with petals whose tips are spiky and whorled, the willowherb with four notched petals and eight stamens. The comfrey, a tall stout perennial of the borage family, is also common along the river bank: its flowers are usually mauve but sometimes creamy-white, and are bell-shaped and set in forked and curling clusters. Umbellifers such as cow parsely vie for height, and display ever-exploding fireworks of white flowerets within inches of our faces. And then, prickly and grotesque, teasels rear their enormous spiny heads of tight-packed composite purple flowers.

Just over half a mile from Bablock Hythe is the site of the old weir described so charmingly by Boydell (49, page 258). No one reading it can fail to hear the roar of falling water or see the sun's sparkle on the cascade. The names of these vanished weirs are endlessly confusing, and they often went by the name of the man who ran them for milling or fishing. The Harts seem to have been a prominent family of river professionals – we have already seen them in Stage 7 – and now we have two Hart's Weirs in close proximity, which Boydell himself confuses. This first one was also known as Ark, or Ark Island, Weir.

Soon after the site of Ark Weir we come to Northmoor Lock, built in 1895 at a point where no previous weir had been. But the weir is constructed in the traditional manner, for the flow of water is regulated not by sluices but by paddles set between poles, or rymers, as already described to us by Dr Plot (37, page 204). The lock is in the parish of *Northmoor*, a small village three-quarters of a mile off. Northmoor is a marshland village and, like several others near the Upper Thames, could only be built after earlier communities had succeeded in draining the marshes. It was founded in Norman times, which is when the present church (of St Denis) was built. The church tower is fifteenth-century and by it is an Elizabethan house, built as the rectory by the then owners of the living, St John's College, Oxford. Those were the days when tithes were spent on keeping the parson comfortable rather than the

Paddles and rymers at Northmoor Lock

church in good repair; and a dovecote near it testifies to another privilege enjoyed by the incumbent.

The bells of Northmoor church that rang out to celebrate a very special wedding one day in 1766 could be clearly heard at Hart's Footbridge, our next point of reference. This is where the second Hart's Weir was; it was also known as Rudge's, Rudge being the family involved in the rustic romance as described by Eric de Maré (50, page 259). It all seems so natural nowadays, but two centuries ago class barriers were so strong that such a union was almost unthinkable. Betty was clearly a more receptive subject for social training than Eliza Doolittle, but maybe the local gentlefolk who taught her how to talk proper were more sympathetic than the terrifying Professor Higgins. One wonders what really happened at that first meeting at the ferry; and how many ferry rides were taken before the lovers began to talk of marriage. Surely they took long walks along the towpath, under the benevolent eye of Betty's dad, ferry and fly-fishing forgotten.

Newbridge isn't new: it is very old. And this is how William Morris alludes to it when he passes under it with his beautiful dream girl, a figure who represents the links between human love and love of nature. It is 'new' only in relation to Radcot Bridge upstream. In the first half of the thirteenth century the Benedictines of St Denis in France sent over to their priory at La Nore (as Northmoor was then called) some bridge engineers in the guise of monks known as Pontific Brothers, who built the bridge we see, or, more accurately, parts of it, for it was rebuilt in the fifteenth century and repaired in 1801. The brothers also built long causeways at each end with small arches as vents against floods. Once opened it was put into the charge of hermits who levied tolls and kept it in repair; and it seems to have been a great success financially for only once (in 1462) did they seek help from the king by means of a pontage grant. This is because its position was well chosen, taking advantage of a finger of higher land coming south from around Witney, and useful for the trains of packhorses bringing wool from the prosperous Cotswolds towards Wallingford and Abingdon on their way to London and the

Newbridge

south-east. Immediately above the bridge the Windrush joins the Thames, having come past Taynton and the quarries of the bridge's stones.

It is sad to see the venerable Newbridge under the burden of commercial vehicles with loaded weights hundreds of times greater than anything the Pontific Brothers knew of. But it is good to see it isolated among meadows, with the only houses in sight the two genial inns that flank it. On the left bank is the Rose Revived, a delightful name for an inn that had once been called the Rose, then the Crown: the inn-sign shows roses being revived not in water but in Moreland's real ales. On the right bank is the Maybush right against the bridge, a smaller and older building.

Twice a year for several centuries Newbridge was a scene of animation, crowds gathering in the field behind the Rose Revived for the fairs held on 31 March and 28 September. But in the Civil War these were suspended and a grimmer scene enacted, as recounted by Clarendon (51, page 259), himself the King's anonymous adviser. The Parliamentarians very nearly succeeded in bottling Charles I up in Oxford, but he got out just before their pincers met at Woodstock. Five years later, a force of Levellers being pursued by Cromwell tried to cross the bridge but, finding it guarded, swam across upstream, only to be hounded down by him near Burford.

A broad grass meadow draws us towards the slight slopes of Harrowdown Hill. Beyond the river and the flats is *Standlake* (stony stream), another settlement on reclaimed land, built along the line of dykes which held back the flood-water from the gravel terraces. The river rounds to where a line of pylons, close alongside, seem to have been placed with complete disregard for the river scenery. Beyond them is the farm and church at *Shifford* (sheep ford). Shifford is a deserted village, one of thousands in England. Contrary to popular belief, most of them were not deserted because of the Black Death, but rather from the gradual pressures of economic forces over a long period. In this case it seems that the enclosure of the rich meadows forced a depopulation from what had been quite a substantial village – twenty-three households in 1279. Although the village has gone, the church (of St Mary) has been rebuilt, in the Early English style of 1863, and has a small belfry.

Here also a water channel joins the Thames on the far bank. This is the mouth of an ambitious irrigation ditch known as the Great Brook. It was dug in the 1850s as part of the systematic enclosure of common lands and it stretches for three miles through the flat lands and their elevated dykes.

Half a mile on we come to Shifford Lock and its cut, opened in 1898. The lock-keeper's cottage is one of the most remote on the Thames and until quite recently life here was largely self-sufficient, with home-grown vegetables and livestock. The island between the cut and the mainstream has a forgotten air about it, with small fields and thick hedges, and a rough path running through them to an old ford – Duxford (Duduc's ford). This is a rarity, for bridges and locks have replaced all the other fords on the navigable Thames. It looks delightful: no river craft, high bushy banks and the ford (concrete based) usually with only a few inches of water flowing over it. Beyond is Duxford Farm.

Near the bank, upstream of the cut, and on another gravel ledge just above the alluvium, is the hamlet of *Chimney*. Other than this and Duxford farm buildings there are no houses in sight for the rest of the stage, and only Tenfoot Bridge, a humped wooden footbridge on the site of an old weir, interrupts the natural scene. The path now becomes badly overgrown, though it will by clearance and usage in time be made good. Hard as it may be to imagine now, it was once smooth and firm throughout. Early in the last century a raised dyke was built along the river bank for the towpath, and it also served to prevent flooding. This was the fine gravelled path which James Thorne strode along in 1847, starting at Lechlade (52, page 260). Still, he had his problems also, and it may be that his delays at ferries made his progress no quicker than ours, for though the going may be rougher the continuity is now unbroken.

In this way we come to Tadpole Bridge and if it is raining we can like Emily Cook take refuge in the Trout, and exorcise the ghost of Matthew Arnold who haunted the start of this Stage (53, page 261).

ANTHOLOGY
(48) Rowing upstream, with a beautiful girl, between Bablock
Hythe and Newbridge: from William Morris's *News from Nowhere*,
1891.

She laughed now, but looked very kindly on me. 'Well,' she said,
'meantime for the present we will let it be; for I must look at this
new country that we are passing through. See how the river has
changed character again: it is broad now, and the reaches are long
and very slow-running. And look, there is a ferry!'

I told her the name of it, as I slowed off to put the ferry-chain
over our heads; and on we went passing by a bank clad with oak
trees on our left hand, till the stream narrowed again and deepened,
and we rowed on between walls of tall reeds, whose population of
reed sparrows and warblers was delightfully restless, twittering and
chuckling as the wash of the boats stirred the reeds from the water
in the still, hot morning.

She smiled with pleasure, and her lazy enjoyment of the new
scene seemed to bring out her beauty doubly as she leaned back
amidst the cushions, though she was far from languid; her idleness
being the idleness of a person, strong and well-knit both in body and
mind, deliberately resting.

'Look!' she said, springing up suddenly from her place without
any obvious effort, and balancing herself with exquisite grace and
ease; 'look at the beautiful old bridge ahead!'

'I need scarcely look at that,' said I, not turning my head away
from her beauty. 'I know what it is; though' (with a smile) 'we used
to call it the Old Bridge time agone.'

She looked down upon me kindly, and said, 'How well we get on
now you are no longer on your guard against me!'

And she stood looking thoughtfully at me still, till she had to sit
down as we passed under the middle one of the row of little pointed
arches of the oldest bridge across the Thames.

'O the beautiful fields!' she said; 'I had no idea of the charm of a
very small river like this. The smallness of the scale of everything,

Duxford

the short reaches, and the speedy change of the banks, give one a feeling of going somewhere, of coming to something strange, a feeling of adventure which I have not felt in bigger waters.'

(49) Hart's Weir: from Boydell's *History of the Thames*, 1794.

On approaching Hart's Weir, at the distance of somewhat more than a mile from Newbridge, the banks are so thickly planted, that the river appears to be passing through a wood, whose trees, extending their branches from either side, over-arch the water and form a sylvan canopy. Here the Thames divides itself into one large and two lesser streams, forming as many islands; one of which is inhabited. The weir stretches across from the meadow bank to these islands; and, at a short distance, on a retrospective view of the river, is a principal feature of one of those home scenes, which frequently afford a more complaisant delight to the mind, and awake a more pleasing solemnity of sentiment, than the wide expansive variety of distant prospect. A range of flood-gates crosses the larger current which pours through it in frothy agitation, while the diminutive streams, that divide the islands, tumble over their sluices in unbroken waterfalls. The banks of the islands, which recede a little in the view, are planted with the willow and the alder, intermingled with forest trees of various kinds, which rise boldly above them. Through the frame-work of the weir was seen a bright vapoury gleam, hovering, as it were, over the main channel of the river; while the thick overshadowing alders served to heighten the transient lustre that sparkled on the streamlets which poured down between them: at the same moment, the sickly green of the willows became grey from the brightness of the higher foliage, which, as it played in the breeze, received the glowing rays of a setting sun. The near part of the scene was the whole expanded breadth of the river, where all was eddy and agitated current: – no sound was for some time heard but from the rush of waters; which, as we passed on, was succeeded by the dashing of an oar, the insect-hum of the evening, and the song of the nightingale. Such a picture, where the rude contrivance of humble art is blended with simple objects of unadorned nature, at once turns the pensive mind from the business, the pleasures, and painted pomp of the world, 'to find tongues in trees, books in the living brooks, sermons in stone, and good in everything'.

(50) The peer and the ferry-girl: from Eric De Mare's *Time on the Thames*, 1952.

The place is associated with the true love story of Weir-keeper Rudge's daughter, Betty, and a certain peer of the realm. To Bablock Hythe one sunny day to fish came young William Flower second Viscount Ashbrook, then an undergraduate at Christ Church. Here he found sweet Betty helping her father at the ferry. It was love at first sight. Before long the young milord removed Betty from her cottage, not in the manner of Henry Rex to a bower at the end of a maze, but to a nearby family of gentlefolk to be fitted for a higher kind of life than that to which she was accustomed. The pair were married in Northmoor Church in 1766 and in the register you can still see their signatures. The union, which produced two boys and four girls, seems to have been an unusually happy one, although it did not last very long. William died eighteen years after meeting his Betty and then she, having borne ten years of widowhood, married again, this time a brilliant theological scholar, one Dr John Jones of Jesus College, Oxford. She herself died, 'a courtly old grandame', in 1808. One of her grand-daughters married the sixth Duke of Marlborough and through her the humble blood of the Rudges has enriched that of other aristocratic families.

(51) The capture of Newbridge, 1 June 1644: from Edward Hyde, Lord Clarendon's *History of the Rebellion*, seventeenth century.

On the other side, Waller's forces from Abington did not find the New-bridge so well defended, but, overcoming those guards, and having got boats in which they put over their men, both above and below, they got that passage over the river Isis: by which they might have brought over all their army, and fallen upon the king's rear, whilst he was defending the other side.

It was now high time for the king to provide for his own security, and to escape the danger he was in of being shut up in Oxford. Waller lost no time, but the next day passed over five thousand horse and foot by New-bridge, the van whereof quartered at Ensham; and, the king's foot being drawn off from Gosworth-bridge, Essex immediately brought his men over the Cherwell, and quartered that night at Bletchington, many of his horse advancing to Woodstock; so that the king seemed to them to be perfectly shut in between them; and to his own people his condition seemed so desperate, that one of those with whom he used to advise his most secret affairs, and whose fidelity was never suspected, proposed to him to render himself, upon conditions, to the earl of Essex; which his majesty rejected with great indignation, yet had the goodness to conceal the name of the proposer; and said that 'possibly he might be found in the hands of the earl of Essex, but he would be dead first'.

(52) Walking the towpath between Lechlade and Oxford: from James Thorne's *Rambles by the Thames*, 1847.

The rambler will of course take the path. But as this path is to accompany him – or more properly, as he is to accompany it – or more properly still, as both are to be together all the rest of the journey, it is desirable that he should know what sort of a path it is; and – as I do not intend to take any further notice of it after setting out upon it, but shall go from one side of the river to the other just as if there were no path in the way – why this seems the proper place to give some little information about it. For it would not accord with my plan to mislead the rambler who turns to me for guidance by any want of explicitness. Well, then, it is not, as he may suppose, a narrow winding path, worn out of the soft green grass by the foot of the pensive angler or patient pilgrim, with daisies and celandines and other field-flowers on either side of it, but, on the contrary, it is a broad towing-path for horses, formed of flint-stones and flanked

by a ditch – at least that is its general character. At times the rough
flints give place to sand, at others to mud. He must make the best of
it.

Before starting upon it, however, there is one thing he should
provide himself with, and that is – this is entirely between ourselves,
he might not think of it without this private hint – a store of copper
coins. And for this reason: – the path is not only hard and flinty, but
capricious withal. Whilst you are treading soberly along it, admiring
the beauty of the landscape, it may be, or thinking of your dinner,
or your debts, or – of anything else that is equally pleasant or
pressing – all at once you find yourself at the end of the path, and
discover that it recommences on the other side of the river. To
continue on the side you now are is impossible, or at least not easy,
for there is a brook in front, or perhaps a weir. Now, as you begin to
perceive, there is, or ought to be, a ferry here. And there is a ferry –
sometimes too a ferryman: but if not, the miller's man, or the
miller's maid, will ferry you over. Now it is against these
occurrences (and they happen half a dozen times at least in a day's
walk) that you need the pennies. Thames boatmen, from Cricklade
to the Nore, are always 'short of change'. When a pretty demure
damsel takes the trouble to push the boat across the river for you,
you will of course not care to search for coppers; but when a clumsy
clown does it – it is another matter. But this is only a hint (aside) to
the rambler – he may please himself about attending to it. I have
done my duty as a guide, and my conscience is at ease on the
subject.

(53) Reading poetry at The Trout, Tadpole Bridge: from Emily
Cook's *From a Holiday Journal*, 1904.

Tadpole Bridge, a mile below Rushy, is specially noteworthy as the
site of the 'Trout' Inn – a most comfortable stopping-place, with a
charming landlady, who with her husband does her utmost for her
guests. Four miles from here is the little town of Bampton, with an
old church and pretty vicarage, quite worth the walk thither. This
recommendation is not given on the guide-book principle, and may

therefore be received without suspicion. Guide-books are unanimous and indiscriminate in their wish that you by no means leave any tomb or monument within a circuit of many miles unvisited, whatever else you may have to pass by. Even Murray may be said to suffer from this slightly gloomy tendency. Now tombs, when you are on holiday, are distinctly *not* the things you most yearn for. The average guide-book treats you very much as the child was treated, who, when it asked to go to a pantomime, was told, 'No, but you may visit your grandmother's grave.' We do not propose to recommend all the tombs in the neighbourhood. To the healthy-minded river-tourist quite as much gloom as he can stand will be supplied by a pocket edition of Matthew Arnold's poems. No poet, it need hardly be said, is more beautiful, more enthralling, than Matthew Arnold; but you distinctly need a cloudless day to read him on; a day when 'nothing is so dainty sweet as lovely melancholy'. On one occasion when spending a wet day at this very 'Trout' at Tadpole, we well remember being reduced to a frightful state of depression by a long afternoon of him. By five o'clock we were melted almost to tears, and had to hurry forward our dinner as the only cure for our melancholy. No! Matthew Arnold's view of life is beautiful, but, like that of Ibsen's hero in 'Rosmersholm' hardly exhilarating. He writes ever in the minor key. Was this the price that the author of the 'Scholar Gipsy' had to pay for immortality?

Sheila McKee, landlady of the Trout at Tadpole

Stage 13 **Bampton to Lechlade** 9.8 miles (15.8 km)

Stage 13 is on the whole easier than Stage 12: over a mile of it is surfaced, and there is more pasture open to the river bank. The Stage features Lechlade as an attractive destination, as well as the exquisite groups of buildings at Radcot, Kelmscot and Buscot, and is delightful throughout.

Path Upstream: see also Strip Chart
Buscot Lock to St John's Bridge, Lechlade: alternative route
1.4 miles (2.2 km)
   Follow the left bank for 0.5 miles, then on to a track leading to a road. Left along this to a T junction: then left again to cross St John's Bridge.

Path Downstream: see also Strip Chart
St John's Bridge, Lechlade, to Buscot Lock: alternative route
1.4 miles (2.2 km)
   Cross to the left bank and go along the road to a junction. Turn right and, 350 m on, right again on to a track which leads to the river, and so down to Buscot Lock.

Approach by car
At start: Bampton is in Oxfordshire, on the A4095 between Witney and Faringdon, and Tadpole Bridge (2 miles from Bampton) may be approached on the road between Bampton and Buckland; park near the bridge. *At end*: Lechlade is in Gloucestershire, at the junction of the A361 and the A417; car-park in Lechlade or across the bridge in Riverside Park. *Also*: at Radcot, also on the A4095 between Witney and Faringdon, park near the bridge.

Approach by other transport
No satisfactory public transport, but British Rail station at Swindon is 10 miles from Lechlade, and there are local bus services from Swindon to Lechlade, and from Witney to Bampton. *Taxi*: Witney,

Hunts Cars (0993-5136); Swindon, Tramps (0793-610000).

Refreshment
Pubs: Trout Inn, Tadpole Bridge; Swan, Radcot: Plough Inn,
Kelmscot; Trout Inn, St John's Bridge, Lechlade; New Inn,
Lechlade. *Restaurants*: Crown Inn, Lechlade.

Accommodation
Hotels: Plough Inn, Clanfield, Oxford OX8 2RB (0367-81222);
Faringdon Hotel, Market Place Faringdon SN7 7HL (0367-20536);
New Inn Hotel, Lechlade GL7 3AB (0367-52296). *Guest houses and
small hotels*: Morar Farmhouse, Weald Street, Bampton OX8 2HL
(0993-850162); Portwell Guest House, Market Place, Faringdon
SN7 7HU (0367-20197); Appletree Inn, Buscot, Faringdon SN7
8DA (0367-52592). *Camping*: St John's Priory Caravans, Lechlade
GL7 3EZ (0367-52360).

Admission
Kelmscot Manor, first Wednesday in the month, April to
September; Buscot Park, April to September, afternoons of
Wednesdays to Fridays and of alternate Saturdays and Sundays.

State 13 **Bampton to Lechlade** 9.8 miles (15.8 km)

DESCRIPTION

The Trout at Tadpole – a good name for a pub that owns a fishing reach and a good pub to find at this lonely spot. Tadpole Bridge was built in connection with the Thames and Severn Canal. To provide adequate passage for the barges the required water depth was 1.1 m, and this meant heightening the level at Tadpole ford. So a new bridge was built for the new road between Bampton and Buckland, a single-arch structure with attractive keystones and roundels in relief, some time at the end of the eighteenth century.

Buckland (land held by charter), two miles to the south, is a small village beside a great house of classical design, believed to be by John Wood the younger. To the north is *Bampton* (probably Banna's settlement): Emily Cook (53, page 261) puts it at four miles, but it is only two, though two miles along a road nowadays at the mercy of motor traffic may well seem like four miles. Bampton has no great house but several fine town houses built for merchants or lawyers, for it was a leading market town. It later declined in importance and so preserved its original form, compact and with clean-cut contrast to the flat surrounding fields. The spire of St Mary's is seen from afar and is one of the largest and finest in the area. Octagonal in shape, it soars from the square central tower, supported by eight little flying-buttresses, a graceful architectural conceit of the thirteenth century. But this spire is now dwarfed by the forest of Ministry of Defence communications masts between Bampton and the Thames, which dominate our view for the first half of this Stage. Bampton's big day is Spring Bank Holiday Monday when, with bells on their legs and streamers in their hands, the white-clothed Morris dancers take to the streets in a form of dancing that had almost disappeared before being rediscovered early this century by Dr Cecil Sharp.

A new access road and the tall masts may reduce the sense of remoteness at Rushey Lock, but the scene is otherwise much as seen by Fred Thacker at the beginning of this century just after the new lock and keeper's cottage had been built (54, page 277). In his memorable character-sketch of Tom Weal his reference to the 'former crazy lockhouse and weir' was no exaggeration; for, according to a report of 1857, the weir was then in a frightful state of dilapidation, with only two of the paddle-gates operational and the rest stuffed with hurdles and straw and other debris to keep the water level up. Rushes clogged the waterway also, to judge from the name of the place. Tom Weal's successor keeps Rushey in excellent order, and his hard work in his garden is evident: he also boasts a peacock.

Between Rushey and Radcot Locks we walk through a riverine landscape which, perhaps more than anywhere else along the path, is least changed from past centuries. Although as elsewhere the land has been drained and enclosed, there are few hedges close by us; and although cattle graze in the grass pastures, these have not been systematically cleared but have clumps of hawthorn and brambles on them. The river bank is entirely natural and has at places been broken down where cattle come to drink at little gravelly beaches. The river meanders erratically and our path through the grass cuts the loops.

All along the bank are rows of pollarded willows. These stunted trees, so characteristic of the Upper Thames, have been planted here for a double purpose. They are excellent in maintaining the river bank, being easy to propagate, quick growing, wide rooted and receptive to damp ground. And their shoots yield a perpetual supply of wood – brushwood, firewood, small stakes and materials for hurdles or large baskets – if cut every seven years or so at the top of the bole. But nowadays the cropping of these pollard willows is uneconomic; on close inspection their trunks are often decaying, and soon there will be far fewer of them. True, it is sad to see a tree cut back from its potential to what is in effect a bush set on a pole, but these pollards do have a special visual attraction here on the stripling Thames because in contrast to fully-grown trees they complement the little river by being so small themselves, providing an excellent proportional balance.

A steep humped wooden footbridge maintains the course of several ancient rights of way which converge to cross the river at a lonely spot. It is called Old Man's Bridge, because on the site of Old Man's Weir. The Old Man, I am glad to learn, was not entirely solitary, for somewhere between here and Rushy there was also an Old Nan's Weir.

We soon approach Radcot Lock, which is on the site of Clarke's, or Buck's, Weir, as described by Boydell (55, page 278). His evocation of the scene is so perfect that it is just as well that he was swept through the weir before he had the chance to 'stay and moralize', which might have spoilt the effect for modern readers. Instead, to complement him, we have Robert Gibbings taking to his feet between Old Man's and Radcot Bridges when he needed 'a rest from sitting' (56, page 279).

When I first walked this Stage and crossed the wooden bridge on to the island by *Radcot* (red, or reed, cottage), I thought I was suffering from severe hallucination. Too much contemplation of the past was perhaps going to my brain. For there, quite distinctly, all around the bridge and the garden of the Swan, were scores of people and every single one was in seventeenth-century clothes. All the women were in long dresses and the men in breeches and stockings and a bewildering variety of coats and cloaks, hats and helmets: there were plenty of halberds, pikes, swords and martial ensignia. I was clearly the odd man out, but none of them seemed to notice as I peered closely, unable to find any fault with their authenticity, for all their materials were of wool or linen or leather, with no suspicion of synthetic fibres. Only at the crush of the bar did I get it – the Sealed Knot Society had come to re-enact the skirmish of Radcot Bridge in 1645.

In the Civil War the bridge served as an outpost to *Faringdon*, strongly defended for the King: Faringdon, two and a half miles to the south, whose location we can fix by a high clump of beeches and Scots Pines. These trees disguise the Faringdon Folly, the result of a collaboration of two Geralds: Gerald Berners, fourteenth Lord Berners, owner of Faringdon House, and Gerald Wellesley, later the eighth Duke of Wellington, the architect. Erected in 1936, it is a tall narrow brick tower without any windows except at the top where a Gothic octagon lantern lights a lofty room. Lord Berners, a famous eccentric, conceived the idea (fortunately abandoned) that when dead he would be stuffed and kept up here, seated at a grand piano.

Over the side channel at Radcot is in effect the oldest bridge over the Thames. It dates from the early thirteenth century, probably built to the orders of monks. To make the arches the masons first built stone groins, or ribs. These can be seen on the two pointed outer arches but not on the round central arch, because this arch was broken down in 1388 and soon afterwards was rebuilt by the more advanced method of a removable timber frame. It had been broken for military purposes. Henry Bolingbroke, Earl of Derby and future Henry IV, together with other lords, was in open defiance against his first cousin, Richard II. Richard's supporter and favourite, Robert de Vere, who had been created Earl of Oxford and Duke of Ireland, was hurrying south to join the King and heading to cross the Thames at Radcot. Here the lords laid a trap for him by breaking the bridge and attacking him on the north bank with a superior force. What happened then is graphically recounted in Holinshed's Chronicles (57, page 282), and it is only a pity that Shakespeare, who made such use of Holinshed, did not include the incident in his play.

It is a sombre reflection that if the German Army had successfully invaded England in 1940 or 1941, the Upper Thames would have been held as a defensive line and all the bridges blown up as a matter of course, even if there had not been widespread fighting. Pillboxes at tactical intervals along the left bank in this Stage provide a permanent reminder of the battle that never was.

Old Radcot Bridge retains its medieval appearance thanks to a decision by the Thames Commissioners to build a new channel with a new bridge for the passage of the barges, which is what we now see across the mainstream – a decision made entirely for cost-effectiveness and not for conservation. And by it they built a wharf, now the garden of the Swan, for Radcot had for long been an important point of transhipment for Taynton stone, brought by ox-carts from the quarries ten miles north. Enormous quantities were thus transported, including all that was needed to build St Paul's Cathedral, as well as, of course, the Radcot Bridges.

Our path is often narrowly hemmed between nettles and thistles

Radcot Bridge

but nowhere fails entirely. The river is there beside us, but
sometimes out of sight. There are fewer boats, but not so few as in
1946 when between New Year and May only one single boat passed
through Grafton Lock. Soon after Grafton Lock we come to a
straight reach where a few houses and a small church line the
further bank. The presence of these old buildings denotes that the
Thames is once again alongside a gravel terrace of higher ground.
Here was once the large village of *Eaton Hastings* (river settlement
belonging to the Hastings family), and the church of St Michael and
all Angels is largely thirteenth-century, with fine Norman windows.
In them is some very good Victorian stained glass, one window
being by Burne-Jones. This work of Pre-Raphaelite art provides an
appropriate prelude to our arrival, around the next couple of bends,
at Kelmscot, home of William Morris.

Let us follow the track where it turns from the river and walk the
couple of hundred metres off course to look at this beautiful
Elizabethan manor house, with its gables and mullions and tall
chimneys, all of Cotswold stone, its barn and outhouses and walled
garden. But let us try to approach it in the frame of mind of William
Morris, since the house is a memorial to him: and how better than
by reading the passage in *News for Nowhere* (58, page 283) where
he comes to it in a dream of the future, conducted by a lovely girl?
What is more, they have arrived by river, rowing all the way from
Hammersmith, and we saw them in Stage 12. This fantasy is based
on an actual journey Morris made in 1880, rowing up with a few
friends and relations in a small houseboat called *The Ark*. Despite
several flash locks they made it from Oxford on the final day,
rowing in the darkness from Radcot with a lantern tied to the prow.
William Morris was a polymath and made his influence felt as an
artist, a printer, a designer, a writer and a political activist. Of most
immediate relevance to Thames Path walkers, he was a pioneer in
the conservation of old buildings, and he fulminated against all the
ugly developments along the Thames downstream. He also took a
simple joy in the scenes of nature: here is our Stage 13 on a June
morning:

O June, O June, that we desired so,
Wilt thou not make us happy on this day?
Across the river thy soft breezes blow,
Sweet with the scent of beanfields far away,
Above our heads rustle the aspens grey,
Calm is the sky with harmless clouds beset,
No thought of storm the morning vexes yet.

See, we have left our hopes and fears behind,
To give our very hearts up unto thee;
What better place than this, then, could we find,
By this sweet stream that knows not of the sea,
That guesses not the city's misery,
This little stream whose hamlets scarce have names,
This far-off, lonely mother of the Thames.

Behind the manor is the village of *Kelmscot* (Cenhelm's cottage),
where the feeling of timelessness is sustained: there are several
large farmhouses and a village hall and some cottages built to
Morris's principles. The church (of St George) is Norman, with wall
paintings and medieval glass, and in the churchyard is William
Morris's tomb: his body was carried here on a yellow farm wagon,
decked with vine leaves and willows.

When Morris first came to live here in 1871, he shared the lease
with the artist Dante Gabriel Rossetti. The two soon became
incompatible. Their temperaments were utterly opposed, their
personal habits quite different, Rossetti going to bed at daybreak,
drugged with chloral, and waking at midday. Worse, Rossetti was in
love with Morris's wife, Jane. It seems that the event which made
Rossetti leave Kelmscot and get out of what had become an
impossible situation was that one day, when walking along the
towpath, he imagined he heard some fishermen making insulting
remarks about him. He flew into a rage and shouted such vitriolic
abuse at them that much ill feeling was created in the
neighbourhood against the unconventional occupiers of the manor.

At a little island the Thames is spanned by another footbridge.
This is the site of yet another Hart's Weir, also known as Eaton

Weir. Here the last of the flash locks remained on the navigable Thames, till 1936. The flash was such a small affair that Henry Taunt (another Thames enthusiast and early photographer who travelled about on a two-seater tricycle pedalled by a perspiring assistant) scraped his nose and face on the rail above, when going under it; and Emily Cook describes the delightful sensation of swishing through into the foam-flecked waters down the stream, guided into the channel by a long hook propelled by the weir-keeper, a 'genial fellow, strong as Hercules'. A long line of poplars cutting a straight line beside the looping stream next points our way ahead to Buscot Lock, which has a powerful air about it now that a new weir and channel were opened in 1979.

Buscot (Burgweard's cottage), across the river by the lock, is a model village of 1879, financed by Robert Campbell, who had bought the Buscot estate. He was a rich Australian who introduced modern farming methods well before his time. His main venture was the cultivation of hundreds of acres of sugar-beet for the purpose of producing alcohol. By means of a private narrow-gauge railway, the beet was brought to a distillery near the lock. The fields were irrigated from a large reservoir fed from the Thames by a giant water-wheel across the millstream just beyond the old lock-keeper's cottage. The work-force enjoyed less physically tiring work, shorter hours and higher wages. But he could not make it pay and it largely ruined him. The estate was bought by Alexander Henderson, later Lord Faringdon, whose son Gavin was a great supporter of the Labour Party, and many leading socialists came as weekend guests to Buscot Park, which is a mile or so beyond the village. The large seventeenth-century house beside the river a little above the lock is the Old Parsonage: and beside it is Buscot Church (St Mary's), with a perpendicular tower and containing more stained glass by Burne-Jones.

Just opposite to where a powerful pillbox dominates the steepest river loop yet, we pass the site of an important commercial depot known as the Cheese Wharf. At its prime it must have been a very busy place, for in 1809 nearly 3,000 tons of cheese were shipped

Eaton footbridge

from here to London: at about ten hard round cheeses to the hundredweight this implies about a quarter of a million of them. Just before we reach St John's Bridge, the tiny Leach enters the Thames on the far bank.

The Priory of St John Baptist was responsible for the original bridge, and the priory itself was just north of the Trout Inn, once called the St John Baptist's Head. The old bridge, like Radcot, was the scene of action in the Wars of the Roses and the Civil War: in 1471 Edward IV led his army over it on his way towards the Battle of Tewksbury, and in 1646 Fairfax stormed it and routed the Royalist garrison. Later it was extended to span the new lock cut, for St John's Lock and its close neighbour Buscot Lock were both originally built in 1791.

Here we find Old Father Thames in person, surveying the flow of water through his highest lock from that recumbent posture traditional for river gods, who are thought to lounge around on the mud amid the rushes like satiated hippos. And from here we go across the meadow to Halfpenny Bridge and Lechlade, whose spire has been our visible goal since Buscot. In a matter of three miles we have walked in three counties: just past Eaton Weir we left Oxfordshire for Gloucestershire; from St John's Bridge and past the lock we were back in Oxfordshire for the final time; and the last half mile was in Wiltshire.

ANTHOLOGY

(54) Tom Weal of Rushey Lock: from Fred Thacker's *The Stripling Thames* 1909.

Big slow Tom is a character I remember with affection. Many a talk I have had with him on his white-railed lock in the cool of the evening, watching Bampton spire piercing the lemon clearness above the trees; while Buckland woods darkened into ever deeper purple. The extortions of some of the River inns, his son's trophies and adventures in South Africa, local drownings, his eeltraps, the

Father Thames

winter floods, the former crazy lockhouse and weir: on these he will talk by the hour with many a bit of humour his impeded speech does nothing to diminish. He was born in Perivale; and when the Brent flooded the churchyard and washed away the earth he used with other boys to p-p-poke the coffins with a stick and get the b-b-bones out! He is only 'the b-b-boy' to his capable wife and pretty daughter, who are usually busy in the summer with holiday visitors. My boat lies cosily in a tiny bay in his weir stream beneath the willows; and it has always been with real regret and many a backward look that I have let her float downstream, around the bend and out of sight of this little haven of remoter Thames. The lock is thickly embowered in trees, one a dainty symmetrical little chestnut; and its white fences, and old barn usually decorated with the head of a pike, cling closely in the memory.

(55) Clarke's Weir, now Radcot Lock: from Boydell's *History of the Thames*, 1794.

With a high ridge of land, at some distance to the right, with Farringdon-hill rising beyond it, and a low, flat country to the left, the Thames continues its course from Radcot-bridge to Clarke's, or Buck's-weir, which, on a gentle turn of the stream beyond it, displays a charming little piece of rustic scenery. These weirs, which are very frequent in the upper part of the Thames, and give a very pleasing variety to it, are artificial dams or banks, carried across the river, in order to pen up the water to a certain height, for the service of the mill, the fishery, and the navigation. A large range of frame-work, which resembles the railing of a bridge, rises from the bank below, and supports a number of small flood-gates, sliding in grooves, and connected with a sill in the bottom. When these are drawn up, the whole body of the stream, being collected in a narrow place, rushes through with great rapidity, and gives a temporary depth to the shallows, or, by the power of the current forces barges over them. This machinery never fails, in a greater or less degree, to attract attention. In its most simple state, it affords variety to the view, breaks the line of the river, produces some kind of waterfall, and gives activity and eddy to the current. But these weirs are generally connected with various accessory and diversifying circumstances; the mill, the fisherman's hut, or the cottage of the person who collects the toll, sometimes embowered in trees, but always connected with them, heighten and vary the character of the scene. When the river is high, the overfall of the water forms a large cascade: but, at all times, the upper stream forces its way; in some parts spouting through the apertures of the floodgates; in others, fretting among the mossy timbers, or rushing over the aquatic plants that cling to the frame-work; and thus, broken into a thousand various rills, falls into the lower water, and continues the current of the river. Clarke's-weir is a very picturesque example of the necessary appendages to the upper division of the Thames navigation; and possesses a full proportion of the circumstances which have just been described: – a rude railing, contrived to support a range of flood-gates, stretches across the stream from a group of willows on one side, to a bank with two thatched habitations on the other: they are of singular form, and peculiar neatness, and would be called cottages, if the adjoining out-houses did not raise them to the character of small farms; while other appertinent objects encourage the opinion that the inhabitants employ their industry in two elements; that their alternate occupations were to till the earth, and to fish the water. It is a scene where the eye, tired with the glare of extensive prospect, is glad to repose; it is a spot that inspired the wish to stay and moralise; – but the stream bore us on its accelerated wave, to look again on the expansive view from which we had been too shortly separated; and took its course, with little variation of prospect, through Rushey, or Rudge's-lock, to Tadpole, or Kent's-weir.

(56) A stroll along the bank from Radcot: from Robert Gibbings *Till I End My Song*, 1957.

Yet still higher on the river I spent some pleasant days at the Swan by Radcot Bridge. 'The house is yours,' said Mr Bowl the landlord, when I put my bag inside his door. 'You go where you like and ask for what you want: a couple of extra eggs for breakfast or a pot of tea at any time. There's boats in the boat-house, help yourself, and if you want to make a splash in the river there's deep water under the diving stage by the bridge.'

I didn't want extra eggs, boats, or splashes; I was content to sit in the garden and watch, appropriately enough, the swans, seventeen of them, riding so proudly the wind-ruffled water, or gliding effortless where no ripple but of their own making disturbed the reflected light. Kingfishers streaked up- and down-stream, swallows splashed as they swooped at drowning insects, wagtails pied and grey ran to and fro about the lawn. When I needed a rest from sitting I would wander along the towpath to the lock and just beyond it the bent-back wooded span known as Old Man's Bridge. Big insolent steers in one meadow, in the next younger cattle more polite, moving aside to let me pass. Fishermen and fisherwomen all the way on folding stools, fixed as photographs. Across the river copses of willows, reed beds, and rushy pools among intermingling streams and rills, difficult country to travel for man or beast.

There is little sensation of distance when crossing a field – one just moves from side to side of it, from hedgerow to hedgerow, with every varying footfall, with ever varying invitation. On a road, whose interest is merely incidental to its purpose, the same fraction of mileage seems many times as long. Sometimes in the fields there is a beaten track, in summer dry and hard as it winds drunkenly from gap to stile; but in winter its inconsequence seems reasoned and sedate, as it skirts areas of flood water and the pools that well up from the sodden soil.

Of all beaten tracks the towpath by a river must be one of the richest in association: in the past hard toil for horses, men, women, and even children; to-day a right of way to 'the width of the waters, the hush of the stream'.

River loop near Buscot

(57) The fight at Radcot Bridge between the supporters of
Richard II and the Earl of Derby (Henry IV), 1388: from Raphael
Holinshed's *Chronicles*, 1577.

But Thomas Molineux determined to fight it out, since the lords
were not yet all come together at that place, but only the earl of
Derby and certain others. Nevertheless, after he had fought a while,
and perceived it would not avail him to tarry longer, as one
despairing of the victory, betook him likewise to flight, as the Duke
of Ireland had led him the way: and plunging into the river, which
was at hand, it chanced that Sir Thomas Mortimer being present
amongst others at the same place, willed him to come out of the
water unto him; for if he would not, he threatened to shoot him
through with arrows in the river where he stood. 'If I come (said
Molineux) will you save my life?' 'I will make you no such promise
(said Sir Thomas Mortimer) but notwithstanding, either come up,
or you shall presently die for it.' 'Well then (said Molineux) if there
be no other remedy, suffer me to come up, and let me try with
hand-blows, either with you or some other, and so die like a man.'
But as he came up, the knight caught him by the helmet, plucked it
off his head, and straightway drawing forth his dagger, struck him
into the brains, and so dispatched him.

In the meantime, the duke of Ireland (as you have heard) seeking
to escape by flight, came to the river's side; but finding the bridge
broken, he galoped till he found another bridge, where he found a
number of archers ready to stop his passage. When he saw that he
was thus inclosed with his enemies on the one side, and the river of
Thames on the other, he thought to put all in adventure; and casting
away his gauntlets and sword (to be the more nimble) gave his horse
the spurs, and lept into the river; but missing the ford, and not able
to land his horse on the further side, he forsook him, and swimming
over so well as he might, got to the bank, and so escaped. It was
now night, and therefore his enemies having no knowledge of the
country, followed him not; but his horse, helmet, cuirasses,
gauntlets, and sword being found, it was thought verily that he had
been drowned.

(58) Approach to Kelmscot Manor: from William Morris's *News from Nowhere*, 1891.

As I stood there Ellen detached herself from our happy friends who still stood on the little strand and came up to me. She took me by the hand, and said softly, 'Take me on to the house at once; we need not wait for the others: I had rather not.'

I had a mind to say that I did not know the way thither, and that the river-side dwellers should lead; but almost without my will my feet moved on along the road they knew. The raised way led us into a little field bounded by a backwater of the river on one side; on the right hand we could see a cluster of small houses and barns, new and old, and before us a grey stone barn and a wall partly overgrown with ivy, over which a few grey gables showed. The village road ended in the shallow of the aforesaid backwater. We crossed the road, and again almost without my will my hand raised the latch of a door in the wall, and we stood presently on a stone path which led up to the old house to which fate in the shape of Dick had so strangely brought me in this new world of men. My companion gave a sigh of pleased surprise and enjoyment; nor did I wonder, for the garden between the wall and the house was redolent of the June flowers, and the roses were rolling over one another with that delicious superabundance of small well-tended gardens which at first sight takes away all thought from the beholder save that of beauty. The blackbirds were singing their loudest, the doves were cooing on the roof-ridge, the rooks in the high elm-trees beyond were garrulous among the young leaves, and the swifts wheeled whining about the gables. And the house itself was a fit guardian for all the beauty of this heart of summer.

Once again Ellen echoed my thoughts as she said: 'Yes, friend, this is what I came out for to see; this many-gabled old house built by the simple country-folk of the long-past times, regardless of all the turmoil that was going on in cities and courts, is lovely still amidst all the beauty which these latter days have created; and I do not wonder at our friends tending it carefully and making much of it. It seems to me as if it had waited for these happy days, and held in it the gathered crumbs of happiness of the confused and turbulent past.'

She led me up close to the house, and laid her shapely
sun-browned hand and arm on the lichened wall as if to embrace it,
and cried out, 'O me! O me! How I love the earth, and the seasons,
and the weather, and all things that deal with it, and all that grows
out of it – as this has done!'

Kelmscot Manor

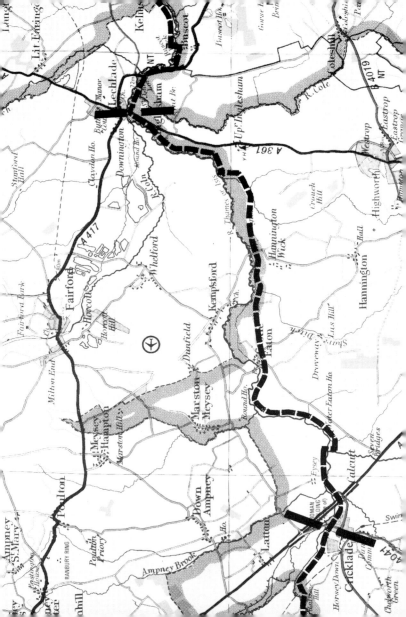

Stage 14 **Lechlade to Cricklade** 9.9 miles (16 km)

Until the sections of new riverside path have been cleared, much of this Stage will be really rough; and the alternative routes are unsatisfactory, being largely on roads including a mile of main road without a verge. But, once cleared, this will become the best Stage for naturalists, since navigation ceases upstream of Lechlade and the surrounding area is entirely agricultural. Lechlade and Cricklade provide two pleasant poles to the Stage.

Path Upstream: see also Strip Chart
Inglesham footbridge to Hannington Bridge
   250 m above the footbridge the path leaves the right bank. *It then leads to the access road to Inglesham Farm and Church, and from it regains the river bank, which it follows for 1.4 miles. At a stream turn left away from the river and, 300 m on, turn right on to a bridleway.* Follow this ahead along the line of hedges for 1.4 miles to where the route becomes paved; shortly after, where it joins a small road at a corner, turn right for Hannington Bridge.
   The alternative route to this section (3.8 miles, 6.1 km) is as follows: as above, then pursuing the path past Inglesham to the A361. Right along this road for 1.2 miles to Upper Inglesham. Right on to a village road and 200 m on, past Manor Farm, right again on to a bridleway. After 0.5 miles this is joined by the proposed route: then as above to Hannington Bridge.

Hannington Bridge to Castle Eaton Bridge
   100 m from the right bank at Hannington Bridge take the footpath opposite a cottage ahead along a watercourse and then across fields to Blackford Farm. Follow Blackford Lane to its end, then right into Castle Eaton and right again along the village street, passing the church, to the bridge.

Castle Eaton Bridge to Water Eaton footbridge: alternative route
2.1 miles (3.3 km)
   At Castle Eaton follow the village street around to where it joins

the small road leading to Seven Bridges and the A419. After 1.2 miles on this small road, just after Lower Part Farm, take a footpath obliquely right across fields to Water Eaton Farm and from there to Water Eaton Footbridge.

Path Downstream: see also Strip Chart
Water Eaton footbridge to Castle Eaton Bridge: alternative route 2.1 miles (3.3 km)
   On the right bank at Water Eaton footbridge take a footpath towards Water Eaton Farm: then ahead by a footpath across fields towards Lower Part Farm. Here gain the small road to Castle Eaton, turning left to enter the village street.

Castle Eaton Bridge to Hannington Bridge
   Along the village street, past the church; then left at a road junction. 200 m on, turn left on Blackford Lane to Blackford Farm. Then ahead by a footpath through fields to the road just by Hannington Bridge.

Hannington Bridge to Inglesham footbridge
   From the right bank go along the small road for 300 m to where it turns right. Here turn left on to a small road leading to a bridleway, which leads along the line of hedges. *1.4 miles on, turn left for 300 m to regain the river. Then follow the bank for 1.4 miles to Inglesham. Go behind the complex of buildings by means of the access road and then a footpath* to regain the river 250 m above Inglesham footbridge.
   The alternative route to this section (3.8 miles, 6.1 km) is as follows: as above, but continuing along the bridleway for a further 0.5 miles to Upper Inglesham. Left along the A361 for 1.2 miles. Just after the access road to Inglesham, left on a footpath across a field, and then as above to Inglesham footbridge.

Approach by car
At start: Lechlade is in Gloucestershire, at the junction of the A361 and the A417; car-park in Lechlade or across the bridge in

Riverside Park. *At end*: Cricklade is in Wiltshire, off the A419 between Swindon and Cirencester; car-park. *Also*: at Castle Eaton, on a small road off the A419 between Swindon and Cricklade; park near the bridge.

Approach by other transport

No satisfactory local transport, but British Rail station at Swindon is 7 miles from Cricklade, and there are local bus services from Swindon to Cricklade and Lechlade. *Taxi*: Swindon, Tramps (0793-610000); Cricklade, Blackwell's Car Hire (0793-750225).

Refreshment

Pubs: New Inn, Lechlade; Red Lion, Castle Eaton; Vale Inn, Cricklade. *Restaurants*: Crown Inn, Lechlade; White Hart Hotel, Cricklade.

Accommodation

Hotels: New Inn Hotel, Lechlade GL7 3AB (0367-52296);Cricklade Hotel and Country Club, Common Hill, Cricklade SN6 6HA (0793-750751). *Youth hostel*: Little Holme, Upper Inglesham, Highworth SN6 7QY (0367-52546).

DESCRIPTION

Lechlade (passage by the Leach) is in Gloucestershire, and on entering this, our first riverside town since Oxford, we realize how far we have come. Walking up the street from the bridge or standing at the corner of the Market Place, it is stone which dominates, brick is only occasional; and some of the stone has the distinctive honey colour of the Cotswolds. A rustic appearance pervades and it would not seem surprising if, with a clatter of hooves and a blast of the horn, the Oxford mail coach emerged from St John's Street; or, with ponderous tread, a couple of oxen pulled a farm cart along Burford Street, led by a white-smocked peasant. Gazebos, or little summer houses, provide an architectural whimsy to the old town, mostly tucked away in gardens but one in Burford Street. For the leading families they provided a pleasant means of observing local happenings such as fairs, markets or stage-coach arrivals from the security of their own gardens; but one suspects that they also became status symbols. Lechlade was, from its origin in Norman times, essentially a place of transhipment. At its wharf goods were transferred from Thames barges to carts and wagons; even, in earlier days, on to small, flat-bottomed craft on the Leach or the Coln. At its inns (there were no less than ten of them in the eighteenth century) stage-coach passengers collected and travellers spent the night on their way between London and Wales.

Like us they would have seen the spire of St Laurence's church long before their arrival, and now, like us, they would stand below it and gaze up the ledged lines of the battlemented and pinnacled tower to where the octagonal spire reaches for the sky. The church is fifteenth-century and its interior is lit by large windows in aisles and clerestory, and brightened by painted roof bosses. Beyond the church is the finest of Lechlade's houses, Church House, with a large formal garden overlooking the river; beside the church a chestnut avenue leads through the churchyard towards a footpath across the fields to St John's Bridge. This avenue is called Shelley's Walk from his poem written here on a summer evening: the first verse sets the scene:

The wind has swept from the wide atmosphere
Each vapour that obscured the sunset's ray;
And pallid Evening twines its beaming hair
In duskier braids around the languid eyes of Day:
Silence and Twilight, unbeloved of men,
Creep hand in hand from yon obscurest glen.

Lechlade town bridge has always been known as Halfpenny Bridge
because when it was built in 1792 the tolls were 6d for a carriage, 2d
for a horse and ½d for pedestrians; though (big deal) churchgoers
and mourners were allowed to cross free. This toll on foot travellers
caused much local resentment, especially during the years of
depression after the Napoleonic Wars, and was withdrawn in 1839.
The hump-backed bridge, still with the toll house on it, is made of
stone from Eastleach. Beside the main arch is a small towpath arch
which duly leads us into the start of the Stage.

The old commercial wharf at Lechlade is still busy with boats, for
beyond this reach the Thames becomes unnavigable for
motor-cruisers, and many of them moor here at the termination of
their journeys and are re-supplied by the chandlers at the wharf. In
the past this is where many barges began their voyages down to
London. Two hundred years ago the return journey of a sixty-tonner
cost the bargemaster £26 or more in wages and in tolls for locks,
bridges and ferries, and took nearly a fortnight. But since the barge
itself cost only about £150 and a full one-way load could earn £60,
there were good opportunities for quick profits.

On our bank a meadow has been made into a riverside park, after
which comes the final section of the Thames towpath. Just beyond a
footbridge the Coln joins the Thames. At this point, early in
September 1815, a clinkered skiff was paddled around in uncertain
fashion. It bore four young people: the poet and rebel, Shelley; his
lover Mary Godwin; Charles Clairmont, her foster brother; and
Thomas Love Peacock, a friend of Shelley who had written a long
poem called 'The Genius of The Thames'. Besides being a strong
walker, Shelley loved messing about in boats and water exercised
on him a fascination that was to have a tragic sequel. They had
intended to continue on to the Thames and Severn Canal: but when

they tried to enter it were told that the charge would be the same as
for a commercial barge on a season ticket, £20, an enormous sum in
those days. So they tried instead the unnavigable Thames, but very
soon retreated to Lechlade. Peacock's reference to the expedition
(59, page 298) describes the extraordinary change that came over
Shelley, and his poetic imagination gained too, for we can clearly
detect the Thames in the 'revolt of Islam':

> The boat flew visibly – three nights and days,
> Borne like a cloud through morn, and noon, and even,
> We sailed along the winding watery ways
> Of the vast stream, a long and labyrinthine maze.
> A scene of joy and wonder to behold
> That river's shapes and shallows changing ever,
> Where the broad sunrise filled with deepening gold
> Its whirlpools, where all hues did spread and quiver

The Round House on the far bank indicates where once the Thames
and Severn Canal joined the Thames. Hard as it may be to imagine
now, this canal at its inception was one of the most important
engineering and commercial enterprises in England, comparable to
the Channel Tunnel today. It had long been mooted, and it opened
in 1789 (60, page 300). The intention was to facilitate trade between
the West Country and London, and divert cargoes from the English
Channel. But it was from the start bedevilled with problems. Its
construction was expensive and complicated, for in a distance of 28
miles it needed forty-three locks and a tunnel 3,490 m long. And it
constantly suffered from water seepage. The Upper Thames from
Lechlade down to Oxford also acted as a restraint because of its
flash locks and dubious clearances. The trade itself never developed
in the way expected: it was always unduly weighted eastbound, and
degenerated into local traffic of coal and other bulk commodities.
And all too soon there came the challenge of the railways. The
canal in effect died a natural death within a hundred years of its
birth, but then was given a new lease of life by the newly fledged

Halfpenny Bridge, Lechlade

Gloucestershire County Council, which most unwisely took responsibility and injected a large capital sum. This was, of course, quite hopeless, and the canal closed soon after, the eastern section in 1927. Fortunately, the ubiquitous Thacker had walked along it a few years earlier and noted its romantic stagnation (61, page 300).

A sad story. But let us imagine the scene here when the canal was in its prime. A barge is emerging from the canal lock. It is of a design different from the Thames barges, for it has been made over in the west, at Brimscombe: a bluff rounded bow, curved sides and square stern, and a removable mast with a russet square sail. A single horse precedes it, on this its downstream journey. It is carrying a mixed cargo of tin, iron, copper and lead, as well as a few perishables such as cheese and cider. And maybe, tucked away, are some of the exotic consignments mentioned in old company books, such as carotels of currants, firkins of butter, bobbins of flax, pockets of hops, casks of purative squills, stakes of timber, hampers of vegetable alkali from Spain, or loaves of sugar.

As to the Round House, it was one of five specially designed for the canal as an economical dwelling for lock-keepers. The ground floor was the stable for canal horses, the first floor was a living-room and kitchen, and the top floor a bedroom. Above that, this (Inglesham) Round House had a flat lead roof to form a rainwater cistern. Such circular simplicity, like a lighthouse, did not always earn the approval of the staff. An applicant, newly engaged to be married, went with his girl to inspect a Round House. She adamantly protested it wasn't good enough for married life, and the company gave in and provided her with an external kitchen and stair, and converted the stable into a living-room.

Churches ought to induce a sense of mystery and wonder and not merely be places where we can tick off various styles or monuments from our copy of Pevsner or the Shell Guide. Unarmed by either of these I arrived at Inglesham church one still Sunday evening. The massive door was ajar and I walked into one of the strangest experiences, for the whole place appeared as it might have done in the early nineteenth century before restoration. Not only were the Jacobean box pews and Elizabethan pulpit still in place, but the flagstones were rough and uneven, the altar simple and unemphasized, and the wooden roof and screens unvarnished. It seemed as if the black-robed parson had just finished his one-hour sermon to a dozing congregation, with the squire firmly segregated in his prominent pew. And all around were the thirteenth-century walls and plain glass windows. It was too late in the evening to be able to read anything for there was no electricity, so only afterwards did I learn that St John Baptist's, Inglesham, was restored by the Society for the Protection of Ancient Monuments under the aegis of William Morris, and has since become redundant to church needs. These two facts are what makes it so essentially different, though in no way should we disparage Victorian restorations altogether. Without them most of our churches would have fallen into decay and in them the spirit of the medieval church is often better evoked than by this fossilization of Erastian protestantism at Inglesham. *Inglesham* (Ingin's dry ground) is a vanished village, and all that is near the church is a farmhouse which was formerly a priory.

By now we see a different Thames, undredged and uncleared, flowing through reeds and rushes. These water plants with their greens of different shades, some submerged and bending, some tall and erect, now begin to dominate the aquatic scene. The sedges are present in great variety, their tall spiky leaves protruding from the water. More spectacular are the reed-maces, including bulrushes with their chocolate-brown flowers tightly packed into sausage-shaped spikes. Then there are burr-reeds and flags and hemp agrimony, water-lilies and water-violets. From the river, with its increasingly steep and overgrown banks, no house is to be seen for three miles to Hannington (cock's hill settlement) Bridge, built in 1841, with its three arches and adjoining farmhouse.

The solitude is next broken by the vision of *Kempsford* on the far bank. The stately perpendicular tower of St Mary's rises in isolation above the rough hedgelines amid a clump of trees, like a painting by Constable. No wires, no cars, no housing – indeed, no people – are there to shatter the illusion. Yet actually behind the village is RAF Fairford, a huge military complex with a runway nearly two and a half miles long. From Fairford parachute troops took off for airborne invasions of Europe in the war: it then for a time became a US Air Force Base, and later was used for testing Concorde.

Kempsford (Cynemaer's ford) first appears in history in AD 800 as the scene of a Saxon tribal battle: a force of Hwiccians crossed from the north but were defeated by the men of Wiltshire with whom we will identify since Stage 14 is entirely in that county. After the Norman Conquest the manor was held by the Chawarth family till Maud, their heiress, married Henry of Lancaster, a nephew of Edward I. Their son, Henry Duke of Lancaster, later gave it to a religious foundation who held it till the reformation, when it was bought from the Crown by the Thynne family. The Thynne's manor house stood between the church and the river, and the earlier manor house had been just to the south of it, though in neither case was this the principal residence of these territorial magnates. Such are the bald facts, though legend has taken over from history at Kempsford with tales of a vanished castle, of John of Gaunt, of Chaucer, of ducal horseshoes and suspected lovers and I know not what.

At *Castle Eaton* St Mary's church overlooks the Thames, its stone tower and wooden bell-turret capping an expanse of slate roof. The iron bridge, though fairly innocuous, unfortunately replaced an old stone one, and was originally painted red, which added insult to injury.

Hedges and ditches: these prosaic words disguise the wealth of natural life that still exists amid intensive agriculture, and I know of no better description of this than Alfred Williams' when he passed by here earlier this century (62, page 301): Luss Hill, by the way, is the small protruberance a mile and a half south of Kempsford and Castle Eaton. Some of the ditches are very ancient, predating the fields themselves which in these parishes date from enclosures of around 1800. Ditches had been used for many centuries not only to drain the water meadows but also to help them flood in winter and prevent the surface getting too severely frozen, so assisting the grass to grow in early spring. On the great meadows, hundreds of hectares in size, the flocks of sheep and herds of cattle would graze, watched over by children: in 1587 there were 5,447 sheep in the Kempsford parish meadows.

Inglesham Church

Just above the footbridge at Water Eaton the Ray joins the
Thames: and before the Eysey footbridge we pass higher ground,
on the top of which once stood a chapel. Here we are within 500 m
of the line of the canal, which has followed the Thames at a discreet
distance to the north. Pastures bring us under the bridge of the new
road bypassing Cricklade and in so doing re-establishing the line of
the Roman Road known as Ermine Street, heading for Cirencester.
And so into Cricklade.

ANTHOLOGY
(59) Shelley's boating expedition up the Thames in 1815: from
Thomas Love Peacock's *Memoirs of Shelley* (edited Brett-Smith,
1909).

At the end of August, 1815, we made an excursion on the Thames
to Lechlade, in Gloucestershire, and as much higher as there was
water to float our skiff. It was a dry season, and we did not get much
beyond Inglesham Weir, which was not then, as now, an immovable
structure, but the wreck of a movable weir, which had been
subservient to the navigation, when the river had been, as it had
long ceased to be, navigable to Cricklade. A solitary sluice was
hanging by a chain, swinging in the wind and creaking dismally. Our
voyage terminated at a spot where the cattle stood entirely across
the stream, with the water scarcely covering their hoofs. We started
from, and returned to, Old Windsor, and our excursion occupied
about ten days. This was, I think, the origin of Shelley's taste for
boating, which he retained to the end of his life. On our way up, at
Oxford, he was so much out of order that he feared being obliged to
return. He had been living chiefly on tea and bread and butter,
drinking occasionally a sort of spurious lemonade, made of some
powder in a box, which, as he was reading at the time the *Tale of a
Tub*, he called *the powder of pimperlimpimp*. He consulted a
doctor, who may have done him some good, but it was not
apparent. I told him, 'If he would allow me to prescribe for him, I

The Thames near Castle Eaton

would set him to rights.' He asked, 'What would be your
prescription?' I said, 'Three mutton chops, well prepared.' He said,
'Do you really think so?' I said, 'I am sure of it.' He took the
prescription; the success was obvious and immediate. He lived in
my way for the rest of our expedition, rowing vigorously, was
cheerful, merry, overflowing with animal spirits, and had certainly
one week of thorough enjoyment of life.

(60) The opening of the Thames and Severn Canal: from *The
Gentleman's Magazine*, December 1789.

A boat, with the union flag at her mast-head, passed laden for the
first time to St John's bridge, below Lechlade, in the presence of
great numbers of people, who were assembled on the occasion; and
who answered a salute of twelve pieces of cannon from Buscott
Park by loud huzzas. A dinner was given at five of the principal inns
at Lechlade, and the day ended with ringing of bells, a bonfire, and
a ball.

(61) Last days of the Thames and Severn Canal: from Fred
Thacker's *The Thames Highway*, 1920.

Now this watercourse, opened with such jubilant enthusiasm and
lofty hopes, is the almost unmolested haunt of the dragon fly and
menacing great bullocks; more filled if possible with drowsy peace
and solitude than even the infant River itself. Its towpath will ofen
afford a route between selected communities more direct than the
ordinary roads; but the only vessels that awake a momentary surge
upon its placid, limpid waters are an occasional barge repairing the
bridges, or an infrequent dredger. Such of its wharves as I know are
silent and untenanted; and the dwellers in its round houses and by
its locks concern themselves but rarely with navigation. Its
milestones are overgrown with thyme and bryony; and in its weeds
the wolfish pike hang motionless, watching their prey. Occasionally
pleasure craft travel this way; but they say the tolls are almost

prohibitive. Its waters are clear; every curve opens up some fresh
scene of quiet loveliness; there is the reflection of the sky and the
sailing clouds; and I am grateful for the memory of many a solitary
tramp along its lonely banks.

(62) Luxuriance in hedges and ditches near Castle Eaton: from
Alfred Williams' *Round about the Upper Thames*, 1922.

The hayfield was situated about half-way between Lushill and
Castle Eaton, in the valley of the Upper Thames, near where the
four counties of Wiltshire, Berkshire, Gloucestershire, and
Oxfordshire come into conjunction. A hard road ran through the
field, bordered by a high hedge on one side. Here the beautiful wild
rose, shell-pink and creamy-white, with sweet crimson-pointed buds
and wax-like petals, infolded, or curved outwards underneath,
expanded like a saucer, or depressed like an umbrella, hung in
luxuriant trusses and clusters from the top of the hedge down to the
ground, shedding a soft radiance, and emitting a faint tea perfume.
Between the rose boughs, along the shallow ditch, crept the
dewberry with occasional blossoms and exquisite bluish fruit; here a
teasel, light green in foliage, with prickly buds and thin rings of
purple flowers growing from tiny cells like honeycomb, stood boldly
up alongside a stately thistle, to the large head of which a drowsy
humble-bee was clinging, though all her companions had long ago
departed homewards to their nest in the mossy bank.

Running along at the bottom of the field was a deep ditch, like a
brook, one of those made to conduct the water readily into the
Thames, and relieve the river in flood-time. Here, bordering the tall
flags, and shaded with boughs of guelder rose laden with milk-white
flowers, were banks of forget-me-not and brooklime; the
snow-white watercress leapt out of the ditch upon the bank, while
here and there shone a yellow iris, or a tall spike of pink valerian
showed above the reeds and added to the beauty of the border. In
the bed of the ditch, if you could have peered through the dense
flags, plants, and grasses, you would have seen the moorhen with
her brood of tiny young wading and swimming in the shallow water.

As it was, they were out of sight, and their presence would have been unsuspected if the mother bird had not indiscreetly uttered a loud 'cirr-rr-rr', thereby discovering their whereabouts. In the oak tree, standing down the hedgerow, a trim-looking magpie hopped deftly in and out among the branches. On one side the tall taper top of the rick, nearly completed, was visible in the farmyard; on the other the stately tower of Kempsford church rose above the elm-trees and peered majestically over all the valley round about.

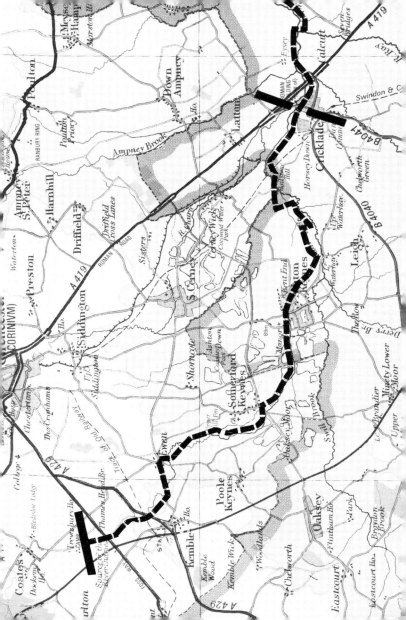

Stage 15 **Cricklade to Thames Head** 11.5 miles (18.5 km)

SPECIFICS

Stage 15 differs in character from all the other Stages because for much of it the Thames is no longer a proper river but merely an intermittent stream. 3 miles are on new tracks between the gravel lakes of the Cotswold Water Park. For the rest, it is mostly grass fields, which at times can be flooded. We pass through the fine old stone village of Ashton Keynes and close by those of Somerford Keynes, Ewen and Kemble.

Path Upstream: see also Strip Chart
Cricklade High Bridge to the former railway bridge
   At Cricklade High Bridge take the small road near the right bank for 0.3 miles, then right by a footpath between housing and through a field to the bridge at the end of Westmill Lane. *Then ahead up the right bank to a footbridge, which cross*: the alternative is to cross at Westhill Lane bridge and go up the left bank. Follow the left bank to the former railway bridge and up to the embankment.

Former railway bridge to Waterhay Bridge
   This is a bridleway throughout. Go along the former railway northwards and away from the left bank, for 300 m. Then turn left and continue by a circuitous route between gravel lakes, regaining the river at one point and then again near Waterhay Bridge.

Waterhay Bridge to Church Walk, Ashton Keynes
   (If joining from the road, go through a farm gate to the right of the road as you stand on Waterhay Bridge looking north.) From the bridleway just north of Waterhay Bridge go to the hedgeline and take the footpath to the left of it for 0.3 miles. The path crosses a ditch and continues over a field to a sports ground and to a small road. Cross this into a driveway which reduces to a path to reach Back Street, Aston Keynes. Along this, then across High Road into Church Walk.

Church Walk, Ashton Keynes, to Neigh Bridge, Somerford Keynes
   At the end of Church Walk take the path ahead between houses.
Then ahead across a road. Keeping to the line of the Thames, and
ignoring other paths, go through woods and then past gravel lakes
and cross to the left bank to gain a track past the windsurfing centre
at Lower Mill Farm. Turn left along Spine Road for 200 m, then
right for 150 m to Neigh Bridge.

Neigh Bridge, Somerford Keynes, to Parker's Bridge,
Kemble-Ewen road

   *From Neigh Bridge the path is up the left bank, past Kemble Mill,
Old Mill Farm and Upper Mill Farm: it then switches to the right
bank to Ewen Bridge. Go right up the road into Ewen*, then left for
0.5 miles along the road to Parker's Bridge. Unless an alternative
route is waymarked, the easiest alternative is to walk this section
entirely on small roads, through Somerford Keynes, then branching
left for Ewen: 2.9 miles, or 4.7 km.

Parker's Bridge, Kemble-Ewen road, to the Source
   At Parker's Bridge go up the left bank of the river bed to the
A429 road bridge. Beyond, pursue the path, initially by the right
bank, but then across a field ahead towards a hedge, continuing by
the edge of the field a little away from the bed, then heading
towards a stile to cross the A433. After this it is 0.4 miles more
along another field edge, then through a field, then to the Source,
marked by a heap of stones. (From the Thames Head Inn, the
Thames Path may be approached either where it crosses the A433
400 m in the Cirencester direction, or by a path beside the railway
and then across it to the Source.)

Path Downstream: see also Strip Chart
Source to Parker's Bridge, Kemble-Ewen road
   (From the Thames Head Inn the Thames Path may be
approached either where it crosses the A433 400 m in the
Cirencester direction, or by a path beside the railway and then
across it to the Source.) From the Source – marked by a heap of

stones – follow the gentle declivity of the fields down for 0.4 miles to the A433. Across this, the path continues to the right of a field, later coming beside the river bed on approaching the A429 bridge. From here go down the left bank to Parker's Bridge.

Parker's Bridge, Kemble-Ewen Road, to Neigh Bridge, Somerford Keynes

   Go along the road into Ewen *and take the first turning right, to Ewen Bridge. From here go left along the right bank of the river bed, crossing to the left bank before Upper Mill Farm, and so on, past Old Mill Farm and Kemble Farm, to Neigh Bridge.* Unless an alternative route is waymarked, the easiest alternative is to walk this section entirely on small roads, through Ewen bearing right for Somerford Keynes: 2.9 miles, or 4.7 km.

Neigh Bridge, Somerford Keynes, to Church Walk, Ashton Keynes

   From Neigh Bridge to the Spine Road and left along it for 200 m; then right along the access road past the windsurfing centre at Lower Mill Farm. Cross the river bed and continue on a path on the right of it, soon entering woods, later crossing a road, and ahead into Church Walk, Ashton Keynes.

Church Walk, Ashton Keynes, to Waterhay Bridge

   Cross High Road into Back Street. Just after it turns right, go left on to a footpath by Kent End Farm and behind houses. Cross a small road, then ahead over a sports ground and by a field to a hedgeline. Cross a ditch and continue to the right of the hedgeline as far as a crossing track, close by the north side of Waterhay Bridge.

Waterhay Bridge to the former railway bridge

   (If joining from the road, go through a farm gate to the right of the road as you stand on Waterhay Bridge looking north.) Find the new bridleway track leading nearest to the river. This leads between gravel lakes, frequently changing direction. Where it comes to the former railway embankment, go on to this rightwards, coming to the bridge within 300 m.

Former railway bridge to Cricklade High Bridge
   Go down the left bank as far as the next bridleway bridge. *Cross
it, and continue down the right bank to the bridge at the end of
Westmill Lane*: the alternative is to continue down the left bank and
cross at the Westmill Lane bridge. Here find a footpath ahead by a
field into housing, then left along a road by the river to Cricklade
High Bridge.

Approach by car
At start: Cricklade is in Wiltshire, off the A419 between Swindon
and Cirencester; car-park. *At end*: Thames Head is in
Gloucestershire, on the A433 between Cirencester and Tetbury;
park by the Thames Head Inn. *Also*: at Ashton Keynes and
Somerford Keynes, on small roads south of Cirencester and west of
Cricklade; park near Church Walk at Ashton Keynes or by Neigh
Bridge at Somerford Keynes.

Approach by other transport
Train: British Rail station at Kemble. *Bus*: local bus services from
Swindon to Cricklade and from Cirencester to Kemble. *Taxi*:
Cricklade, Blackwell's Car Hire (0793-750225); Cirencester, Radio
Cars (0285-68031).

Refreshment
Pubs: Vale Inn, Cricklade; Plough Inn, Ashton Keynes; Bakers
Arms, Somerford Keynes; Thames Head Inn, Thames Head.
Restaurants: White Hart Hotel, Cricklade; Wild Duck, Ewen.

Accommodation
Hotels: Cricklade Hotel and Country Club, Common Hill,
Cricklade SN6 6HA (0793-750751). *Guest houses and small hotels*:
Cove House, Ashton Keynes SN6 6NS (0285-861221); Old Manor
Farmhouse, Ashton Keynes SN6 6QR (0285-861770); Wild Duck,
Ewen (0285-77310). *Camping*: Cotswold Caravan Park, South
Cerney GL7 5UQ (0285–860216).

Stage 15 **Cricklade to Thames Head** 11.5 miles (18.5 km)

Cricklade is the highest town strictly on the Thames, and at
Cricklade High Bridge the river graduates in two important ways,
one legal and one geographical.

Legally, on flowing under the bridge, it 'goes public': that is to
say, anyone who wishes can go on it, though effectively this is
practicable only for canoes down as far as Hannington Bridge.

Geographically, just above the bridge a branch of the Churn joins
the Thames. Since the Churn is longer by ten miles at the point of
confluence, some have claimed for it the seniority. In fact, at its
source at Seven Springs in the Cotswolds just south of Cheltenham,
a tablet reads *Hic tuus O Tamesine Pater Septemgeminus Fons*
(Here, O, Father Thames, is thy sevenfold spring). And in 1937 the
local member of parliament asked that the maps should be altered
to sanction this assertion. His suggestion was brushed aside, not
merely because coincidentally the Minister of Agriculture happened
to have Thames Head in his constituency, but on the more serious
grounds that the Churn has always been regarded as a separate
river. All the same, as we shall see, the source of the Thames is
particularly ambiguous and elusive and one cannot but regret that
the Churn, with its definitive source and its delightful little valley
down to Cirencester, is merely a tributary.

The dry etymological facts which demolished the claims of the
Churn can likewise easily deal with the fanciful notions of early
historians and poets about Cricklade, namely, that it derives from
Greeklade and was a seat of learning before Oxford: (actually, it
means the river passage by the hills). But all the same it does have
an ancient history, having been an important Saxon town on the
frontiers of Wessex. In 878 Alfred forded the Thames here in his
war against the Danes, and in 1016 Canute came with his army on a
raiding sweep through the Midlands. It then became a market town,
and a rotten borough, and sank into agricultural quiescence; and
William Cobbett's account of Cricklade and its surrounding fields in
1821 provides a salutary antidote to thoughts of the Merrie England
of the Morris dancers (63, page 318). But towering over this scene

of wretchedness was, as now, the magnificent perpendicular tower of St Sampson's, and the High Street had already its double line of well-built stone houses, so not everything can have looked bad as the great radical rode through on that November day.

An inscription by the High Bridge records that it was rebuilt in 1854 by the Feoffees of the Cricklade Waylands, a long established charitable trust which has benefitted local services. Another communal benefit is North Meadow (in old Wiltshire dialect 'Nar Mead') a large area of 45 hectares which we see on the far bank. Grazing rights are granted from between 12 August and 12 February, but for the other six months no animal or person may wander on to it except on certain footpaths. This policy produces not only a commercial crop of excellent natural non-chemical meadow hay, but also a brilliant display of wild flowers beneath the lark-infested summer sky. The chief pride of the meadow are the snakes' head fritillaries, with their blotched and chequered flower heads, but there are also many others such as marsh marigolds, water crowfoot, buttercups and celandines. Indeed, in looking at North Meadow I am reminded of the passage in Spenser's 'Prothalamion', written 400 years ago, where he describes the wild flowers, ending with the ten times repeated line which must be the most famous poetic reference to the Thames:

> Of every sort, which in that meadow grew,
> They gathered some; the violet, pallid blue,
> The little daisy, that at evening closes,
> The virgin lily, and the primrose true,
> With store of vermeil roses,
> To deck their bridegrooms' posies
> Against the bridal day, which is not long:
>   Sweet Thames!, run softly, till I end my song.

Beyond North Meadow two decrepit bridges span the infant Thames. The first is what remains of the Latton aqueduct of the North Wiltshire Canal, whick linked the Thames and Severn Canal

Backpacker at Bournelake Farm bridge

to the Wiltshire and Berkshire Canal. The second and larger bridge with iron span carried the Swindon-to-Cirencester railway link which in this section (from Cricklade to South Cerney) has now been converted into a fine bridleway linking the Cricklade Leisure Centre with the Cotswold Water Park. There are also various barriers on the river. Besides the official Thames Water weir beside North Meadow there are various unofficial anti-canoe barbed-wire devices to protect fishing.

After the meadows below Hailstone Hill, marred by a house at its top but graced with a rustic footbridge at its base, we emerge into quite different scenery. In the flat land in this area gravel extraction has taken over from farming. Once extraction has been completed, hundreds of little lakes have been formed. Most have been developed into recreational areas by private owners or local authorities, under the control of the Cotswold Water Park. Besides aquatic activities, walkways and bridleways have been created, one of which we now use on our way to Waterhay Bridge. This soon deviates from the river, near an old double-arched farm bridge at Bournelake, and passes between two lakes. These lakes are at present used only for fishing and so waterfowl are much in evidence, swans putting on an impressive performance as they take off and land in their movements from lake to lake.

At Waterhay Bridge Father Thames plays a typical demigod's trick: he goes invisible. The water flowing under this new roadbridge is not that of the Thames but of the Swillbrook, into which some Thames water has flowed a mile or so upstream. Meanwhile the Thames's official course is for almost a mile and a half along a ditch which scarcely ever has water in it. The purists who devised the Thames Path have opted for this route which passes first through fields and then along Back Street, Ashton Keynes.

Ashton (ash tree settlement) *Keynes* is a distinguished village with a framework of old Cotswold stone houses and an infill of derivative modern ones. Various streams, or veins, of the Thames pass through it, notably along High Road where some twenty houses or farms have little access bridges across one; and we come beside this

Church Walk, Ashton Keynes

stream as we enter Church Walk, the most exquisite corner of the village. At its entrance is a stone column, and there are three others off our route: these all had stone crosses at their heads and were used for medieval processions. Appropriately the church is dedicated to the Holy Cross: it was extensively and effectively restored in 1877, though most of the masonry is medieval and the tower is fifteenth-century. By means of a narrow passage we leave Church Walk and, before crossing a road, can detect to our right the line of a moat that once surrounded a Saxon monastery here. Just after the road are the grounds of the manor house of Ashton Keynes, and we cross a wooden bridge over a sluice where some of the Thames flows into the Swillbrook.

There follows half a mile or so of wooded seclusion of the sort that prevailed before the gravel workings. Under the shade of the alders and willows the water dock, willowherb, purple loosestrife and teasel crowd the banks and the rushes obscure the stream, that is, if Father Thames has not disappeared yet again, for in autumn his bed is often completely dry. The combined effects of the gravel lakes and mechanical irrigation have disrupted him: no longer is he the central, unifying flow to which the streams converge by natural force of gravity, but merely one of several channels of water as regulated by the Thames Water Authority. Like many modern fathers, his control over his children is pretty minimal.

The Cotswold Water Park again becomes apparent as, now in Gloucestershire, we walk past lakes 42 and 44 used by Cotswold Leisure Water Sports who now occupy Lower Mill Farm. Windsurfing is an exciting new sport, ecologically very satisfactory, though it obviously is rather cramped on these lakes which cannot provide the ultimate thrill of the open sea. The erect figures with their bright sails plane and turn about, and it is easy to see which are the beginners.

Somerford, like Ashton, is called Keynes because it was once owned by the powerful Norman family of that name, still famous thanks to George Maynard Keynes. There are plenty of drystone walls and ashlar houses and glimpses into gardens. The church, of

Church and Manor at Somerford Keynes

All Saints, has the rare distinction of being on the site of a stone Saxon church of the eighth century, and still has one of the original doorways – tall, primitive and narrow – whose squared stones may well have come from the ruins of Roman Cirencester. Close beside it is a Tudor manor house.

Neigh Bridge is above Lower Mill but below Kemble Mill, Old Mill, and Upper Mill. All these are within half a mile or so of each other and testify to the practical use that millers put the infant Thames to. All were originally for grinding corn and, though none are now in use, Lower Mill was still operating in the 1960s for grinding cattle feed. The farmer at Upper Mill, Fred Timbrell, personifies the continuity with past times. He comes from a well-established local family, running his mixed enterprise from his homestead by the river. His big barns dominate the scene, which is also affected by the line of high tension wires that pass over the valley between here and Ewen. The stream bed is straight for half a mile, spanned by a wooden footbridge: actually it is a channel made by the millers, and the Thames's earlier bed is to our left.

Ewen (a spring) is a smaller village, so small that it has no church, but plenty of thatched cottages. Its westernmost building is Mill Farm, where was once the first mill on the Thames, as described by the Halls (64, page 319). Part of the charm of their *Book of the Thames* are the delightful engravings, vignettes which adorn almost every page, and with this passage we have the comfrey. But the most spectacular of the floral displays in this locality is not on the banks or fields but in the Thames itself. For the crowfoot grows so profusely in the river bed that in May and June the masses of large white flowers with yellow centres cover it completely like a blanket or a dress; and all the fanciful notions of the pastoral poets about Isis as a bride on her way to meet the manly Thame at once seem entirely natural. Looked at more closely, the water-crowfoot is interesting in that its leaves take on two separate forms: if floating, they are broadly lobed; if submerged, cut into thread-like divisions.

We pursue the Thames, or his bed, up to the A429, which cuts through a former railway embankment, though the station of a real live railway is less than half a mile off. To our left is *Kemble* (possibly from the British god Camulos) on its little hill, with the spire of All Saints, resting on a thirteenth-century tower, guiding us on our steeple-chasing way. And now we enter the meadow where the river most usually rises, and where he has a distinctive birthplace. Set in the middle of a humpy grass expanse and sheltered by some trees is the Lyd (loud) Well, mentioned in Domesday Book. It has a drystone wall beside it to form a little pond, and here, watched over by a giraffe-like wind pump, the infant bubbles out of the ground with happy plops and gurgles.

But we are not quite finished yet, for in winter and spring, as an intermittent winterbourne, he rises nearly a mile further on. His course is marked by baby bridges, more like stepping stones, and leads towards two embankments at the locality of Thames Head.

The embankment to our right is of the old Thames and Severn Canal, whose entrance we saw at Inglesham. The house on it is on the site of a vital element of the canal, the Pump House. From the start it was realized that a pump would be needed to boost the head of water, and in 1792 a Boulton and Watt single-acting beam engine of 58 h.p. was installed here, which lifted the water from 21 m at ten strokes a minute. The pump was always a bone of contention with the local farmers and millers, who understandably complained that it seeped off their water: but in truth it seems that it only affected a small area and did not appreciably lower the water levels.

The embankment ahead is in some ways more recent, in others infinitely older, for though built for the A33 it lies along an ancient Roman road known as the Foss Way, running from Bath (Aqua Sulis) to Cirencester (Cerinium). Cirencester is only a mile and a half along it, so these fields on either side of the Foss Way must have been extensively worked in Roman times, and the springs used as sources of water.

Once across this we penetrate to where the elusive Father Thames promises, like a fading actor, 'positively my last performance'. Guided towards our destination by a final steeple, that of *Coates* (cottages), we walk along the base of a slight valley and arrive at the Source, 109 m above sea level.

Thames Head is a classic instance of an anticlimax, and no one can fail to feel disappointment, especially those who have walked from far, even from Kew. Here is merely a stone block beside a

patch of earth, hard in summer, muddy in winter, and occasionally
fresh with water. To add to the unsatisfactory nature of the scene,
the mound just beyond the stone is the embankment of the former
canal, now only half a mile from its own great climax, the 3,490-m
Sapperton Tunnel under the watershed of England on the ridge of
the Cotswolds. This embankment cuts Trewsbury Mead, on which
we stand, from its home base, the ancient mound known as
Trewsbury Castle. And the railway embankment across the
meadow completes the imprisoned aspect of the scene. An attempt
was made by the Thames Conservancy in 1958 to dignify the site by
placing here a statue of Father Thames, protected by a railing: but
the poor old fellow was the butt of all sorts of cruelty, like a
medieval peasant in the stocks, and so in 1974 was removed to St
John's, Lechlade, (as we have seen). Still, there are bushes and
flowers, as recorded by Robert Gibbings (65, page 320). And at
least a bicentennial ash stands over the source, inscribed with the
letters TH. A willow would have represented better the banks along
the Thames. An oak would better stir any patriotic English heart.
But an ash is perhaps the most appropriate tree to guard Thames
Head because in pagan times it was associated with a certain
primeval power, as were springs of water, cleft rocks, sulphuric
earth and suchlike.

   Perhaps a sense of mystery is the most important qualification for
visitors to Thames Head, a moment of wonder at the simplicity and
complexity of nature and of the forces which combine to create a
river, quite irrespective of what may be subsequently done to
control or alter its flow and course, and quite apart from any
historical associations. The Thames is nowadays in many ways an
artificial river, but at least its source is entirely natural.

ANTHOLOGY
(63) Appalling conditions at Cricklade: from William Cobbett's
Rural Rides, 1821.

I slept at a Dairy-farm house at Hannington, about eight miles from
Swindon, and five on one side of my road. I passed through that

villanous hole, Cricklade, about two hours ago; and, certainly, a
more rascally looking place I never set my eyes on. I wished to
avoid it, but could get along no other way. All along here the land is
a whitish stiff loam upon a bed of soft stone, which is found at
various distances from the surface, sometimes two feet and
sometimes ten. Here and there a field is fenced with this stone, laid
together in walls without mortar or earth. All the houses and
outhouses are made of it, and even covered with the thinnest of it
formed into tiles. The stiles in the fields are made of large flags of
this stone, and the gaps in the hedges are stopped with them. –
There is very little wood all along here. The labourers seem
miserably poor. Their dwellings are little better than pig-beds, and
their looks indicate that their food is not nearly equal to that of a
pig. Their wretched hovels are stuck upon little bits of ground *on the
road side*, where the space has been wider than the road demanded.
In many places they have not two rods to a hovel. It seems as if they
had been swept off the fields by a hurricane, and had dropped and
found shelter under the banks of the road side! Yesterday morning
was a sharp frost; and this had set the poor creatures to digging up
their little plots of potatoes. In my whole life I never saw human
wretchedness equal to this: no, not even amongst the free negroes
in America, who, on an average, do not work one day out of four.
And, this is 'prosperity', is it? These, O Pitt! are the fruits of thy
hellish system! However, this Wiltshire is a horrible county. This is
the county that the *Gallon-loaf* man belongs to. The land all along
here is good. Fine fields and pastures all around; and yet the
cultivators of those fields so miserable! This is particularly the case
on both sides of Cricklade, and in it too, where every thing had the
air of the most deplorable want.

(64) The first mill on the Thames, at Ewen: from Samuel and Anna
Hall's *The Book of the Thames*, 1859.

Soon after we leave the valley in which the Thames is born, and
where its infant wanderings are but promises of strength, the river
becomes well defined, and of no inconsiderable breadth and depth;

its waters have gathered force, and are turned to profitable use. A mile or so of pleasant walk along its banks, and we reach THE FIRST MILL ON THE THAMES: at least it was and probably still is – the earliest effort to render it subservient to the wants of man, ministering to industry and producing wealth. The mill is sufficiently rude in character to be picturesque: it is in an open court, fronted by an old pigeon-house, and occupied by a pleasant and kindly miller, who reasonably complains that the engine of the canal frequently leaves him without water to move his wheel. He was, however, busy during our visit, and seemed well pleased to aid the artist in his efforts, apparently much interested in the progress of his work.

While the artist was thus employed, we had leisure to rove about the adjacent meadows, and to examine the numerous wild flowers and water plants which, in this vicinity, assume forms more than usually large. Among the most prominent was the Comfrey (*Symphytum officinale*), which appears in great abundance on the river-bank, rearing its bold form above the lower herbage. When in blossom – every branch decorated with clusters of pendant bell-shaped flowers, varying in every shade of colour from white to deep purple – the comfrey is one of the most ornamental among the many floral beauties that grace the waterside; and it once held a high place in the herbal of our forefathers for its great healing virtues: but its reputation for these qualities, whether deserved or not, has passed away, in common with that of most of our native medicinal herbs, to make way for drugs of foreign lands, which, if sometimes less efficacious, are at least more novel and costly.

(65) The Thames Head: from Robert Gibbings' *Sweet Thames Run Softly*, 1940.

The meadow was carpeted with vetches and clover, purple harebells and the yellow rock-rose, and I followed along as I was told, past the straggly bushes and the dead tree, to neither of which did I pay any attention, until I found the big ash, with the initials just

Water crowfoot covering the Thames by Parker's Bridge

decipherable in its bark. Immediately in front of this tree was the well, and on either side a thorn bush festooned with wild clematis, better known as old man's beard. It was the sort of thorn bush under which, in Ireland, if you had a mind to it, you might see the 'wee folk', but in Trewsbury Mead I didn't see as much as a fairy ring, though I did find some giant puff-balls twelve and fourteen inches in diameter, and looking like lumps of dough. It is said that when these are young and still snowy white, they make good eating if cut into slices, smeared with egg and breadcrumbs, and fried in butter. But for me that is a risk not yet undertaken. Behind the ash the ground sloped up to the banks of the disused Thames-Severn canal, whose dry bed, filled with thistles and the froth-like blossoms of meadow-sweet, makes a happy playground for young rabbits.

Early engravings of Thames Head show a fountain of water, as powerful as a burst water-main, welling up into a lake whose banks are bordered by tall rushes and the reed-mace; but today the well is no more than a circle of loose stones, and there is no water in it. It was difficult to realize that over fifteen hundred years ago Roman legionaries had knelt there to drink, and Roman matrons and their children had carried jars of water from it to their camp on the adjacent hill.

SIX UNOFFICIAL CIRCULAR ROUTES

Six unofficial circular routes

RICHMOND PARK LOOP, from Stage 1: 3.3 miles (5.3 km). Together with 3.7 miles of Stage 1 it provides a circular route of 7 miles (11.3 km). This loop is mostly on the edge of Richmond Park, though including 1.5 miles through the streets of Kingston: it also passes through the Georgian enclave of Petersham. The Kingston entrance to Richmond Park is only open in daylight hours.

Route outbound
0.5 miles upstream of Richmond Bridge, at the end of the riverside gardens by a plaque denoting Devonshire Lodge, leave the towpath for a path ahead across Petersham Meadows and then between hedges and past Petersham Church to Petersham Road. Left along road for 150 m, then right through gate into Richmond Park. Through park, always keeping to path at lower edge of bank, for 1.1 miles to cross a park road by Ham Gate; then for 0.9 miles still along the lower edge of the hill, and close to the park wall, to Kingston Gate. Into Park Road and immediately right into King's Road. King's Road passes to the right of the Richmond Park public house and later crosses Richmond Road. 200 m beyond, where King's Road veers left, continue straight ahead by King's Walk (with the power station immediately on the left) to regain the river at a point 0.2 miles downstream of Kingston railway bridge.

Route inbound
0.2 miles downstream of Kingston railway bridge, immediately after passing the power station, turn right up King's Walk and then straight on up King's Road to its extremity at Park Road. Left at Park Road into Richmond Park at Kingston Gate. Keep along gravel path near to park wall on the left and at the lower edge of a hill for 0.9 miles, to cross a park road by Ham Gate. Then straight ahead along a track for 1.1 miles, always at the lower edge of the bank, to leave the park at the Petersham Gate. Left for 150 m along Petersham Road, then right into a lane passing by Petersham Church and on between hedges and so across Petersham Meadows to rejoin the towpath at the entrance to the gardens, 0.5 miles upstream of Richmond Bridge.

WINDSOR PARK LOOP, from Stage 3: 5.3 miles (8.5 km). Together with 5.1 miles of Stage 3 it provides a circular route of 10.4 miles (16.7 km). This loop is mostly in Windsor Great Park, including the full 2.3 miles of the Long Walk between the Castle and the Copper Horse. It also goes through the center of Windsor and past the entrance to the Castle. Windsor Great Park is only open in daylight hours.

Route outbound
On Runnymede make for the Kennedy memorial and take the path uphill behind it, continuing ahead up Oak Lane to the A328. Turn left up this road for 100 m, then half right into Castle Hill Road. At a fork, half right again and ahead along Bishopsgate Road and past the Fox and Hounds public house to Bishopsgate into Windsor Great Park. Ahead for 400 m to a fork: take the park drive to the right, which leads to the end of the Long Walk. Walk along the Long Walk to its extremity in front of the Castle, then left into Park Street and then the High Street, and then downhill by Thames Street to Eton Bridge.

Route inbound
At Eton Bridge walk into Windsor up Thames Street and then past the Castle entrance into the High Street and on into Park Street. Enter Windsor Great Park and walk away from the Castle along the Long Walk to its extremity. Where the park road forks at the end, take the left hand drive. 0.7 miles on, turn left on to the drive leading to Bishopsgate, leaving the Great Park. Walk along Bishopsgate Road for 0.7 miles, passing the Fox and Hounds public house and rejecting roads to the right and the left. Then at a fork branch left on to Castle Hill Road, which leads to a main road, the A328. Walk down this to the left for 100 m, then turn right into Oak Lane and on down a path to the Kennedy memorial, and across Runnymede to regain the river.

BISHAM LOOP, from Stage 5: 4.7 miles (7.6 km). Together with 4.5 miles of Stage 5 it will provide a circular route of 9.2 miles (14.9

km), but *only* when the proposed footbridges at Bourne End and above Temple have been opened. This loop is largely along sections of alternative routing in Stage 5. Half of it is on the chalk slopes of Winter Hill, mostly through beechwoods. The other half is past Bisham and Temple, nearly a mile of it on small roads.

Route outbound
Take the Stage 5 alternative route from Bourne End railway bridge as far as the point where it is noted that the Bisham Loop diverts. Here cross the road and continue along a path at the lower edge of the wood. The path leads to the cottages of Bisham-under-Wood, and then crosses the A404 (exercise great caution) to a small lane which leads to a road junction by a war memorial. From here pick up the Stage 5 alternative route which starts at Marlow Bridge, as noted, and follow it to the site of the proposed footbridge.

Route inbound
Take the Stage 5 alternative route from the site of the proposed footbridge above Temple as far as the point where it is noted that the Bisham Loop diverts. Here cross the road for a small dead-end lane which shortly reduces to a path which crosses the A404 (exercise great caution) to the cottages of Bisham-under-Wood. Pass between the cottages to a path leading leftwards and then left again along the lower edge of Quarry Wood. At a road pick up the Stage 5 alternative route which starts at Marlow A404 Bridge, as noted, and follow it to its end at Bourne End railway bridge.

RIDGEWAY PATH LOOP, from Stage 8: 6.3 miles (10 km). Together with the 6.5 miles of Stage 8 it provides a circular route of 12.8 miles (20.5 km). This loop follows the official Ridgeway Path in its short section close beside the Thames between Goring and Grim's Ditch within a mile of Wallingford. Apart from 1.5 miles largely between housing at the Goring end, it is mainly through pleasant agricultural land slightly away from the river, though with a mile of towpath; and it passes through two attractive villages, South Stoke and North Stoke, as well as the buildings of Carmel College at Mongewell. The going is easy throughout, mostly on earth though with paved sections.

Route outbound

At Goring enter Thames Street: where it turns right, continue ahead and uphill by a narrow path, then ahead along a small road. At a junction by Cleeve Mill continue ahead along a track between the river and the railway, which becomes surfaced as an access road, later reducing to a path through fields to South Stoke. Ahead through South Stoke, past the church, then left by a lane and track to regain the river. Follow the towpath upstream and under the railway bridge to the former Littlestoke ferry point. Here the route continues slightly away from the river as a track through fields and woods to North Stoke, approached through the churchyard. In the village turn left and then ahead again through fields to Mongewell Park. Passing to the right of the buildings of Carmel College continue ahead by a paved path, crossing the line of Grim's Ditch (where the Ridgeway Path turns right) and ahead to a farm. Here find the track ahead between farm buildings, then in a field turn left by a path to the river; then up the bank to Wallingford Bridge.

Route inbound

At Wallingford Bridge cross to the left bank and follow it for 0.5 miles, then turn from the river towards farm buildings. Pass between these, then ahead by a paved path, crossing the line of Grim's Ditch (where the Ridgeway Path comes in from the left) to arrive at Carmel College. Keeping to the left of the college buildings and car park, find the track ahead through fields to North Stoke. Turn right in the village, then through the churchyard continuing ahead by a path, regaining the river at the former Littlestoke ferry point. Follow the towpath downstream and under the railway bridge to where it ceases, then by track and lane into South Stoke, turning right at a junction and passing the church,

ahead through the village, then ahead on a path through fields.
Always keeping between the river and the railway, the route
develops into an access road, then a track, then a small road again.
Soon after passing Cleeve Mill it leaves the road as a narrow path
half right, to enter Thames Road in Goring.

DORCHESTER LOOP, from Stage 9: 2.7 miles (4.3 km) Together with
the 2.4 miles of Stage 9 it provides a circular route of 5.1 miles (8.3
km). This short loop comprises the villages of Shillingford, a section
of towpath, and the ancient earthworks known as the Dyke Hills: it
also crosses the little river Thame and passes by the edge of
Dorchester, with its magnificent abbey church. Unfortunately, it
also comprises 0.4 miles on the verge of the A423. It is easy going
throughout.

Route outbound
At Shillingford Bridge go to the end of the embankment on the left
bank of the river. Turn left on to a driveway: where it divides, take
a footpath half right. Beyond the walls of Shillingford Court, turn
left by a footpath to Wharf Road, then right up to the A423. Left
along this for 0.4 miles, then left by a footpath to regain the river.
Follow the towpath upstream and cross the footbridge over the
Thame: then turn right, away from the Thames, on a footpath
through pastures to the edge of the Dyke Hills. Rejecting the path
ahead into Dorchester, turn left along the path beside the Dyke
Hills: this soon turns left through the earthworks. Then cross the
field directly to Day's Lock.

Route inbound
From the left bank at Day's Lock take a footpath across the field
away from the river: this leads through the earthworks of the Dyke
Hills, then along the edge of them. Where it turns left into
Dorchester, turn right on to a footpath through fields to regain the
river. Cross the footbridge over the Thame and follow the towpath
downstream for 0.8 miles; then turn left to the A423 by a footpath.
Right along the A423 for 0.4 miles, then right into Wharf Road,

Shillingford. Just before reaching the river, turn left by a footpath between houses, then right on to another enclosed path. At end, half left on to a driveway which leads to Shillingford Bridge.

OXFORD LOOP, from Stage 11: 3.9 miles (6.3 km). Together with 3.5 miles of Stage 11 it provides a circular route of 7.4 miles (11.9 km). This loop is half through the centre of Oxford and half through the open space of Port Meadow. The route through Oxford goes directly past the University Buildings and several famous colleges, and is mostly by small lanes and roads between these and in a residential area known as Jericho, largely avoiding traffic. Christ Church Meadow is only open in daylight hours.

Route outbound
Cross the river at Folly Bridge and go along St Aldate's for 300 m, then turn right into the Christ Church Memorial Garden, and then ahead into Christ Church Meadow. Pass in front of the Meadow Buildings, then turn left along a path and then a passage between Corpus Christi and Merton Colleges. Then across Merton Street up Magpie Lane past the back of Oriel, to the High Street. Cross the High Street into Catte Street, passing All Souls to the right and the Radcliffe Camera and the University Buildings to the left, then left into Broad Street and past Trinity. At the end, by Balliol, turn right into St Giles' and then, by St John's, left into Beaumont Street. At the end by Worcester College, turn right into Walton Street, left into Worcester Place, right into Walton Lane, and left into Richmond Road, which leads into Nelson Street. Then half right into Canal Street. At a small public garden at the end of this street, cross by a footbridge over the Oxford Canal, then right and along the towpath to the next bridge. Here leave the canal and take the small road to the left to the entrance of Port Meadow. At Port Meadow strike any line, with the river to the left, to reach the far end at Lower Wolvercote by the car-park close by the river. Cross the bridge over a weir stream and then, after the Trout Inn, Godstow Bridge over the mainstream, to regain the towpath.

Route inbound

Cross Godstow Bridge over the mainstream and then, after the Trout Inn, another bridge over a weir stream. From the car-park at Lower Wolvercote strike any line across Port Meadow, with the river to the right, to reach the far end where a track leads away from the river to a gate. Go through the gate on to a road over the railway and then, 100 m on, descend from the road to the right on to the towpath of the Oxford Canal. Follow this downstream: then cross it by the first footbridge and go through a small public garden and into Canal Street on the right, and continue to the end of this street. Then half left into Nelson Street, which becomes Richmond Road. Right into Walton Lane; left into Worcester Place; right into Walton Street. By Worcester College, left into Beaumont Street. Across St Giles' and turn right in front of St John's; then, by Balliol, left into Broad Street and past Trinity. At end, right into Catte Street and past the University Buildings to the right and later All Souls to the left, to the High Street. Cross the High Street into Magpie Lane, passing the back of Oriel. Cross Merton Street into a passage between Merton and Corpus Christi into Christ Church Meadow. Where the wall on the right ends, turn right and pass the Meadow Buildings of Christ Church into the War Memorial Garden. At St Aldate's turn left to cross Folly Bridge and regain the towpath.

Selected further reading

ANDERSON, J. R. L., *The Upper Thames*, Eyre and Spottiswoode, 1970

BURSTALL, PATRICIA, *The Golden Age of the Thames*, David and Charles, 1981

CHAPLIN, PETER, *The Thames from Source to Tideway*, Whittet Books, 1982

DE MARÉ, ERIC, *Time on the Thames*, Architectural Press, 1952

EMERY, FRANK, *The Oxfordshire Landscape*, Hodder and Stoughton, 1974

GIBBINGS, ROBERT, *Sweet Thames Run Softly*, Dent, 1940

HALL, S. C., *The Book of the Thames*, Charlotte James, 1975

HOUSEHOLD, H., *The Thames and Severn Canal*, David and Charles, 1969

JEBB, MILES, *The Thames Valley Heritage Walk*, Constable, 1980

JENKINS, ALAN, *The Book of the Thames*, Macmillan, 1983

JEROME K. JEROME, *Three Men in a Boat*, Penguin, 1970

MORRIS, WILLIAM, *News from Nowhere*, Penguin, 1984

PEEL, J. H. B., *Portrait of the Thames*, Robert Hale, 1967

PHILLIPS, GEOFFREY, *Thames Crossings*, David and Charles, 1981

PRICHARD, MARIE, and CARPENTER, H., *A Thames Companion*, Oxford University Press, 1981

ROLT, L. T. C., *The Thames, from Mouth to Source*, Batsford, 1951

THACKER, FRED S., *The Thames Highway*, David and Charles, 1968

Index